A2 LAW FOR OCR

Jimmy O'Riordan

OCR

RECOGNISING ACHIEVEMENT

Heinemann Educational Publishers
Halley Court, Jordan Hill, Oxford OX2 8EJ
Part of Harcourt Education

Heinemann is a registered trademark of Harcourt Education Limited

© Jimmy O'Riordan 2003

First published in 2003

07 06 05 04 03
10 9 8 7 6 5 4 3 2 1

British Library Cataloguing in Publication Data is available
from the British Library on request.

ISBN 0 435 551078

Designed and typeset by J&L Composition, Filey, North Yorkshire

Original illustrations © Harcourt Education Limited, 2003
Illustrated by Simon Smith
Printed in the UK by Scotprint
Cover photo: © Photodisc/Randy Allbritton

Acknowledgements
Every effort has been made to contact copyright holders of material reproduced in this book. Any
omissions will be rectified in subsequent printings if notice is given to the publishers.

There are links to relevant websites in this book. In order to ensure that the links are up-to-date, that
the links work, and that the sites are not inadvertantly linked to sites that could be considered
offensive, we have made the links available on the Heinemann website at www.heinemann.co.uk/
hotlinks. When you access the site the express code is **1078P**.

Contents

Introduction

This book has been written specifically for OCR students studying A2 law. I have worked exactly to what is in the syllabus and other advice from the examination board. I have tried to cut out all unnecessary details and focus on the key concepts and cases that are required for this challenging A2 course and success in your examinations. I have listened carefully over the years to the pleas from students about what suits them best in their reading. As a result I have tried to write in simple English so that the concepts themselves are easily understood, broken down concepts into bite-size chunks, provided key points at the beginning, advice about what to look for at the start of each unit and put revision questions at the end of each unit. There are fuller exam style questions at the end of the criminal law and contract law sections. I have tried to avoid long streams of text that simply send students away from their books and tried to make the book as user friendly as possible.

Each unit has revision questions to test your knowledge and exam questions with detailed answer guides. To supplement this book it is important that you read quality newspapers and watch relevant television programmes on law. Law is ever changing and by keeping up to date you will test your knowledge and application and also give yourself up-to-date examples to use in your essays. The work of A2 does draw upon much of your AS law studies particularly the synoptic module. The synoptic module is examined in detail at the end of the book.

As usual I have my lovely wife Catherine to thank for looking after our two growing toddlers, Alexander and Elizabeth. I am as always extremely grateful for the time she has given up to help me with this project. I would also like to thank my students at High Pavement Sixth Form College who have provided great insights into legal issues, as well as Peter Welsby and Dave Spriggs of the law department and the superb librarians Jane Parker and Kerry Piggot. Also many thanks to all those at Heinemann who have given me so much support and encouragement, particularly Nigel Kelly, Vicky Cuthill and Sarah Ross.

Jimmy O'Riordan
March 2003

Criminal law 1

Principles of criminal liability

1 *Actus reus*

2 *Mens rea*

3 Strict liability

4 Participation

5 Preliminary crimes

Offences against the person

6 Murder

7 Manslaughter

Actus reus

Key points

1 Meaning of *actus reus*
2 Proof of positive acts
3 Omissions as *actus reus*
4 Principles of causation and *sine qua non*
5 Factors affecting chain of causation

Why do I need to know about *actus reus*?

Criminal law studies the most serious offences against members of society. In legal terms the guilty act itself is known as the *actus reus*: this is the physical element of the crime but it is only one part of any crime that needs to be

Intervening event

proved. This unit looks at the definition of crime and the physical elements of an act of crime. The other part of the crime concerns the guilty mind, which you will study in Unit 2. The study of legal cases will be vital to your overall understanding of this complex part of the law. It is important that you relate the law you learn carefully and thoughtfully to the case studies you will be presented with. This means that you must have a thorough understanding of the basic concepts and principles of English criminal law. The law in this area is often subject to change so keep up to date by reading quality newspapers and following important cases in the news.

1 Meaning of *actus reus*

Criminal law deals with serious offences against the state or society. As these offences are often severe, the proof needed must be of a higher quality than that needed in other branches of the law. In the case where a defendant pleads not guilty, the prosecution must prove that the defendant is guilty 'beyond reasonable doubt'. If the prosecution can prove this, the jury will return a verdict of guilty and the judge then sentences the defendant. If the defendant pleads guilty then the jury is not used: the judge listens to the case and passes a sentence.

Where a criminal law is broken, the state will sometimes consider prison – prison is the harshest punishment used against an individual. Under recent guidance produced as a result of the Human Rights Act 1998, judges must consider all other options before imposing a prison sentence.

Criminal law covers a wide range of offences from traffic violations and shoplifting to major crimes such as armed robbery and murder. Minor criminal cases are heard in the Magistrates' Court. The more serious criminal cases are heard in the Crown Court. The Auld Report is proposing that many more criminal offences will be switched from the Crown Court to the Magistrates' Court. This may also mean increased powers for the magistrates.

All criminal offences consist of two distinct parts: the first is the *actus reus* and the second is the *mens rea* (this will be looked at in the next unit).

The term *actus reus* means 'the guilty act'. It forms part of a Latin phrase meaning:

'the act is only guilty if the mind is also guilty.'

Actus reus is a key concept in criminal law and it must be present for there to be a criminal offence. *Actus reus* involves the physical elements to crime rather than the mental. For example, it involves the physical lifting of a stolen item or the pulling of a trigger on the gun that leads to the injury of a human being. At this stage it is not important to look at what prompted the person to commit these guilty acts or their state of mind.

2 Proof of positive acts

In the vast majority of cases a defendant is only guilty if they have voluntarily committed a positive illegal act, that is, the act must be deliberate. Ignoring someone drowning in a river is not regarded as a criminal offence although possibly as an immoral one: throwing someone in and then letting them drown *would* be seen as a criminal offence. The defendant has committed a positive act by throwing the person into the river. In some legal systems there is a duty on citizens to act as good Samaritans. The English system allows citizens to choose.

The *actus reus* may consist of a number of elements (including a positive act but not necessarily). These might include:

● conduct

● consequences

● circumstances.

Rape, for example, involves a positive act by the rapist, that is, unlawful sexual intercourse, but it also requires a circumstance, which in this case is the lack of consent from the person raped. Crimes where the act is the key element in the crime are known as 'conduct crimes'.

Murder requires a consequence. The victim of the crime must die – this is a consequence. There is also another circumstance in the case of murder, which is that the death must occur under the Queen's peace. Death of another human being whilst the country is at war may be classified as a 'legitimate' death under conditions of warfare. The offence of murder does not require a conduct element, only that death occurred of another human being. Crimes where the end result is the key element are known as 'consequence crimes'.

3 Omissions as *actus reus*

Omissions, actus reus and duty of care

The *actus reus* is generally a voluntary act, but there are circumstances where an omission will also be considered to be *actus reus*. One such situation is when a duty of care is created.

Legal case: *R v Gibbins and Proctor (1918)*

The case of *R v Gibbins and Proctor (1918)* illustrated the duty of care that existed by the presence of a parent/child relationship. Gibbins, the girl's father, allowed his daughter to starve to death and he and the woman he was living with were found guilty of murder. The father's duty of care made his omission the *actus reus* of the crime.

Sometimes a duty of care exists via legislation, as in reporting road accidents. This is often referred to as statutory duty. Other duties of care may exist between teachers and pupils, doctors and patients, and even between motorists and other motorists. An omission may form part of a criminal case if there had been a contractual obligation that formed a duty of care. The *actus reus* would then be failure to carry out the contractual duty.

Legal case: *R v Pittwood (1902)*

A gatekeeper on a railway level crossing failed to close the gate after allowing a car through. Some time later a passing train killed the owner of a second vehicle and the gatekeeper was found guilty of manslaughter. The court stated that a person might incur criminal liability from not carrying out part of a contract. His omission to close the gate became the *actus reus* of the crime.

The Pittwood case illustrates a situation where a contract created a duty. The following case shows where a person holding a public office may face criminal charges through an omission.

Legal case: *R v Dytham (1979)*

Dytham was a police officer on duty near a nightclub. A person was thrown out of the club and a fight started which eventually involved a large number of men. The person thrown out of the nightclub died as a result of injuries he sustained. Dytham did not intervene and when the trouble was over he drove away. He was convicted of wilfully omitting to carry out his duty by neither stopping the fight nor apprehending the offenders. The Court of Appeal confirmed his conviction.

The Dytham case is covered by the common law offence of misconduct whilst acting as an officer of justice.

There are two important factors that must be present if a person is to be charged with failure to act.

● The crime must be one where it is possible to commit it by not acting.

Some crimes may be committed by omission. *Gibbins and Proctor (1918)* and *R v Pittwood (1902)* show this to be the case, in the first case murder and in the second case manslaughter. Other offences cannot be committed by omission. Crimes such as burglary and robbery clearly need the defendant to commit a positive act and cannot therefore be committed by omission. Burglary requires the defendant to act as a trespasser and then steal or go on to steal. The offence of robbery requires the defendant to inflict violence or put the victim in fear of violence whilst they commit theft.

● The defendant must have been under a duty to act

The defendant must be under a duty to act, which is recognised by the law. If I believe that my neighbour is under a duty to act if he sees someone climbing through my kitchen window to commit an offence of burglary this is not going to be recognised in law. He does not have to call the police although in the long run it might be in his interests to do so to bring about similar responsible neighbourly behaviour from me. The following case illustrates the legal issue.

Legal case: *R v Khan and Khan (1998)*

Two drugs dealers Khan and Khan supplied heroin to a fifteen year old girl who overdosed and died. Khan and Khan failed to summon medical assistance. They returned the day after and found the youngster dead. She had consumed double the dose she should have. During the trial the judge had not properly directed the jury in regard to whether the defendants had a duty to act. He informed the jury that the issue was one of 'manslaughter by omission'. This was incorrect since manslaughter could only be produced by an unlawful and dangerous act or gross negligence. The Appeal Court decided that the judge should have established whether a duty of care was *capable of being produced* by the facts of the case and then it would be the job of the jury to *actually decide whether it was or not*. A retrial was ordered as a result of the first trial judges misdirection.

If a person establishes a duty of care when will that duty cease? Can the carer or employee ever be free from their responsibility? Clearly in an employment contract duty of care situation when the contract ends and the employee moves to another job their previous duties will cease. When children leave school or home and become independent beings the responsibility of those teachers or parents will cease.

The following case shows a duty of care released under very stressful circumstances.

Legal case: *Airedale NHS Trust v Bland (1993)*

Mr Anthony Bland was one of the victims of the Hillsborough disaster, which claimed over 90 lives during a football match in 1989. Mr Bland was severely injured during the crush at the football ground and entered a deep and long lasting coma. The Hospital Trust caring for him sought permission from the courts to stop life support, which included artificial feeding. The House of Lords were asked to deliver judgement in this most distressing case and decided that it would be lawful in these circumstances for the hospital to cease all intervention and allow Mr Bland to die. Effectively the hospitals duty of care towards Mr Bland was removed. Lord Goff made some important points during the judgement including the point that futile treatment may not be in the best interests of the patient and omission to provide such treatment would not be seen as a failure of duty to care.

As we have seen in English law we are not under a duty to care for anyone in normal circumstances. Duty of care for another can however be voluntarily taken on. The following case illustrates an assumption of such a duty of care. As with *R v Miller (1983)* if we put ourselves into certain circumstances we are then duty bound to act responsibly and fulfil our obligations.

Legal case: *R v Stone and Dobinson (1977)*

John Stone aged 67 and his girlfriend Gwen Dobinson aged 43 assumed care of Stone's sister who was aged 61. The sister suffered from an eating disorder which eventually led to her being confined to her bed. Stone and his girlfriend made some attempts to call for help but were unable to properly use the telephone. The sister did not help them and made attempts to prevent them from calling for help since she believed she would be taken away. Eventually the sister died and the court heard the terrible physical condition she was in due to the neglect she had suffered partly as a result of her own actions and partly due to Stone's inability to care for her. The court found Stone and his girlfriend guilty of manslaughter through gross negligence. Gross negligence is negligence which a jury thinks is deserving of a criminal conviction.

Group activity

Do you think that Stone and his girlfriend should have been found guilty? What factors might the court have taken into account when deciding their outcome?

Stone and his girlfriend were not charged with murder since their intention was not to kill the sister. Their incompetence and pathetic attempts to care for her and summon help amounted to gross negligence and therefore a charge of manslaughter. In the case of *R v Gibbins and Proctor (1918)* however the court felt that the intention by this pair was to kill the unfortunate seven year old girl. A different situation entirely.

People are not generally required to 'act the hero' and save others from burning buildings. If they have themselves created the dangerous circumstance, however, then they have a duty towards possible victims. The following case illustrates this situation.

Legal case: *R v Miller (1983)*

A squatter smoking a cigarette accidentally set fire to his mattress so he moved into the next room without putting the fire out or alerting anyone else. He was found guilty of arson under the Criminal Damage Act 1971. His omission became the *actus reus* of the crime.

The defendant must have control over their actions or their omissions. If they act out of reflex or because of some other force acting on them, it cannot be seen as voluntary and they are not guilty. An example was given in the case of *Hill v Baxter (1958)* where a driver was being stung by a swarm of bees. Clearly, driving a car in these circumstances would be extremely difficult and you could not be held liable for your actions.

Group activity

A strong and fit swimmer walking past a lake sees a toddler in the water struggling. The swimmer who is late for an appointment keeps on walking, giving no assistance to the helpless child and the youngster drowns. The swimmer is not criminally liable: he has done nothing wrong as far as the law is concerned.

1 What are your views on the case above?

2 Can you think of any reasons why the law does not force a duty of care on all of us to help our fellow citizen?

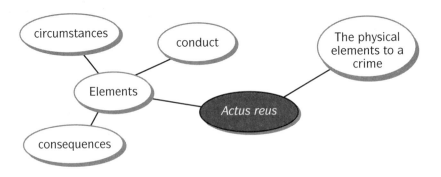

Actus reus

4 Principles of causation and *sine qua non*

Cause in fact

If a criminal case is to be proved then it must be shown that the conduct of the defendant caused the consequence. This is known as *sine qua non*, which means that the act caused the consequence. There must be a clear and unbroken link between conduct and consequence. The 'but for' rule is used to help out in these cases as shown in the following.

Legal case: *R v White (1910)*

This case involved a son attempting to poison his mother but the mother died of a heart attack unconnected to the potassium cyanide put into her drink. The son was not convicted of murder, as it was not the defendant's act that caused the consequence despite his ambition to see her dead. He was, however, found guilty of attempted murder. The 'but for' rule would not apply because the woman would have died anyway.

It may be proved that conduct caused the consequence but there may be no criminal liability. For some cases the issue of remoteness comes in, in other words, the act is too distant from the consequence. For others there may have been an intervening act by a third party, which breaks the chain of causation. This is known as *novus actus interveniens*.

Cause in law

Contribution

To prove legal cause the defendant must contribute to the consequences: it must be more than minimal but it does not have to be substantial. It may also be the case that others were involved but the defendant may still be held liable.

If an act leads to a consequence, the defendant may be found guilty even if the act is not the main contribution to the consequence. The act may even amount to less than the main contribution. Consider the following case.

Legal case: *R v Pagett (1983)*

This case illustrated conduct and consequence working together. Pagett used his girlfriend as a shield when firing a gun at the police. The police returned fire and killed the girlfriend. Pagett was found guilty of her unlawful death even though it was police bullets that killed her. It was stated that holding the girl in front of him and firing at the police were both unlawful and dangerous acts that contributed to the *actus reus*. His contribution was not the main cause of her death but she would not have been put into the position 'but for' him. He was found guilty of her manslaughter.

5 Factors affecting chain of causation

Even if secondary events take place, which seem to make matters worse, the courts may show a degree of firmness as shown in the following case.

Legal case: *R v Smith (1959)*

A British soldier in Germany named Smith stabbed another soldier. The injured victim was dropped twice on the journey to hospital and then received inadequate medical care. The court ruled that despite the appalling treatment the victim had received at the hands of the medical unit, Smith was still guilty of the death. The events did not break the chain of causation.

In the above case Smith began the chain of events that led to the death of the victim and the intervening acts did not break this chain of events according to the court. It may be said that courts are fairly reluctant to allow a defendant 'off' due to intervening acts breaking the chain of causation. The following important case reflects this tendency of the courts.

Legal case: *R v Blaue (1975)*

An eighteen year old girl was attacked and stabbed in the lung. She was taken to hospital but refused a blood transfusion due to her religious beliefs. The attacker, Blaue, was convicted of manslaughter on the grounds of diminished responsibility. He appealed against this conviction on the grounds that it was the girl's own act that caused her death. The appeal was dismissed and the judge stated offenders 'must take their victim as they find them'. The intervening act did not break the chain of causation.

Group activity

Taking your victim as you find them is also known as 'the thin skull rule'. The criminal cannot blame the victim for having some sort of weakness that results in a more serious injury than intended. Do you think this is unfair on the defendant?

A number of other cases involving medical intervention illustrate the court's general views.

Legal case: *R v Cheshire (1991)*

The attacker shot the victim in the leg and stomach, wounding him seriously. The victim was taken to hospital where he developed complications from his medical treatment and died eight weeks later. The Court of Appeal stated that only 'in the most extraordinary and unusual case' would medical treatment be regarded as the cause of the victim's death. The intervening act did not break the chain of causation.

Medical advances have posed problems for the courts. It is now possible to keep people 'alive' for long periods of time although it might be fair to say that it is only their body rather than their mind that is still functioning. A case that clarified this difficult area of law came in 1981.

Legal case: *R v Malcherek (1981)*

A husband stabbed his wife repeatedly and she was put on a life-support machine. The medical team switched off the life-support machine when it was decided that recovery of the victim was not going to happen. Malcherek put forward the defence that it was the action of turning off the machine that caused death. The Court of Appeal decided that the intervening act did not break the chain of causation and that Malcherek was responsible for the death and not the doctors. The Court of Appeal went on to say that they thought the argument that Malcherek had not caused the death was 'bizarre'.

Foreseeability

The defendant will be found guilty of all events they could reasonably have foreseen from their actions. If, for example, a man with a gun is threatening a victim and the victim, whilst trying to escape, is seriously injured, the defendant will be held responsible. They should have foreseen that this was a possibility of their actions.

Intervening acts and a break in the chain

As seen, there have been several cases where the chain of events was not broken despite people intervening. The chain of causation can be broken by the following circumstances:

- actions of a third party (not the victim or the defendant)
- the victim's own contribution to events
- a natural event that could not be foreseen.

Quick revision questions

1 Define criminal law.

2 Define *actus reus*.

3 What elements make up the *actus reus*?

4 Why was *R v Gibbins and Proctor (1918)* important as far as omissions were concerned?

5 Give two examples where statutory law has placed a duty of care on the defendant.

6 How is the 'but for' rule used with *actus reus*?

7 What does 'taking your victim as you find them' mean?

8 How did the legal case *R v Malcherek (1981)* explore the issue of causation?

9 Give three circumstances that break the rules of causation.

10 Explain foreseeability.

Exam question

Explain the importance of *actus reus* in criminal law illustrating your answer with relevant cases. [50 marks]

Exam answer guide

Knowledge and understanding [20 marks]

- ✓ Define *actus reus* – the guilty act
- ✓ Outline need for proof of voluntary positive acts
- ✓ Mention elements such as conduct, consequence and circumstance
- ✓ Outline importance of omissions such as *actus reus* and need for duty of care – Quote cases such as *R v Gibbins and Proctor (1918)*, *R v Pittwood (1902)* and *R v Miller (1983)*
- ✓ Give details of causation (*sine qua non*) by quoting *R v White (1910)* and *R v Pagett (1983)* and intervening events by quoting *R v Smith (1959)*, *R v Blaue (1975)*, *R v Cheshire (1991)* and *R v Malcherek (1981)*

Analysis and evaluation [25 marks]

- ✓ Discuss central importance of a guilty act and omission to the commission of an offence
- ✓ Discuss issues that arise from each of the quoted cases. For example whether decisions in *R v Smith (1959)* and *R v Malcherek (1981)* cases were correct
- ✓ Discuss the issue of 'no need to help victim in trouble' the (good Samaritan issue) Should this be changed?
- ✓ Comment on differences between cause in fact and cause in law
- ✓ Evaluate fairness to the defendant when intervening factors make a situation worse
- ✓ Comment on actions of a third party and victims own contribution to events.

Presentation [5 marks]

- ✓ Structure your work in a logical and well-planned way. Employ good quality and clear English in your writing. Make use of punctuation and correct spelling in your answers.

Intent – Direc/ obliq
Recki: – sub/obj)
Sit – abs/re?
Negligend :

Mens rea

Key points

1 General principles of intention
2 Direct intent, oblique intent and foresight of consequences
3 Specific intent and basic intent
4 Subjective recklessness and objective recklessness
5 Gross negligence
6 Transferred malice

Why do I need to know about *mens rea*?

For most crimes it is not enough just to prove that the person committed the guilty act, there is also a need to show a guilty state of mind as well. *Mens rea* means 'guilty mind'. There is a strong link between the last unit on *actus reus* (the guilty act) and this one on *mens rea*. Both are required to be proved before a person is found guilty of a criminal offence. There are some fascinating cases used in the exploration of these ideas so make sure you know and learn them. Think about the people involved and the fairness of the situations they find themselves in. You can even apply these ideas in day-to-day events in your own life. Get familiar with the concepts!

A criminal offence consists of two parts

1 General principles of intention

The *mens rea* of an offence is the guilty mind associated with that offence: it involves the mental elements involved in a crime. Both the guilty act and the guilty mind must be present if a person is to be convicted of a criminal offence. *Actus reus* and *mens rea* are required.

The shop where goods may have been stolen might have the incident recorded on CCTV. They may possess the videotape and take it to court as proof of the defendant's guilt. The court, however, must be satisfied that the person had it in their mind to take the goods without paying for them. Possible defences might include:

- a medical condition or medication, which lowers your ability to concentrate
- fatigue, which may increase absent mindedness
- stress caused by family or work problems
- old age
- pre-menstrual syndrome (PMS).

The court may take these factors into consideration when deciding whether a person deliberately attempted to steal from the shop. These are known as extenuating circumstances, situations that may temporarily affect a person's judgement.

Legal case: *R v Madeley (1990)*

Richard Madeley, the presenter of the popular TV show *Richard and Judy*, found himself in court charged with shoplifting from a major supermarket. The store had witnesses and other evidence to 'prove' the guilty act took place. The court accepted the star's defence that overwork and stress had led him to forget to pay for the goods. The *actus reus* was proved but not the *mens rea*.

Each criminal offence has its own *mens rea*. The minimum level of *mens rea* for that offence must be proved if the prosecution is to win its case.

Group activity: *R v Hart (2002)*

The driver of a Land Rover skidded off the motorway and ended up on railway tracks. The vehicle caused a major train crash at Selby killing ten people. Mr Hart was charged with dangerous driving. He had been on the Internet/phone for most of the night but maintained that he was normally competent to drive under such conditions. He was found guilty and jailed for five years. The maximum for dangerous driving would have been ten years.

1 Should Mr Hart have been jailed?

2 Did *mens rea* exist in this case?

Coincidence of *actus reus* and *mens rea*

When *actus reus*, the guilty act, and *mens rea*, the guilty mind, come together and both can be proved there is a criminal offence. The two must come together or be close to one another in time.

Legal case: *R v Taaffe (1983)*

Mr Taaffe was intercepted by customs and his car was searched. Small packages of cannabis were found. When questioned, Mr Taaffe revealed that he thought it was money being illegally imported into the UK against currency regulations. This was not a crime at the time even though he thought it was. He had the *mens rea*, theoretically, for an *actus reus* that was not a guilty act. He was convicted of illegally importing cannabis. The Court of Appeal and the House of Lords both confirmed that without the *mens rea* for importing cannabis no offence had been committed. The *actus reus* was present since the drugs had been imported, but not the *mens rea*.

The following case explores some of the issues of coincidence of *actus reus* and *mens rea*.

Legal case: *Fagan v Metropolitan Police Commissioner (1968)*

Police Constable David Morris observed Vincent Fagan driving erratically. The police officer directed Fagan towards the kerb and stood a couple of metres in front of the car. Fagan parked the car tyre on the police officer's foot. The police officer asked Fagan to move the car but Fagan told the police officer he would have to wait. Fagan was again asked to move and eventually did. Fagan stated he moved onto the policeman's foot accidentally, that he had no intention and did not behave recklessly. If this were so there would be no *mens rea*. However, Fagan continued to keep his car tyre on the policeman's foot. If an act continues then the *mens rea* can occur at a later time. Refusing to move when told was seen as the *mens rea*.

The Fagan case involves what is known as the Continuing Act Theory. The *mens rea* was not present at the beginning of the *actus reus* but appeared during it. The eventual coincidence of *actus reus* and *mens rea* produced a criminal offence.

2 Direct intent, oblique intent and foresight of consequences

When a person desires the result of their actions it is known as direct intent. If a person traces the movements of their victim, plans when to attack them and carries out an attack that results in the consequences they had planned, this would be called direct intent.

If the person carries out the attack but produces another consequence that they did not intend but knew was likely to occur, this is known as oblique intent. In other words, if the attacker plans to murder his victim by exploding a bomb under their car and as a side effect destroys nearby houses then the oblique intent is the demolition of the houses. This was very likely to happen if an explosive device was detonated in a street full of houses.

From these two issues of direct and oblique intent comes the question of foresight of consequences. This is an important aspect of cases where the court has to decide matters of intention. The key questions that arise are:

● Does the defendant know that their actions may cause a particular consequence even if they do not want that consequence?

● Can foresight of consequences be taken as evidence of intention?

There are a number of interlinked cases where this concept has been explored and developed. The courts were clearly not entirely happy with the earlier cases and tried to improve the clarity of the argument in each subsequent case.

Legal case: *R v Maloney (1985)*, *R v Hancock and Shankland (1986)*, *R v Nedrick (1986)* and *R v Woolin (1998)*

R v Maloney (1985)

The defendant shot and killed his stepfather in a 'game' that went tragically wrong. Both were drunk and trying to decide who had the fastest draw. It was decided by the court that foresight of consequences was only evidence that could be used to decide intent, it did not prove intent.

R v Hancock and Shankland (1986)

Two defendants attempting to intimidate a fellow worker during a strike threw a concrete block from a bridge onto the victim's passing car, killing the victim. The court focused on the probability of the consequence when using it as evidence to decide intent.

R v Nedrick (1986)

The defendant poured petrol through the letterbox of a house to frighten the woman living there. The result was the death of a child. From this particular case two questions emerged, which it was hoped would help clarify the intent.

1 Was the result a virtual certainty of the action?

2 Did the defendant realize that the result would be a virtual certainty of his action?

Unless the jury was happy that the answer to both questions was 'yes' they could not assume the defendant's intention.

> *R v Woolin (1998)*
>
> A defendant threw his three-month-old baby at his pram. The baby missed the pram and crashed into the wall, dying of his injuries. The courts were not happy with the two questions used in the Nedrick case but still wanted the jury to 'find' intention but only if they thought the result was a virtual certainty from the actions of the defendant and that they felt he knew this to be the case.

The key points that come from the above cases seem to be:

- foresight of consequences cannot be read as intention

- the more likely the consequence, the more likely the intention.

The definitions of intent that are being used by the courts are very complex. Do not be put off by these cases: they are difficult for most lawyers, judges and juries, not to mention students.

3 Specific intent and basic intent

Specific intent

Specific intent is also known as intent and it is the highest level of *mens rea*. In other words, the defendant must have clearly had this in his mind and not committed the offence by accident or carelessness, it must have been his unmistakeable goal. It must be proved by the prosecution in cases of murder and grievous bodily harm with intent.

Put legally, specific intent involves proving whether a person committed an act with purpose of the consequence or had the knowledge that the consequence was virtually certain to occur as a result of their actions (see *R v Mohan (1976)*). The concept is seen more fully in the following case.

Legal case: *Hyam v DPP (1974)*

Pearl Hyam was jealous of Mrs Booth as she thought that the woman was about to get married to her former boyfriend. To scare her off she set fire to her rival's house. Mrs Booth escaped but two of her children were killed. Pearl Hyam was charged with manslaughter, but was she guilty of murder? Did she intend to kill the two children? If she were only guilty of manslaughter, what would it have taken to prove the *mens rea* for murder?

Crimes of specific intent are difficult to prove by the prosecution since the level of *mens rea* is very high. Crimes of specific intent include:

- murder

- wounding with intent

- causing grievous bodily harm
- theft
- robbery
- burglary.

Basic intent

For crimes of basic intent the prosecution can find the defendant guilty if they prove either intention **or** recklessness. This makes their job easier since recklessness is a lower level of *mens rea*. Crimes of basic intent include:

- involuntary manslaughter — Unlawful m/s
    Gross negligence m/s
- rape
- wounding
- inflicting grievous bodily harm
- actual bodily harm
- assault and battery
- criminal damage.

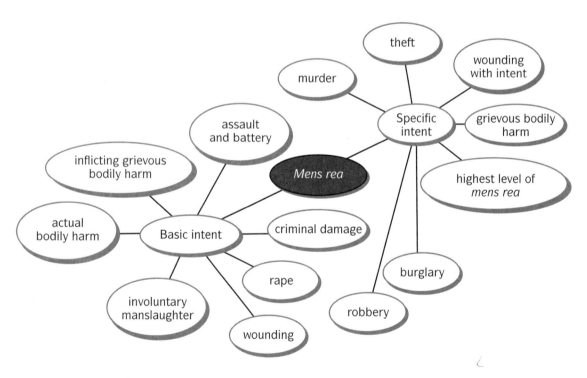

Mens rea

4 Subjective recklessness and objective recklessness

Two important tests are used in law, the subjective test and the objective test.

The subjective test

The subjective test considers what was in the **defendants mind**. Would the defendant have realised what they were doing was wrong? This test does not consider what the ordinary person would think.

The objective test

The objective test considers what was in the **ordinary persons mind**. Would an ordinary person have realised the thing done was wrong? This test does not consider what the defendant was thinking.

Two examples to consider for subjective and objective

1 The subjective test might consider what was in the mind of someone who was taking drinks from a bar whilst working as a barman. If they did not believe it was wrong because they thought everyone one else was doing it they might have committed no offence. The jury would consider what was in their mind when they were doing this.

2 The objective test might be used when an ordinary person was asked whether they thought driving through a very busy area with lots of schools and shops at high speed was dangerous. They might think it was dangerous even though a defendant might honestly think it was perfectly safe. They would probably be found guilty of an offence.

Group activity

List three examples of when a subjective test could be used and three examples of when an objective test could be used.

Subjective recklessness

Subjective recklessness involves the taking of an unjustifiable risk. The defendant recognizes that there is a risk but continues nonetheless with his actions.

Subjective recklessness is a lower level of *mens rea* than specific intention. The accused is judged from what he believed to be the case. Did the defendant realize that what he was doing involved some risk of harm to someone else? It is linked to crimes such as common assault, actual bodily harm and malicious wounding, or most crimes that include recklessness as the *mens rea*.

The following case highlighted the issues around the idea of subjective recklessness.

Legal case: *R v Cunningham (1957)*

The defendant tore a gas meter from the wall of a cellar in order to steal the money contained inside. The gas leaked from the exposed pipes through the cellar wall and drifted up into the next house where it injured a woman. The defendant did nothing to stop the gas escape. The word 'maliciously' was used in the case to try and convict the defendant and became defined as either:

- intending the harm that resulted, or
- being reckless and realizing there was a possibility that the harm would result.

The second point came to be known as 'subjective recklessness'.

There was no assumption in the above case that Cunningham was trying to injure the woman next door. The court, however, did assume that he should have realized that his actions may have led to an injury but continued with his actions anyway. The defendant behaved recklessly in taking an unjustified risk and he, the subject, should have known better, hence subjective recklessness. The case is so often quoted that subjective recklessness is often called 'Cunningham recklessness'.

Objective recklessness

Objective recklessness is used where the defendant does not realize that there is a risk of certain undesirable consequences but an ordinary person would have realized the risk. As a result, this is seen as a lower level of *mens rea* than subjective recklessness, where the person was assumed to understand the risks involved.

This test of what should have been realized employs the idea of what an ordinary, prudent person would have realized. The following case is the classic illustration of this issue and the legal term is often called 'Caldwell recklessness' after the defendant, Caldwell.

Legal case: *MPC v Caldwell (1982)*

Caldwell was employed by a hotel and held a grievance against the owner. During a drunken episode he set fire to the hotel. He was charged with arson under the Criminal Damage Act 1971 and also with reckless behaviour leading to the endangering of life. The key point of this the case was not whether Caldwell realized that this was reckless behaviour, but whether an 'ordinary, prudent person' would have realized that it was reckless. The objective test was being employed.

The Caldwell case attempted to define the word 'recklessness'. A result of the case was a sharper definition of the term 'reckless', which was now to be considered:

- the defendant has given no thought to the consequences of his actions, or
- he realizes the risk from his actions but continues all the same.

5 Gross negligence

There are degrees of negligence in life. Failure to put a warning sign on a wet floor may be classified as negligence if a person slips and hurts themselves; failure to close the doors of a ship as it leaves harbour with hundreds of passengers on board may also be classified as negligence. Clearly, the second case is of a different order to the first. If there is a consideration that criminal charges are relevant, the negligence is now known as gross negligence. There are some key cases that illustrate the issue.

Legal case: *R v Adomako (1994)*

An anaesthetist did not realize that the oxygen supply to a patient in his care had been cut off. The patient's brain was damaged and he died. It is the jury who decides whether this amounted to gross negligence. The judge said this offence was 'supremely a jury question' given the risk of death involved in such a breach of duty.

In *R v Adomako (1994)* the House of Lords gave a list of what might be considered gross negligence:

- lack of concern to the possibility of an obvious injury
- foresight of the risk but a resolve to still run that risk — *forsaw it but went out to do it anyway*
- foresight of the risk coupled with a weak attempt to avoid it that still amounts to a high degree of negligent behaviour
- inattention to an important matter that relates to the defendant's duty of care.

All of these judgements are left to the jury to decide.

6 Transferred malice

If a person commits an unlawful act against one person that actually injures another, can he get away with the unplanned injury? The courts think not and have developed a term called 'transferred malice'. For example:

If person A intends to run down pedestrian B in his car but accidentally crashes into pedestrian C, the driver person A will be held responsible for C's injuries. Liability cannot be denied as the *mens rea* is transferred. *R v Latimer (1886)* illustrates the concept of transferred malice.

Legal case: *R v Latimer (1886)*

When Latimer attempted to strike his intended victim he missed and hit a woman nearby who was seriously injured. He was held liable for her injury as the *mens rea* was transferred from his intended victim to his actual victim.

The offences involved in transferred malice must be of the same nature. Latimer could be charged with injuring the woman as he had intended to injure his original victim. If they are different, a case could still be made using recklessness as the *mens rea* of the offence. So if Latimer had broken a nearby window as he struck his victim, he might be said to be behaving recklessly. The leading case of *R v Pembliton (1874)* underlines the need for similar offences to be involved if transferred malice is to be proved.

Legal case: *R v Pembliton (1874)*

Pembliton was involved in a brawl outside a pub. He threw a stone at one of his fighting partners but missed and the stone went through a large window. The court decided that the *mens rea* was related to assault but the *actus reus* related to criminal damage. He was found guilty of neither.

There is draft statutory provision for this situation. If the defendant has knowledge or intention that their actions may lead to a similar offence against a person other than the intended victim, this in itself will be an offence.

Legislation

Section 17(2) Offences Against the Person Bill 1998

A person's intention, or awareness of risk, that his act will cause a result in relation to a person capable of being the victim of the offence must be treated as an intention or (as the case may be) awareness of a risk that his act will cause that result in relation to any other person affected by his act.

'In relation to any other person affected by his act' refers to the unintended victim.

Quick revision questions

1 Describe *mens rea*.

2 What is the relationship between *mens rea* and *actus reus*?

3 What are specific intent, direct intent and oblique intent?

4 What is subjective and objective recklessness?

5 How do the cases of *R v Cunningham (1957)* and *MPC v Caldwell (1982)* illustrate subjective and objective recklessness?

6 Give three examples of gross negligence.

7 Who decides whether an offence constitutes gross negligence?

8 What is transferred malice?

9 What does the case *Taaffe (1983)* show about the coincidence of *mens rea* and *actus reus*?

10 What does the case of *Fagan v Metropolitan Police Commissioner (1968)* show about the coincidence of *mens rea* and *actus reus*?

Exam question

Comment on the importance of *mens rea* to criminal offences. How do the courts examine this concept? [50 marks]

Exam answer guide

Knowledge and understanding [20 marks]

✓ Define *mens rea* and general principles of intention

✓ Outline the need for coincidence of *actus reus* and *mens rea*. Quote *Fagan and Metropolitan Police Commissioner (1968)*

✓ Define direct intent and oblique intent and foresight of consequence

✓ Distinguish between basic and specific intent

✓ Outline subjective and objective recklessness. Define each test. Quote *R v Cunningham (1957)* and *MPC v Caldwell (1982)*

✓ Outline gross negligence using *R v Adomako (1994)* and transferred malice using *R v Latimer (1886)*

Analysis and evaluation [25 marks]

✓ Distinguish between direct and oblique intent and assess cases used to develop the idea of evidence of intention such as *R v Moloney (1985)*, *R v Hancock* and *Shankland (1986)*, *R v Nedrick (1986)* and *R v Woolin (1998)*

✓ Analyse the importance of subjective and objective reckless in determining necessary *mens rea*. Assess the effectiveness of *R v Cunningham (1957)* and *Metropolitan Police Commissioner v Caldwell (1982)*

✓ Assess the list of what might be considered gross negligence by the House of Lords in *R v Adomako (1994)*

✓ Give your view on the issue of transferred malice via *R v Latimer (1886)*

Presentation [5 marks]

✓ Structure your work in a logical and well planned way. Employ good quality and clear English in your writing. Make use of punctuation and correct spelling in your answers.

Strict liability

Key points

1 Strict liability and absolute liability
2 Strict liability and statutory law
3 Strict liability and the courts
4 Reasons for and against strict liability
5 Due diligence defences

Why do I need to know about strict liability?

Strict liability puts another perspective on the link between *actus reus* and *mens rea*. You will need to understand the situations where limited *mens rea* or even no *mens rea* can still produce a successful prosecution. Strict liability remains a

Strict liability

controversial area because it does not require a deliberate intention to commit an offence, fault does not have to be proved. The areas covered by strict liability include day-to-day activities we all use or take part in. Questions on strict liability require knowledge of relevant legal cases. This knowledge is also an important aid in understanding and applying this concept.

1 Strict liability and absolute liability

Strict liability

Strict liability involves offences where the *mens rea* to some elements of the *actus reus* do not have to be proved. The defendant will be found guilty even if he did not mean to commit the offence. The defendant will be found guilty even if he did not have a guilty mind for all of his actions.

The reasons for strict liability are:

- it would be impossible to ever prove the *mens rea* of the defendant in some types of offences

- there is a greater benefit to the public even if it may appear a little unfair on the defendant

- the consequences of the offence would be so serious that a very firm line must be taken

- having such an offence makes people extra careful in their behaviour.

Normally the prosecution must prove the defendant had a guilty mind (*mens rea*) for the guilty act (*actus reus*). The following case illustrates the accused committing an act where the prosecution does not have to prove the *mens rea* for at least some elements of the *actus reus*.

> ## Legal case: *R v Prince (1875)*
>
> The defendant was found guilty under the Offences Against the Person Act 1861 when he took a sixteen-year-old girl 'out of the possession of her father'. He believed the girl to be eighteen. The prosecution did not have to prove that the defendant did or did not know the girl was only sixteen, only that he had taken her from her father. Strict liability applied with regard to the age of the girl and the defendant was found guilty.

The types of offences that are covered by strict liability are often ones that relate to public health or safety such as food quality, the condition of the cars that are driven, speeding offences and parking violations. It would be very difficult to prove *mens rea* in such cases and so this is dispensed with as a matter of public policy. The benefits seem to outweigh the costs.

The following case illustrates the seriousness of strict liability cases and the pressures put upon professionals to take the utmost care in the course of their work.

Legal case: *Pharmaceutical Society of Great Britain v Storkwain (1986)*

The pharmacist in this case supplied a restricted drug to an addict on a forged prescription. He was found guilty of an offence despite no fault on his part. Strict liability was relevant since he was the one who supplied the drug.

Absolute liability

Some offences do not require any element of *mens rea* to be proved. This is known as absolute liability. The only thing that needs proving is the *actus reus*.

Legal case: *Winzar v Chief Constable of Kent (1983)*

The defendant was taken to the hospital on a stretcher but ejected because he was drunk. Later he was found in a seat inside the hospital. The police were called and the police car was parked outside on the hospital forecourt, the defendant was carried by the police to the car. Winzar was found guilty of being drunk on the highway (hospital forecourt). Absolute liability meant he was still guilty even though he had not put himself on the highway.

Legal case: *R v Larsonneur (1932)*

The defendant was deported from the Republic of Ireland under police guard and was found in the UK. She was arrested at Holyhead when the boat arrived and charged with being in the UK without permission. She was eventually convicted of the offence even though she had not voluntarily travelled to the UK.

Group activity

Comment on the Winzar and Larsonneur cases. Do you think it was fair that both were convicted of offences when essentially it was the police who put them into the situation in which they found themselves?

2 Strict liability and statutory law

Most of the strict liability offences are statutory offences. These offences were mostly passed during the nineteenth and twentieth centuries as business and commerce started to expand and there were worries about public safety in a number of areas including the following.

The sale of food to the public

This included shops and restaurants. The way food was produced and processed had changed and the possibility for contamination and the poisoning of members of the public had increased. Even with this legislation the UK has had problems in recent times with BSE, listeria, and even metal poisoning in bottled water.

Sale of goods to the public

Businesses are not allowed to falsely describe their goods in advertisements or put misleading prices on their goods in the shops. The Trade Descriptions Act 1968 is a key part of legislation, keeping the standards of service to customers up to scratch.

Health and safety

One of the most important pieces of legislation in recent years is the Health and Safety at Work Act 1974. This forces employers to operate a safe working environment with regular safety checks and the provision of safety equipment and training. Even with these provisions many thousands of people are injured and hundreds killed every year at work.

Presumption of *mens rea*

For most criminal cases there is a presumption that the prosecution must prove that the accused had some level of *mens rea*. Courts on the other hand are prepared to see the legislation as strict liability and disregard the presumption of *mens rea* if the statute states this to be the case or implies it through the wording of the legislation. This is an example of statutory interpretation.

Legal case: *Callow v Tillstone (1900)*

A butcher had contacted a vet to ask his professional opinion on a piece of meat. The vet stated that the meat was fit for consumption but this was later found to be untrue. Although the butcher had gone to some trouble to verify the state of the meat he was still found guilty.

The Callow case highlights one of the problems of strict liability. It was presumed that *mens rea* was present even though the butcher had taken reasonable steps to avoid committing an offence of this nature.

When looking at strict liability cases some elements of the *actus reus* may require no *mens rea*, whilst for other elements of the *actus reus* there may be a requirement for *mens rea* such as intention or negligence.

Legal case: *Sweet v Parsley (1970)*

Ms Sweet was a schoolteacher who let rooms in her home to students. The students had the property to themselves for the most part, although Ms Sweet had a room in the house that she sometimes used on occasional overnight stops. The students were users of cannabis and other drugs. Ms Sweet was convicted under the Dangerous Drugs Act 1965 of managing premises for the use of illegal drugs. The case eventually went to the House of Lords where she won her appeal against her conviction. The Law Lords decided that direct knowledge of illegal drug taking on the premises was required.

A more recent case, *B v DPP (2000)*, is one where the issue of strict liability was again highlighting some of the difficulties involved in this legal concept, and also underlining concerns if strict liability was not used in certain cases. *B v DPP (2000)* goes against the trend for assuming a strict liability.

Legal case: *B v DPP (2000)*

The defendant was a fifteen-year-old boy at the time of the offence, and the victim a thirteen-year-old girl. The defendant had committed an illegal sexual act with the girl but he claimed that he thought she was fourteen or even older. Magistrates hearing the case decided that strict liability applied and convicted the defendant. The Divisional Court supported the magistrates but the House of Lords eventually quashed the conviction. It ruled that *mens rea* was required as to the age of the child. There would have to be an intention to molest the thirteen year old or recklessness as to whether she was underage or not. This could then be linked to the *actus reus* for a conviction.

Group activity

Using the case of *B v DPP (2000)*, explore the issues surrounding the use of strict liability in such legal areas. Look at the possible consequences if strict liability was not used and consider the position of the defendant if it is used.

Strict liability

3 Strict liability and the courts

Judges have not been particularly interested in creating strict liability precedents. Very few common law offences do not require *mens rea* and the few that do exist include the following.

Criminal libel

Editors of newspapers may be held strictly responsible for libellous articles that are published with or without their knowledge.

Blasphemous libel

This common law offence is once more a topical issue since the attacks on the World Trade Centre on 11 September 2001. The government has attempted to bring in changes to the law of blasphemy so that it includes Muslims and people of other faiths. Until now the common law offence of blasphemy has only covered Christians. A moral campaigner called Mrs Mary Whitehouse last used it successfully.

> ### Legal case: *Lemon v Gay News Ltd (1979)*
>
> *Gay News*, a publication of Gay News Ltd, published an illustrated poem that described sexual abuses of Christ after his crucifixion. Mrs Mary Whitehouse brought a private prosecution against the editor, for publishing this material. The publication of the blasphemous words meant strict liability under this common law.

Criminal contempt of court

Contempt of court is a common law that covers behaviour that interferes with the running of the court system. It can include unruly behaviour in court such as shouting or being drunk, disobeying the judgement of the court or anything that obstructs the court's work. The old common law of contempt has changed due to the Contempt of Court Act 1981, but it remains a strict liability offence.

4 Reasons for and against strict liability

This area of law is controversial as defendants often feel unfairly treated by the courts. There are also important social and policy reasons to keep strict liability offences.

Reasons for keeping strict liability

- The public are protected and reassured that businesses and organizations are striving to make their services clean and safe.
- Businesses and organizations are 'encouraged' to have high standards, which benefit the community as a whole.
- Businesses and organizations know exactly where they stand with respect to the law.
- Courts can deal with offences more quickly since the *mens rea* does not have to be proved.

- The main offences are statutory and relate to matters of public concern such as pollution, road safety and food safety. Important policy messages are sent out through strict liability offences.

Reasons against keeping strict liability

- The defendant may not consider absence of *mens rea* fair.
- It might not act as a deterrent as most businesses are probably keen to have high standards anyway.
- People who otherwise take great care with their actions and have taken all reasonable steps to avoid breaking the law could find themselves in court facing criminal charges.

5 Due diligence defences

Due diligence means that the defendant has acted on mistaken facts and not that the defendant has taken all reasonable steps to avoid the offence. The defendant must prove due diligence defences. In some cases the defence may only be possible if both elements are present, that is,

- a third party supplied false information and

- the defendant took all reasonable steps to avoid the offence.

Section 24 of the Trade Descriptions Act 1968 allows such a defence. Although there are due diligence defences in a number of statutory areas, the courts have not followed this lead in common law cases.

Quick revision questions

1 What are strict liability offences? *Actus reus*

2 Why do strict liability offences exist?

3 Why is *R v Prince (1875)* an important case?

4 What are the key areas covered by strict liability statutory offences?

5 How does a case of absolute liability arise? *= involuntary strict liability → act is invol Larsenov winza*

6 Name three common law strict liability offences.

7 What does the *Callow v Tillstone (1900)* case highlight? *no due dilig*

8 Give the key details of *Sweet v Parsley (1970)*. *- Show*

9 Give three reasons for and against strict liability. *→ no mainenum*

10 What is a due diligence defence?

→ Criminal libel
→ blasphemous libel
→ criminal contempt of court
- Public nusane.

On balance strict liability delivers more good than harm. Discuss. [50 marks]

Exam answer guide

Knowledge and understanding [20 marks]

✓ Define strict and absolute liability

✓ Give examples of situations that are covered by strict liability and absolute liability

✓ Quote cases such as *R v Prince (1875)*, *Pharmaceutical Society of Great Britain v Storkwain (1986)*, *Winzar v Chief Constable of Kent (1983)* and *R v Larsonneur (1932)*

Analysis and evaluation [25 marks]

✓ Assess need for strict and absolute liability using cases quoted. Refer to public policy issues that are supported by decisions in courts

✓ Give your opinion on whether gains outweigh costs. Show reasons for and against and comment on your overall position

✓ Evaluate the position of due diligence defences. Should these limit liability or would this destroy clear message of strict and absolute liability?

Presentation [5 marks]

✓ Structure your work in a logical and well planned way. Employ good quality and clear English in your writing. Make use of punctuation and correct spelling in your answers.

Callow v Tilstow
Absolute liability – R v Larsonneur 1933
            R v Constable of Kent 1983

common / statute / ─
                    → Lemon v Gay News
                      Blasphemous libel

presumption of mens rea = R v Sweet v Parsley 1970
                          B (a minor) v DPP 2000

Rebutting of m.s. Gammon (Hong Kong)
        – statute law – "Wood v Alphacell 'caus?'
        – True or quasi crime – Reg – Gammon
                        True – B(a minor)

        – size of punishment

UNIT 4

Participation

Key points

1 *Actus reus* for the liability of an accessory
2 *Mens rea* for the liability of an accessory
3 Aid and abet
4 Counsel
5 Procure

Why do I need to know about participation?

Those who commit the principal offence are known as perpetrators or principal offenders. There may be those who encourage and support these offenders – these are known as secondary offenders, accomplices or accessories. This unit looks at the involvement of secondary offenders and the various ways they can

Aid and abet

assist in the commission of a crime. This unit can be used to underline and develop your understanding of the first two units in this module on *actus reus* and *mens rea*.

1 *Actus reus* for the liability of an accessory

Perpetrators and accessories

Those who directly commit a crime are known as perpetrators or principals. Others, called accessories, accomplices or secondary offenders, help the perpetrators to commit their crimes. Accessories to a crime might include:

- those who give inside information on when money will be available on a premises

- those who keep lookout in case the police arrive

- those who act as getaway drivers

- those who provide support for criminal activities.

The question of how the courts should view the actions of accessories is included in Section 8 of the Accessories and Abettors Act 1861.

Legislation

Section 8 Accessories and Abettors Act 1861

Whosoever shall aid, abet, counsel or procure the commission of any crime is liable to be tried, indicted and punished as a principal offender.

The wording of the legislation gives considerable leeway to the courts in deciding how much of the blame should be apportioned to the accessory. They may have played a significant role in which case they will face a similar treatment as the perpetrator. On the other hand, their role may have been so minor that the court discharges them.

Innocent parties

A person who commits the *actus reus* may not have the *mens rea* for the crime. It may be the case in some circumstances that another person has encouraged them to commit the offence who will then assume responsibility for the crime. Young children have at times been schooled in the art of shoplifting and their age means an absence of criminal responsibility. This responsibility falls instead on the parent, guardian or accessory who encouraged them to break the law.

Perpetrators with no *mens rea*

Even if the perpetrator has no *mens rea* the accessory may still attract liability. If, for example, a person is threatened with violence to commit an offence, they might not be held liable due to the defence of duress: the accessory would attract liability in this case. It is important to bear in mind that an *actus reus* must have happened if there is to be this transfer of responsibility from the perpetrator onto the secondary party.

There are a number of cases that illustrate this point.

Legal case: *Thornton v Mitchell (1940)*

A bus driver asked his conductor to reverse the bus and as the conductor was not paying attention, two people were injured. The driver was acquitted as he had not been careless and as a result no *actus reus* could be committed. The consequence of this was that the conductor was not guilty of the *actus reus* as a secondary party because the *actus reus* was non-existent.

Legal case: *R v Bourne (1952)*

The defendant had forced his wife to commit unlawful sexual acts with a dog. She was found not guilty using the defence of duress, as she was not the perpetrator. Bourne, however, was liable as a secondary party to the crime.

---

2 *Mens rea* for the liability of an accessory

The *mens rea* for accessories is:

- that they must have intended to assist or encourage the carrying out of the offence,
- and have knowledge or be reckless to the existence of the circumstances which produced the offence.

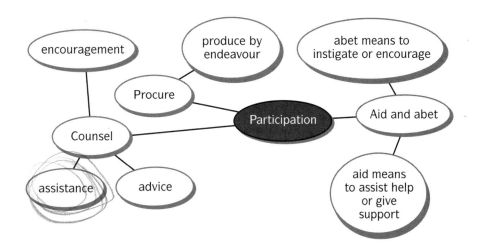

Participation

3 Aid and abet

These two words are often found together although they do have separate meanings:

- aid is to assist, help, or give support
- abet is to instigate or encourage.

The slightest encouragement could be classified as aiding and abetting, for example, a nod or the blinking of the eyes. If the encouragement is intentional then it can be classified as aiding and abetting. If aiding and abetting occurs at the time of the offence, it is this that distinguishes it from counselling.

Legal case: *R v Coney and others (1882)*

A bare-knuckle fight took place by the side of the road. Three defendants, who were watching but not encouraging the fighters, were prosecuted for aiding and abetting assault. The judge had told the jury that people, by their mere presence, could be seen as aiding and abetting the offence. The appeal court disagreed on two grounds:

1. Only intentional encouragement can be aiding and abetting.
2. Mere silence, standing by and watching an offence cannot necessarily be taken as aiding and abetting. A more active involvement is required.

Group activity

Should people be convicted by their mere presence at such an event as bare-knuckle fighting? Should there be an onus to stop such behaviour and should it be legally enforceable?

4 Counsel

Counselling amounts to the provision of:

- advice
- assistance
- encouragement.

These elements must occur before the commission of the offence. The time element marks this example of participation out from aiding and abetting, which happens at the time the offence is being committed.

5 Procure

Procure means to 'produce by endeavour'. In other words, the person accused of procuring an offence brings it about or causes it to happen. Look, for example, at the following case.

Legal case: *R v Millward (1994)*

Millward instructed an employee to drive a tractor and trailer onto a public road despite knowing that the vehicle was in a dangerous condition. The employee was unaware that the vehicle was dangerous and an accident was caused that resulted in a death. The employee was found not guilty of driving recklessly but Millward was found guilty of procuring the *actus reus* of the offence.

Millward clearly had a strong part in bringing about the death, as he was the one who ordered the employee onto the road knowing that the vehicle was unsafe. He was therefore charged with responsibility for the consequences. It must be noted that Millward did not 'endeavour' to produce the death, but there was a causal relationship between his reckless instructions and the actions of the perpetrator.

Quick revision questions

1 What is the difference between perpetrators and accessories?

2 What is another name for a secondary party?

3 What might accessories do to help in the commission of an offence?

4 What piece of statutory legislation covers accessories?

5 What is an innocent party?

6 Is an accessory liable if the perpetrator has no *mens rea*?

7 What is the *mens rea* for an accessory?

8 Define aid and abet.

9 What is counselling in the context of accessories?

10 What does procuring mean?

Exam question

Examine the ways in which a secondary party can help in the commission of a crime. [50 marks]

Exam answer guide

Knowledge and understanding [20 marks]

✓ Define participation and the various forms it takes

✓ Define secondary and principal offenders

✓ Outline the position of accessory when a perpetrator has no *mens rea*

✓ State the *mens rea* for accessories

✓ Distinguish between aid and abet, counsel and procure

Analysis and evaluation [25 marks]

✓ Analyse the need for legislation to charge accessories

✓ Assess the position of innocent parties

✓ Show links between participation and *actus reus* and *mens rea*

Presentation [5 marks]

✓ Structure your work in a logical and well-planned way. Employ good quality and clear English in your writing. Make use of punctuation and correct spelling in your answers.

UNIT 5

Preliminary crimes

Key points

1 Incitement
2 Conspiracy
3 Attempts

Why do I need to know about preliminary crimes?

There are three offences you must know in this area: incitement, conspiracy and attempts. Each has its own *actus reus* and *mens rea* and also its own legal and moral challenges. The three offences have grown up in response to the ways that crimes are committed in reality. The idea of a single criminal acting on their behalf and successfully achieving their criminal aims is only half of the story. When reading criminal case studies look out for the possibility of these three situations.

Incitement

encouraging

1 Incitement — common law

Incitement is a common law offence and it involves one person encouraging another to commit a crime. The offence itself does not need to be committed for incitement to be possible.

If the incitement is tried in a Crown Court then the judge has the power to sentence the inciter of a crime to a greater punishment than the principal offender. The message that is being sent out is that those who incite crime may at times be more blameworthy. This may be related to gang leaders who organize and send out criminals to commit offences without themselves committing the crime. The leader may possibly be seen as more guilty, as without their organizational skills the offence would probably never have happened.

Incitement to commit a summary offence will itself be tried in the Magistrates' Court. The sentence handed down will be no more than the maximum penalty for the incited crime.

Actus reus

The *actus reus* of incitement could be any of the following:

- advice
- financial payment
- threats
- persuasion
- pressure
- goading.

The incitement could be through writing, speech, or through signs.

A classic case of incitement was the following.

Legal case: *Invicta Plastics Ltd v Clare (1976)*

A company had produced a device that could detect police speed traps. It sent out a signal that located the radar used by the police. The company was found guilty of advertising a product in a magazine that would have led to an offence against the Wireless Telegraphy Act 1949. The advertisement actually informed the public that this would be illegal, but the court still believed that the advertisement constituted an offence of incitement to break the law.

The *mens rea* of incitement involves the defendant intending that the offence should take place and knowing the circumstances that constitute an offence.

2 Conspiracy — statutory law not common

Conspiracy is essentially, but not exclusively, covered by statutory law.

Legislation

Section 1(1) Criminal Law Act 1977

If a person agrees with any other person or persons that a course of conduct shall be pursued which, if the agreement is carried out in accordance with their intentions, will necessarily amount to or involve the commission of any offence or offences by one or more of the parties to the agreement, he is guilty of conspiracy.

Actus reus

The *actus reus* of conspiracy is agreement. As soon as those involved with the conspiracy have agreed on their intentions then the offence has occurred: it does not matter that the perpetrators do not carry through with their plan. Also, if one of the conspirators withdraws from the offence but the crime is committed by those remaining, the defence of withdrawal might not necessarily stand. There are defences against conspiracy, the main ones being:

- spouses are involved in the agreement
- persons under the age of criminal responsibility are involved in the agreement
- the victim is involved in the agreement.

The conspirators need to have communicated the agreement with at least one other conspirator. They do not have to have been in contact with all the conspirators.

Mens rea

The *mens rea* of conspiracy occurs when the parties:

- agree that a course of conduct shall be pursued,
- and if the agreement is carried out according to their intentions, will involve the commission of any offence or offences by one or more of the parties involved in the agreement.

The defendants will still be found guilty even if the offence they had planned would have been impossible. If, for example, a contract killing is arranged on a wife's husband but the husband dies of a heart attack the day before the assassination, the conspirators will still be found guilty providing the agreement has taken place between them.

The sentence is the maximum of the crime that was committed by the conspirators.

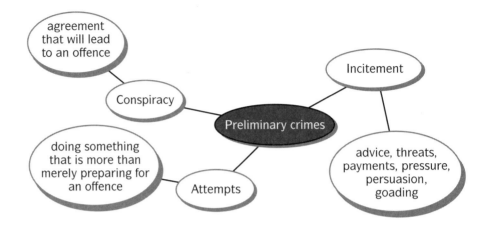

Preliminary crimes

3 Attempts

One of the best-known cases of attempt is the following.

Legal case: *R v White (1910)*

A son poisoned his mother with potassium cyanide, but before the poison could take effect and kill her she died of a heart attack. He was not liable for her death but was convicted of attempted murder rather than murder.

The issue raised in this case is an interesting one. Should an unsuccessful criminal benefit because of their bad luck or their own incompetence in carrying out the crime? Some crimes do require an end result. For example, murder requires the victim to die and robbery requires appropriation. Should the criminal be guilty of nothing? In most cases the victims will have suffered; the intended murder victim may be injured or traumatized; the robbery victim may be assaulted or terrorized by the act. Even if the victim is unscathed, the criminal will be guilty of an attempt to commit the particular crime, which in itself is a criminal offence, and possibly other lesser charges. Of particular interest here is the element of *mens rea* attached to the offence. It will be of a similar order whether the crime is successfully committed or not.

Group activity

In some states of the US the normal approach to sentencing is half of the main offence in attempt cases. Should the criminal suffer the same sentence for a successful and unsuccessful crime in the UK or should the UK adopt the US system?

On a practical level the police would have to wait for a crime to be successfully completed before they could arrest and bring the defendant before a court. This would be of little use to the murder victim or, say, the sub-postmaster faced with a violent and dangerous gang attacking his family and business. If the police have a tip off they will want to catch the criminals and achieve a successful prosecution. This may mean allowing the criminal to pursue the committing of the offence. Arresting a gang in the morning before they set off for a 'job' may mean difficulty in proving the case: arresting them on the doorstop of the post office wearing balaclavas and carrying shotguns is catching them red handed and much more likely to end in a successful prosecution. A problem looked at later is where does preparation end and crime begin? The courts sometimes have difficult cases in this area and decisions are not always obvious.

Actus reus

This has proved an extremely complex area for the courts to resolve. There is help in terms of statutory provision, but courts have also to look at individual cases and bring their greatest attention onto what is and what is not an attempt.

Statutory provision

Statutory legislation exists to cover the issue of attempts.

> ### Legislation
>
> **Criminal Attempts Act 1981**   s(¹)
>
> If, with the intent to commit an offence to which this section applies, a person does an act which is more than merely preparatory to the commission of the offence, he is guilty of attempting to commit the offence.

A·Gretng I(9a2)
(1aa8)

Gulletar
Geddes
Campbell·

The issue then revolves around the words 'merely preparatory'. If there is no evidence that it has gone beyond 'merely preparatory', the judge must instruct the jury to acquit. If the judge believes there is evidence that it has gone beyond 'merely preparatory', they must give the decision over to the jury to decide. The statutory law must be considered first but courts can use previous persuasive cases if appropriate.

Common law tests of attempt
Proximity test

There are a number of tests that might be used to establish whether an attempt has happened or whether they are merely preparatory acts. The proximity test endorsed by the Law Commission involves proving 'acts are immediately connected with' the attempt as opposed to 'acts remotely leading towards the commission of the offence'. The proximity test was used in the following case.

Legal case: *R v Robinson (1915)*

Robinson was a jeweller who had insured his stock against theft. He decided to claim on the policy by hiding the stock around the shop. He tied himself up and then called the police. His scheme was uncovered and he was prosecuted for obtaining money from his insurers to the value of £1200. His defence argued that since he had not obtained, filled in, or sent the claim off, he was not guilty of the offence. The Court of Appeal agreed and quashed his sentence. His acts were not 'immediately connected' with the main offence. However, he might be found guilty of wasting police time!

Rubicon test

'Crossing the Rubicon' is a saying which comes from the crossing of a small river by the Roman emperor, Julius Caesar, which separated Italy from Cisalpine Gaul. The crossing of the river committed him to war with Pompey and the Senate. In terms of attempts, it is the action which commits one to a course of action and to liability in the courts. It can be seen in the following case.

Legal case: *R v Widdowson (1986)*

Widdowson wanted to hire a van but used a false identity since under his own name he would not have been able to. He had not, however, submitted the form to the hire company although he had filled it in with his false details. The Court of Appeal felt that what he had done so far did not amount to a substantive offence and his conviction was quashed, submitting the form would have convicted him.

Series of acts test

An academic called Stephens put forward the view that attempt would consist of a series of acts, which led to the offence and it only became an attempt and not the full offence because it was interrupted.

Legal case: *R v Boyle and Boyle (1986)*

Boyle and Boyle were convicted of attempted burglary as both were found beside a door whose lock and hinges had been broken. A policeman had interrupted them in the commission of their offence. It seems reasonable that they would have continued with their series of acts ending in a charge of burglary if the policeman had not intervened. Their conviction was upheld on appeal.

Gullefer test

The problem about determining when the merely preparatory begins and ends were explored in *R v Gullefer (1990)*. Stephens' series of acts test did not resolve the continuing problem about merely preparatory acts being seen as part of a series leading toward but not quite reaching the act itself.

Legal case: *R v Gullefer (1990)*

A man had put a bet on a dog running at Romford greyhound track and it was clearly losing. In a bid to void the race, he leapt over the fence trying his best to cause a commotion in the hope that the race officials would cancel the race and thus all bets. He was arrested and charged with theft. The court, however, found that as he had not yet submitted his betting slips he had not committed the act of theft. His actions had been merely preparatory. Lord Lane commenting in the case said that it was the facts in each individual case that determined when the preparatory acts stopped and the crime itself began.

Geddes test

The issue of mere preparation and actual offence moved a bit further with the surprising case of *R v Geddes (1996)*.

Legal case: *R v Geddes (1996)*

Geddes had entered a school and was found lurking in the boys' toilet. He ran off but left behind a bag containing rope, masking tape and a large knife. The jury convicted Geddes of attempted false imprisonment but on appeal his conviction was quashed. The Court of Appeal found that Geddes had not moved from preparation into execution of his offence. Reasons included the fact that he had not contacted any of the boys. Two questions were posed by the court:

1 Had Geddes moved from preparation to implementation?

2 Had Geddes done something tangible to show that he was trying to commit the offence or were his actions simply putting himself into the position to commit the act?

Mens rea

The *mens rea* of attempt is the intention to commit the substantive offence. It is the *mens rea* which often converts what might seem very ordinary activities into an attempt to commit an offence. Standing in a queue of people at a bus stop might be simply waiting for a 25b, or it might mean an attempt to steal a purse. The *mens rea* will distinguish the mundane activity from the criminal activity.

Quick revision questions

1 Define the crime of incitement.

2 What is the punishment for incitement?

3 Give three examples of incitement.

4 Outline the key issues in *Invicta Plastics Ltd v Clare (1976)*.

5 Define conspiracy.

6 What are the main defences against conspiracy?

7 What criminal issue does *R v White (1910)* illustrate? — *Attempted Murder*

8 Outline the key elements of the Criminal Attempts Act 1981. —

9 Explain the main common law tests used to establish attempts. —

10 Explain the *mens rea* of attempts. *proximity test last Act*

[handwritten left margin: If with intent to commit an offence to which this section applies a person does an act which is more than merely preparatory the commission of the mass of...]

[handwritten: Same as the offence if with intent to comm]

Exam question

Incitement to commit a crime is as serious as conspiracy to commit a crime. Comment. [50 marks]

Exam answer guide

Knowledge and understanding [20 marks]

✓ Define incitement. Quote *Invicta Plastics Ltd v Clare (1976)*

✓ Outline examples of the *actus reus* of incitement such as advice, financial payment, threats, persuasion, pressure and goading. State the *mens rea* of incitement

✓ Define conspiracy. Quote Section 1 (1) of the Criminal Law Act 1977

✓ Outline the *actus reus* and *mens rea* of conspiracy

Analysis and evaluation [25 marks]

✓ Assess the level of guilt for conspiracy and incitement. Evaluate which one might be regarded as more serious

✓ Discuss whether one ends in the commission of crime more often than another

✓ Ensure that you give your opinion on which one is more serious

Presentation [5 marks]

✓ Structure your work in a logical and well-planned way. Employ good quality and clear English in your writing. Make use of punctuation and correct spelling in your answers.

UNIT 6

Murder

Key points

1 Definition of murder
2 *Actus reus* of murder
3 The *mens rea*/malice aforethought of murder
4 Chain of causation
5 Defences of diminished responsibility, provocation and suicide pact

Why do I need to know about murder?

Understanding of the elements of this offence is very important. The three main parts are conduct, circumstance and consequence. Another important issue is the variety of defences the defendant may offer the court to escape the mandatory (compulsory) life sentence this crime attracts. These defences will be looked at at the end of this unit. Although this is an emotive area, keep a clear and detached

Murder

view and stick to the facts of the case and the law you have learned. Make sure you understand the differences between murder and the two types of manslaughter. The law changes often in this area so it is important to keep up to date with developments and new cases.

1 Definition of murder

Murder is one of the most appalling crimes that human beings commit, but at the same time one of the most fascinating. The victim is no longer able to explain events or act as a witness as to events leading up to the crime, and cannot defend themselves against accusations of provocation or blame. Another alarming point is the number of cases where the murderer has a close relationship to the murdered victim, and family members or close friends are often found guilty of this offence. There are also terrorist attacks on commercial and military targets, the murder of public officials, such as police officers, and even head teachers, such as Phillip Lawrence.

The crime of murder is a common law offence. The penalty if the defendant is found guilty is life in prison, regardless of the circumstances. This is known as a 'mandatory sentence'. This makes murder a very unusual offence, and some argue very unfair, for certain groups of people who may respond to stressful situations in unusual ways.

Murder is also known as 'homicide'. The word 'homicide' refers to unlawful killings. The key statutory provisions surrounding homicide are contained in the Homicide Act 1957. The Act does not give a legal definition of murder but focuses on the defences available to those who are charged with this offence. To find a definition of murder you will need to look at judgements made in courts over a period of time up to the case of Woolin (1998), which was heard in the House of Lords.

The following was a recent infamous case involving the deaths of many innocent people.

Legal case: *R v Shipman (2001)*

One of the most notorious murderers in Britain was a family doctor from Hyde in Manchester called Harold Shipman. He was found guilty of the murder of fifteen of his patients although there was strong evidence that he may have killed 215. The figure may have been even larger than this. The enquiry into the murders was published in July 2002 and recommended a major shake-up in procedures for family doctors.

2 *Actus reus* of murder

The *actus reus* of murder is:

- an unlawful act that causes the death of another human being,
- under the Queen's peace,
- within a country of the realm.

Unlawful act

The unlawful act could be many things. A direct and intentional physical blow with a heavy object, the deliberate firing of a bullet from a gun, or calculated stabbing with a knife would be regarded as unlawful acts. However, the following might also be included.

- Scaring someone to death. A recent case where an elderly man died from a heart attack caused by villains who had broken into his house and terrorized the victim and his wife was regarded as murder.
- Causing someone to die in an escape bid. A woman who was kidnapped by a rapist who broke into her car, drove the vehicle at a wall to escape from her assailant. If she had died it may have been regarded as murder.

Note that an act or omission is acceptable for the causing death element to the *actus reus* of murder.

Legal case: *R v Gibbins and Proctor (1918)*

Gibbins allowed his seven year old daughter to starve to death. The court believed that he had a duty of care as a father and he was convicted of murder because he failed to feed the girl. Gibbins' live-in lover was also convicted of murder since she had assumed a duty of care by living in the house as a responsible adult. The *actus reus* for both was one of omission. The charge was murder since it was proved that the couple had not merely been incompetent but had the intention to see the child dead.

Death

A problem that the courts have faced as medical and scientific technology has advanced is in deciding when death has taken place or even if it has taken place. A person kept artificially alive for decades may possibly be regarded as alive by some and dead by others. The courts tend to look at brain-stem death as the key determinate, although each case must be looked at individually. Note *R v Malcherek (1981)* (see page 51) where the defendant blamed the doctors for causing death and not his own frenzied knife attack on his wife.

Legal case: *R v Copeland (1999)*

The bombing of a busy Soho public house, The Admiral Duncan, on 1 May 1999 killed three people, including a woman and her unborn child, and injured 79. The case highlighted some unusual features in that the bomber could not be charged with the killing of the unborn child. The only charge that could be made was of child destruction in this instance. If the unborn child had survived, been born and had then died from injuries sustained in the attack, could it have been classified as murder. The murder charge was used against the offender for the death of the mother and the other adults unlawfully killed on that evening.

Human being

The question of what is and is not a human being may seem straightforward, but there are complications that the courts have had to deal with.

- Is a person in a vegetative coma a human being? The medical profession and the legal profession seem to take brain-stem death as a key indicator. When this happens there is no chance of recovery.

- Is a foetus a human being? A human being must be completely separate from its mother's body to become a human being. Killing a foetus is therefore not the same as killing a human being.

- A person who is lying in a hospital bed in a brain-dead state, although with bodily organs 'alive', who was shot by an assailant, is not regarded as a human being for the purposes of a murder trial. The victim must be a living human being.

Infanticide

The sentence for murder is a mandatory life sentence. A mother who kills her child within one year of the birth of the child may not be charged with murder. The offence would be infanticide and an automatic life sentence would not then be applied. The legal system has come to this position to give the judge some flexibility on each case of infanticide. The judge may still impose a life sentence depending on the circumstances of the case.

Year and a day

The 'year and a day' rule was abolished by the Law Reform (Year and a Day Rule) Act 1996. Before this Act was passed the victim of the murderous attack had to die within one year and one day. The advance of medical science meant this could favour murderers who might escape prosecution if victims were kept 'alive' on life-support machines. Recent rulings on this from the Attorney General means that permission must be obtained from him before prosecution can commence on a case more than three years old.

Legal case: *R v Malcherek (1981)*

In *R v Malcherek (1981)* a husband stabbed his wife repeatedly and she was put on a life-support machine. The medical team switched off the life-support machine when it was decided that recovery of the victim was not going to happen. Malcherek put forward the defence that it was the action of turning off the machine that caused death but the Court of Appeal decided that the intervening act did not break the chain of causation and that Malcherek was responsible for the death and not the doctors. The Court of Appeal went on to say that they thought the argument that Malcherek had not caused death was 'bizarre'.

Under the Queen's peace

Is there a difference between soldiers in Afghanistan fighting Osama bin Laden's Al-Qaeda and soldiers in Northern Ireland fighting paramilitary groups? If the government declares war on another country then our soldiers will not be prosecuted. Therefore, if Al-Qaeda troops are killed by Royal Marines, they are seen as legitimate targets of war. Soldiers in Northern Ireland, where the British government does not recognize a war condition as existing, will be subject to Courts Martial or even the Civilian Courts if citizens are killed or murdered while soldiers are on duty.

Legal case: *R v Clegg (1995)*

Private Clegg was found guilty of the murder of eighteen year old Karen Reilly but was released on the orders of the Attorney General, Sir Partrick Mayhew after much public pressure. The soldier had been manning an army checkpoint when joy riders drove through the barricade and Clegg and another soldier fired at the vehicle as it passed. The prosecution maintained that the immediate danger had passed, which effectively destroyed Clegg's claims of self-defence.

Group activity

Comment on the Clegg case. Should Private Clegg have been convicted of murder, manslaughter or neither?

Country of the realm

Those suspected of murder or manslaughter can be tried in the UK even if the offence was committed abroad, providing the defendant is British.

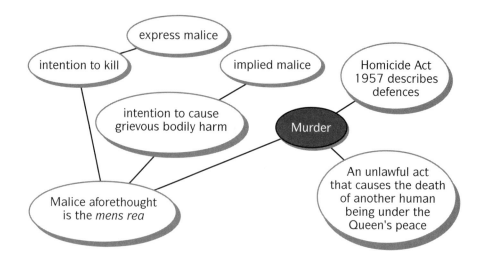

Murder

3 The *mens rea*/malice aforethought of murder

The *mens rea* of murder is commonly known as 'malice aforethought'. It is the intention to kill another human being and consists of two possible elements: the presence of either is enough to prove murder.

1 Intention to kill (express malice aforethought).

2 Intention to cause grievous bodily harm (implied malice aforethought).

Implied malice

For a successful murder conviction the prosecution only needs to prove that grievous bodily harm was intended and death resulted. Intention to murder does not have to be proved. Exploding a bomb in a busy pub on a Friday night would almost certainly have resulted in grievous bodily harm and probably death. Only the former, the grievous bodily harm, has to be proved for the *mens rea* to be established for murder.

Express malice

If the intention to kill can be proved then it is known as 'express malice'. This might be more difficult to prove if the defendant argues that he only meant to inflict grievous bodily harm on his victims. However, the end result is the same – a charge and conviction of murder.

Intention

Intention is a key concept in murder but is also present in other areas such as theft, where the intention is to permanently deprive the owner, and grievous bodily harm, where the intention is to inflict a serious injury. In a charge of grievous bodily harm the offence would be murder only if the victim dies as a result of the attack. In the case of murder the defendant might not have intended to murder, but if they intended serious harm to their victim they could be found guilty of murder if their victim dies as the result of their acts or omissions.

There are two types of intention:

1 Direct intention

The defendant clearly desired the outcome and was happy when it was accomplished – it was the aim of the defendant. If the defendant loads a gun and points it directly at the head of the victim and pulls the trigger, it could be said that the defendant directly intended the death.

2 Oblique intention

If the defendant sprays machine-gun fire at a crowded bus hoping to kill his intended victim, he is very likely to kill other passengers. He may not intend to kill these unfortunate travellers but he still does. This is known as oblique intent.

Oblique intent poses problems for the courts. If the defendant did not intend to kill these bystanders, could it be argued that he acted in a state of recklessness? The following linked cases looked at this issue and the importance of the phrases 'virtual certainty' and 'substantial risk'.

Legal case: *R v Nedrick (1986)* and *R v Woolin (1998)*

R v Nedrick (1986)

Nedrick poured petrol through the letterbox of a woman who he had been arguing with and set fire to it. Her child died in the blaze. The judge directed the jury to find him guilty of murder if they thought 'death or serious bodily harm was a "virtual certainty"'.

R v Woolin (1998)

The defendant killed his son by throwing the three month old at a wall, fracturing the child's skull. The judge directed the jury to look at whether there was a 'substantial risk' that serious harm would be caused to the child. Woolin argued that the judge should have directed the jury with the words 'virtual certainty'. Eventually the House of Lords reduced the charge to manslaughter and stated that the direction in the Nedrick case was to be used.

An important part of the *obiter dicta* to Woolin was the following:

'A result foreseen as virtually certain is an intended result.'

In other words, if the defendant is pretty sure that the person will be killed by their actions, they cannot then use the defence of 'I didn't mean it'.

Evidence of intention

Evidence of intention can be seen in 'foresight of consequences'. In other words, does the defendant realize that their actions will cause a particular event even if they do not want that event to happen?

Legal case: *R v Stephenson (1979)*

A homeless schizophrenic decided to make himself a temporary shelter in a haystack. As he was cold he lit a small fire, which got out of control and caused criminal damage worth £3500. The Court of Appeal ruled that his mental condition made it unlikely that he could have foreseen the consequences of his actions and his conviction was quashed. There was no evidence of intention.

Group activity

What is the difference between 'virtual certainty' and 'substantial risk'? Why did Woolin prefer the judge's direction of 'virtual certainty'?

Mandatory sentences

The only sentence available for murder is life imprisonment. However, the judge has some flexibility on the maximum tariffs handed out. The law takes as a starting point murders between adults who know each other, have argued, with things getting out of hand and ending in a murder. This is the 'typical' murder and it is used as a benchmark when considering other murders. The seriousness of different types of murder is detailed in a Practice Statement issued by the Lord Chief Justice on 31 May 2002. Minimum sentences to be served will be *increased* from the 'typical murder' if it:

- is a professional killing
- is racially motivated
- is politically motivated
- involves vulnerable people such as children or the elderly.

The minimum sentence to be served can also be *reduced* from typical murder if:

- it is a mercy killing
- it is a borderline manslaughter case
- it is an overreaction due to self-defence
- there was a mental disorder (falling short of diminished responsibility).

The Practice Statement also says that it is highly unlikely they will be released when the minimum term is served.

A murderer who is given a life sentence is subject to that sentence for all of their remaining life. If they break the conditions of their licence to be out of prison, they can and are brought back to serve the remaining sentence.

Absence of *mens rea*

If the *mens rea* for grievous bodily harm or murder is absent, the defendant may still be charged with involuntary manslaughter. The defendant cannot be charged with voluntary manslaughter since there may well be an element of *mens rea* present in this offence. These two offences against the person are explored in the next unit.

4 Chain of causation

The defendant must have caused the death of another human being. Sometimes it is argued by defence lawyers that medical treatment has itself contributed to the death of the victim, but the courts are wary of accepting such defences.

Legal case: *R v Smith (1959)*

Two soldiers were fighting and one stabbed the other with a bayonet. Friends of the victim took him to the medical officer, dropping him twice on the way, and once at the medical station they had to wait because the medical officer was busy. The victim died of his injuries but might have survived if he had received prompt and efficient care. The court decided that there was not a break in causation. Only if the second element was so 'overwhelming' to the first could this be considered as breaking the chain of events.

Legal case: *R v Cheshire (1991)*

A similar case to *R v Smith (1959)* is this case, which involved the shooting of Trevor Jeffrey by David Cheshire. Jeffrey was taken to hospital and treated for a stomach wound. He developed a separate medical condition, which led to a tracheotomy and he eventually died from a heart attack, which was caused by his various breathing difficulties. His original wounds had almost healed. The defendant was found guilty and the appeal court upheld this.

In *R v Cheshire (1991)*, the judge stated that only the most unusual medical treatment would break the chain of causation. Judges are free to use either Smith or Cheshire depending on the medical condition of the victim.

Group activity: *R v McKechnie (1991)*

The defendant attacked an elderly man and brain damage was caused to the victim. While the victim was in hospital it was discovered that he had a very serious problem involving a stomach ulcer, which needed immediate treatment. However, treatment could not go ahead because of the victim's head injuries. The victim died of the ulcer complication.

Give reasons why Smith or Cheshire could be used in this case.

Self neglect

If a victim chooses not to receive medical treatment, the defendant can still be convicted of murder. The 'but for' rule could be used – 'but for' the defendant's actions the victim would not have been put into this position. See *R v Blaue (1975)*, page 10.

voluntary manslaughter

5 Defences of diminished responsibility, provocation and ~~suicide pact~~

Provocation is a defence against murder only, which if successful will reduce the charge to manslaughter. It is detailed in Section 3 of the Homicide Act 1957.

Legislation

Section 3 Homicide Act 1957

Where there is evidence that the person charged with murder was provoked (by things done or said or both) the question as to whether it would make a reasonable man do this is left to the jury.

The jury is left to decide whether the person was so provoked that they should escape a murder conviction and its mandatory life sentence.

This statement in Section 3 does not abolish the common law rulings in this area. Devlin gave the classic common law definition of provocation in 1949 in the case of *R v Duffy (1949)*.

Legal case: *R v Duffy (1949)*

'A sudden and temporary loss of self control, rendering the accused so subject to passion as to make him or her for the moment not the master of his mind.'

This definition causes problems for anyone who does not fly into an immediate rage due to some insult or action directed against them. It has been said that women and men react in very different ways and this definition would give protection for men but not for women. Two famous cases that illustrate this issue led to a change in the way that the defence of provocation was perceived.

Legal case: *R v Sara Thornton (1992)*

Sara Thornton was convicted for murder in 1992. Her husband Malcolm had physically and mentally abused her for many years and one night she sharpened a knife from the kitchen and then stabbed him to death after he had once more threatened her. She was found guilty of murder because of the absence of 'sudden loss of control'. The premeditated sharpening of the knife was seen as a significant event.

Legal case: *R v Ahluwalia (1992)*

Ahluwalia had been the long-term victim of an abusive husband and one night she set her husband's bed alight after covering it with petrol. The man died six days later. Ahluwalia was convicted of murder despite arguing that Duffy was an inappropriate test to be used in her case.

The Court of Appeal refused to accept the argument that Duffy did not apply in the case of *R v Ahluwalia (1992)*, as the longer the delay the more unlikely provocation would succeed as a defence. The next case illustrates this point further and also looks at the issue of revenge. The courts are unlikely to accept 'revenge' as a basis for provocation as a defence.

Legal case: *R v Ibrams and Gregory (1981)*

A couple had been intimidated by the woman's ex-boyfriend, John Monk, and they hatched a plan, along with a friend, to deal with him. The plan involved him being persuaded to go to bed with the woman and then to be attacked by Ibrams and Gregory. Monk died during the attack. The court felt that the planning and the time difference between the killing and the last threatening actions by Monk invalidated their defence of provocation.

The Duffy case has been used in cases where there is a long, slow build up to the crime, which ends violently, and also to argue against cases that may involve an element of revenge.

Examples of provocation

The following have been regarded as provocative actions or statements:

- crying babies
- references to lack of sexual ability
- accusations of homosexuality
- adultery
- physical assaults
- long-term mental abuse.

Section 3 of the Homicide Act 1957 directs the judge to allow the jury to decide whether the provocation stated is enough to make a reasonable man have a 'sudden and temporary loss of self control'. The reasonable man may share some of the characteristics of the defendant. Again it is up to the jury to weigh up these issues. If provocation is used, the prosecution must prove beyond a reasonable doubt that the defence is wrong.

Subjective and objective

There is both a subjective and objective element to the defence of provocation.

- **Subjective**

  The subjective question relates to what happened to the defendant. The provocation must have led to a loss of control that was sudden and temporary. As we have seen, this element has caused problems for the courts when women use provocation inspired defences. The sudden and temporary may favour the testosterone filled angry male who sees red, but may not easily apply to women who may have been provoked over a period of time, or where there may be a delay between the last act of provocation and the killing.

- **Objective**

  The objective question relates to what the reasonable man would have done. The courts must be satisfied that the provocation would have made the reasonable man act in the same way. Would the reasonable man have had 'sudden and temporary loss of control' if faced with the same provocation? The law changed after the case of *DPP v Camplin (1978)*.

Legal case: *DPP v Camplin (1978)*

This case involved a fifteen year old who had been sexually abused by an older man. The older man laughed at Camplin who then hit him over the head with a heavy cooking pan. The man was killed. In this case the House of Lords defined the reasonable man as one who shared some of the characteristics of the defendant, that is, gender, age and sexuality.

The reasonable man would now be considered the same sex and age, but also have in common with the defendant some of the elements that might give the provocation its full capacity to provoke.

Diminished responsibility

Section 2 of the Homicide Act 1957 gives a clear definition of diminished responsibility although it can be difficult at times to see when it can be used as a defence.

Legislation

Section 2 Homicide Act 1957

If a person kills while suffering such an abnormality of mind as substantially impaired his mental responsibility for his acts or omissions.

Diminished responsibility has three important characteristics.

- It can only be used as a defence against murder.
- It only reduces the charge to manslaughter.
- Premeditation does not rule out diminished responsibility.

Unlike murder, where the judge has to give the defendant a life sentence, in manslaughter the judge has some discretion over the sentence imposed. The defendant may be committed to life imprisonment, or at the other extreme, may be completely discharged. Others, given the nature of the defence, may be committed to hospital for treatment under the Mental Health Act 1983.

Diminished responsibility has three essential legal elements.

- The defendant has an abnormality of mind.
- The abnormality of mind is related to specific causes.
- This abnormality impairs mental responsibility.

The defendant has an abnormality of mind

It is the job of the jury not of the psychiatrist to decide whether there is an abnormality of mind. Both sides will present medical evidence if it is a murder case and diminished responsibility is being used.

Legal case: *R v Byrne (1960)*

This case introduced the phrase 'abnormality of mind' and means a state of mind so different from that of ordinary human beings that the reasonable man would term it abnormal. It was the Homicide Act 1957 which made this defence possible.

It may be the jury that decides if diminished responsibility is the issue when they feel some sympathy for the killer. On the other hand, Peter Sutcliffe (*R v Sutcliffe (1981)*), the Yorkshire Ripper, was found guilty of murder. His lawyers argued that he had an abnormality of mind, however the judge directed otherwise. The jury found Sutcliffe guilty of murder and therefore morally responsible for his actions. Interestingly, he has spent almost his entire sentence in a mental hospital.

Group activity

Was the jury right to refuse Sutcliffe's plea of diminished responsibility?

The abnormality of mind is related to specific causes

The second part to Section 2 of the Homicide Act 1957 gives guidance about what might be considered as causes of the abnormality of mind. **Only** items on this list can be included and the judges should give guidance to the jury about which evidence should and should not be included. The items include:

- an inherent cause
- abnormality of mind caused by disease
- abnormality of mind caused by injury
- retarded development of the mind

Although the jury have to decide the issue, medical evidence would be crucial in assisting them in their task.

An inherent cause

This could be a number of possibilities.

- Psychopathy relates to people who find it difficult to relate to or understand others and who live in a world where emotional and moral life is not developed.

- Paranoid-schizophrenia. Klein, an emminent psychotherapist, describes this position as 'terrifying persecution feelings coming from disturbances early in childhood'. These overwhelming feelings may bring about very violent or criminal behaviour.

- Epilepsy can have profound effects on a person's mental state that go beyond the well-known attack. At times it is an 'indicator of something wrong with structure or part of the brain', according to the Royal College of Medicine.

- Pre-menstrual syndrome (PMS) can bring about great distress and create out of character behaviour in a small number of women. The jury can take these feelings of tension and stress into account.

- Clinical depression gives those who suffer from it profound feelings of unhappiness and despondency, which may produce irritability and suicidal feelings.

Abnormality of mind caused by disease

Although the medical world accepts that alcoholism and drug addiction can be seen as diseases, the legal world has taken a much more cautious approach.

Courts in England were also slow to accept the concept of 'battered wife syndrome', but the important case of *R v Ahluwalia (1992)* (see page 57) heard in the Appeal Court changed this to a certain extent.

It was argued during the Ahluwalia appeal that if a defendant had been suffering from 'battered wife syndrome' this could have been considered as a defence. This was an important breakthrough but in the specific case of Ahluwalia the court felt that she had not been suffering from such a condition.

Alcohol has a curious position in terms of use as defence. The issue revolves around two questions.

1 Was the person drinking involuntarily? Were they so addicted to the drug that they had no choice in the matter? If this was so then the person should be found not guilty of murder.

2 Was the person capable of resisting that first drink, which led to the second and third, and so on? If this was so then the person should be found guilty. It was a voluntary state they entered into and they should take the consequences.

Alcohol and other drugs can, over time, damage the brain and its functioning. In this case Section 2 of the Homicide Act 1957 would apply and the defendant could claim one of the specified causes, that of 'injury'.

There is also the possibility that regardless of the drink that had been consumed the defendant did have an underlying and unrelated abnormality of mind. In this case a defence of diminished responsibility could succeed. Various possibilities also present themselves.

- The defendant was drunk and killed someone = murder

- The defendant was drunk and killed someone, but had an underlying mental abnormality already = manslaughter

- The defendant had an abnormality of mind caused by drink = manslaughter if brain injury has occurred in the defendant. If it were a disease such as alcoholism then it would probably be classified as murder unless they could not voluntarily resist drink.

Legal case: *R v Tandy (1989)*

After a particularly excessive drinking binge, Linda Tandy strangled her eleven year old daughter. The judge asked the jury to consider whether Tandy's brain had been injured through her previous drinking or whether she had simply become drunk and committed the murder. The jury decided that there was no injury and therefore no defence of diminished responsibility was available to her and so she was convicted of murder.

Abnormality of mind caused by injury

Injury may have occurred due to physical force, during medical procedures or even at birth if the brain had been starved of oxygen. A brain-injured person may enter a plea of diminished responsibility to a murder charge.

Retarded development of the mind

A number of high-profile cases have revolved around defendants who were arrested, prosecuted and convicted on murder charges despite having very low IQ levels. The case of *R v Speake (1957)* was the first to recognize mental deficiency as an 'abnormality of mind'.

This abnormality impairs mental responsibility

The third part to proving diminished responsibility involves the acceptance by the jury of 'substantially impaired mental responsibility' that has arisen from the 'abnormality of mind'. This means that the defendant's responsibility does not have to be completely impaired, but at the same time must not be suffering from some very minor impairment of responsibility. As with other very difficult situations, the jury is asked to decide this issue. The defence must prove on the balance of probabilities that diminished responsibility was present.

Suicide pact

Section 4 of the Homicide Act 1957 makes a provision for those who wish to commit suicide together, a so-called 'suicide pact'. This provision covers two or more people whose aim it is to end their lives collectively. The Act defines this pact as:

'a common agreement whose aim is the death of them all.'

The surviving person could be charged with murder depending on the circumstances of the death/deaths. Section 4 of the Act allows the jury and judge some flexibility in this area and the plea could bring the charge down to manslaughter.

Suicide was once a crime. This no longer the case, but helping another to commit suicide is still illegal. The recent case of Diane Pretty (2002) who took her case to the High Court underlined the problems in this area. Her husband may have been charged with murder/voluntary manslaughter if he had assisted his wife to kill herself. Often the Crown Prosecution accepts a plea of diminished responsibility in cases of mercy killings, aware that juries and the public would be very hostile to a caring relative or friend being imprisoned for the mercy killing of a loved one. Diminished responsibility allows the judge to give a suspended or conditional discharge to the defendant.

The defence must prove a suicide pact existed on the balance of probabilities.

Quick revision questions

1 Where would you find the definition of murder? — common law

2 What does the Homicide Act 1957 detail?

3 What is a mandatory sentence? — life - time imprison   unlawful

4 List the *actus reus* of murder and the *mens rea* for murder. /   result time - death

5 What does the law understand by the words 'unlawful act', 'death' and 'human being'? → fedus, brain dead   there is no death w mr

6 Define the following terms: 'express and implied malice' and 'direct and oblique intention'.   intention to kill   intent to cause Gensh

7 What do the cases *R v Nedrick (1986)* and *R v Woolin (1998)* illustrate?

8 What are the main details of the Practice Statement issued by the Lord Chief Justice on 31 May 2002? →

9 Outline the meaning of abnormality of mind. →

10 Describe the defence of provocation and its limitations.

(Handwritten margin notes, left:)
Actus reus → unlawful killing of a reasonable person in being → with malice aforethought express/implied

(Handwritten margin notes, bottom left:)
Byrne — Abnormality of mind is regarded as anything the the reasonable man would re

Exam question

Why is a charge of murder made so difficult to prove? [50 marks]

Exam answer guide

Knowledge and understanding [20 marks]

✓ Define murder. Use cases such as *R v Shipman (2001)*, *R v Gibbins and Proctor (1918)* and *R v Copeland (1999)*

✓ Describe the *actus reus* and *mens rea*, malice aforethought of murder

✓ Define unlawful act, death, human being, under Queen's peace and country of realm

✓ Illustrate knowledge and understanding of infanticide and 'year and a day' rule

✓ Show the difference between direct and oblique intent

✓ Outline the defences of diminished responsibility, provocation and suicide pact

Analysis and evaluation [25 marks]

✓ The question must be answered with reference to mandatory sentences which judges need to pass when a charge of murder is proved. Only a life sentence is deemed appropriate

✓ Defendants must be seen to have been tried thoroughly when such a socially and legally serious crime is being prosecuted by the state

✓ Consider the importance of defences and the conditions under which they are allowed

✓ Assess the importance of specific intention in terms of the mens rea of murder

✓ Quote and comment on cases such as *R v Tandy (1989)* and *R v Ahluwalia (1992)*

Presentation [5 marks]

✓ Structure your work in a logical and well-planned way. Employ good quality and clear English in your writing. Make use of punctuation and correct spelling in your answers.

Manslaughter

Key points

1 Involuntary manslaughter
2 Constructive manslaughter (unlawful act manslaughter)
3 Gross negligence manslaughter
4 Corporate killing
5 Evaluation and reform of involuntary manslaughter

Why do I need to know about manslaughter?

An unlawful killing, which fits neither into the category of murder nor voluntary manslaughter, may be termed as involuntary manslaughter. Typical examples include irresponsible behaviour that ends in death, or deaths caused by incompetent medical treatment. Involuntary manslaughter can be put into two categories: unlawful/constructive manslaughter and gross negligence manslaughter.

Involuntary manslaughter

These two forms of manslaughter have been created by the operation of the courts rather than statutory legislation. Key legal points need to be explained using appropriate cases.

1 Involuntary manslaughter

Involuntary manslaughter occurs when there was no intention to kill or to cause grievous bodily harm. In other words, there was no malice aforethought, as the defendant did not intend to murder or intend to commit voluntary manslaughter. The critical element to look at is the *mens rea*.

There are two forms of involuntary manslaughter:

1 gross negligence manslaughter

2 unlawful act manslaughter.

One of the problems that exists with involuntary manslaughter is the sheer range of offences that are covered by this term. At one extreme is a drunken car driver ploughing into a queue of people at a bus stop, and at the other extreme someone ignoring an apparently minor health and safety rule that through bad luck leads to the death of a human being. In both cases a charge will be brought if the system feels that the defendant is so blameworthy that the incident may be seen as criminal.

2 Constructive manslaughter (unlawful act manslaughter)

Unlawful act manslaughter is also known as 'constructive manslaughter'. The *actus reus* of unlawful act manslaughter is:

● an unlawful act

● that is dangerous,

● that causes the death of the victim.

The unlawful act must amount to a criminal offence. In other words, both the *actus reus* and *mens rea* must be present. The defendant must also commit an act: an omission is not sufficient.

Unlawful act manslaughter requires the *mens rea* to be such that a reasonable man would believe that the act committed was dangerous, that is, the objective test. The objective test is used for unlawful act manslaughter in the following two cases.

Legal case: *R v Church (1966)*

Church dumped the body of his unconscious lover into a river believing she was already dead. The judge stated that an unlawful act would be one where 'all sober and reasonable people would inevitably recognize that it would subject the other person to the risk of some harm although it does not have to be serious harm'.

Legal case: *DPP v Newbury and Jones (1977)*

The two defendants pushed a heavy paving stone over a bridge as a train was passing underneath and the driver of the train was killed. The defendants appealed on the grounds that they had not intended harm to anyone. The House of Lords used the judgements in *R v Church (1966)* and dismissed the appeal against unlawful act manslaughter on the grounds that the act was *objectively* dangerous, was unlawful, and resulted in death. It must be proved that the defendant had the *mens rea* for the act that caused the death but it does not have to be proved that the defendant knew the act was unlawful or dangerous.

The unlawful act must have caused the death of the victim. The following case illustrates the fact that the victim does not have to be the one intended by the defendant.

Legal case: *R v Goodfellow (1986)*

The defendant firebombed his own house to persuade the council to re-house himself and his family. Unfortunately his wife, a friend of the family and one of his children were killed in the blaze. Goodfellow claimed that he had not aimed the dangerous act at the victims but at the council. The appeal was dismissed, as the unlawful act did not have to be aimed at anyone in particular. The important point was that the unlawful act caused death and a reasonable man would recognize that the act might have subjected someone to the risk of harm.

The *mens rea* of unlawful act manslaughter is:

● fault associated with the unlawful act

● dangerousness.

In other words, the *mens rea* for the unlawful act itself that caused the death.

3 Gross negligence manslaughter

Gross negligence manslaughter has three elements that make up the *actus reus*:

● duty of care

● breach of duty of care

● death of the victim.

The *mens rea* is:

● gross negligence that a jury considers deserves a criminal conviction.

This is an offence where the jury has a great deal of power to decide the fate of the defendant. The following case is often quoted to illustrate gross negligence manslaughter.

Legal case: *R v Adomako (1994)*

The defendant was an anaesthetist who failed to monitor the well being of his patient during an eye operation. The victim suffered a heart attack due to lack of oxygen and although he survived the operation died six months later due directly to his brain being starved of oxygen. The prosecution called two witnesses who claimed that any competent anaesthetist would have spotted the problem within seconds and prevented the patient suffering such an attack. The jury convicted the defendant of gross negligence manslaughter.

Duty of care

Duty of care clearly exists between doctor and patient, but it also exists in many other forms such as:

- teachers to pupils
- train drivers to passengers
- car drivers to other road users
- landlords to tenants.

If the behaviour of any of these groups falls below what is expected of them, there may be a charge of gross negligence manslaughter to answer if someone has been killed. In *R v Adomako (1994)* the House of Lords gave a list of what might be considered gross negligence:

- lack of concern to the possibility of an obvious injury
- foresight of the risk but a resolve to still run that risk
- foresight of the risk coupled with a weak attempt to avoid it that still amounts to a high degree of negligent behaviour
- inattention to an important matter that relates to the defendant's duty of care.

All of these judgements are left to the jury to decide.

Group activity

Using the following groups, how might their conduct fall below what was expected and how should the courts deal with them if someone has been killed? Are the courts the only option?

1 Teachers

2 Train drivers

3 Car drivers

4 Landlords.

Breach of duty of care

It is the job of the jury to decide whether the defendant's conduct departed sufficiently from the standard expected of the defendant. In other words, how serious was the breach of duty? Mistakes can happen and judgements can sometimes be wrong. If a doctor were taken to court every time a patient died there would be no doctors. Who would want such a job? The breach of duty must therefore be a serious breach of duty.

Death of the victim

The defendant must be the one who causes the death of the victim. This may sound obvious, but if a doctor is working as part of a team, it may be difficult to assign blame to one particular person. If a teacher is part of a team where communications have broken down and a pupil dies, it may be difficult to pinpoint the responsibility.

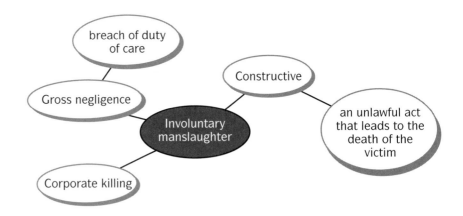

Involuntary manslaughter

4 Corporate killing

Businesses are able to limit their liability to financial disaster by forming companies. A company is a legal construct and company law allows the business to be seen as a separate legal entity distinct from those human beings who have formed it. These companies are owned by shareholders and normally run by professional managers who in turn employ workers to carry out the activities required of the business. Financial liability is fairly clear but liability for criminal activities is less clear.

Actus reus and *mens rea* of corporate manslaughter

One may be able to establish *actus reus* of an offence reasonably easily, but the complication in corporate manslaughter is proving the *mens rea* of a company.

Should the accusation of *mens rea* be made against ordinary workers, against managers or against the shareholders? These questions have come to be known as 'identification'. Lord Reid explored the issue in *Tesco v Nattrass (1972)*.

Legal case: *Tesco v Nattrass (1972)*

Tesco was taken to court under the Trade Descriptions Act 1968 for advertising washing powder for 14p when the actual price was 19p. A branch manager was charged under the Act but the House of Lords felt that it would be more senior people within the structure who would be responsible if there was an offence. The Lords decided that only people who represented the 'controlling mind' of the company could have *mens rea*. If these people had the *mens rea* for the offence then the company had *mens rea* for the offence.

The main problem here is that the proving of a strict liability offence or one where the penalty is not too great generally involves a low level of *mens rea*. Manslaughter involves a much more substantial element of *mens rea* and the courts will find this much more problematic as can be seen in one of the most important cases to come before the courts, *R v P&O European Ferries (1991)*.

Legal case: *R v P&O European Ferries (1991)*

This case was also known as the Zeebrugge disaster. 187 people died when the ferry sailing from Zeebrugge to Dover rolled over and capsized when the bow doors were left open. This allowed thousands of gallons of water to enter the car decks and swing the vessel onto its side. Those inside stood little chance in the confusion and the cold waters. Legal action was brought against the company and those employees directly involved in the negligence. The case against the managers collapsed and the Crown Prosecution Service then dropped its case against individual employees.

There is still a long way to go in the area of corporate manslaughter law and enforcement. The practical difficulties in establishing fault and the huge financial and political power of large companies have allowed them to evade their responsibilities in certain key areas.

✷ 5 Evaluation and reform of involuntary manslaughter

There have been problems in this area of law that have led to great public concern. Some of the issues include the following.

- The law is complex and left to the jury to decide. This causes splits amongst jury members and long deliberation. At times, the complexities can be so overwhelming that jurors make simplistic analysis of the issues and produce less than perfect decisions.

- The range of offences for gross negligence manslaughter is immense. It can cover minor and understandable errors of judgement to very serious reckless behaviour.

- Judges find it difficult to sentence defendants since the charge covers such a wide range of possibilities.

The government and Law Commission have been working on this issue. Proposals include three new offences to update and simplify the law in this area.

1 Reckless killing

This offence would carry life imprisonment and would be caused by someone unreasonably taking a risk that they know will cause death or serious injury.

2 Killing by gross carelessness

This offence would carry a maximum sentence of ten years and would be caused by someone whose conduct falls below what would be reasonably expected or intended, or unreasonably takes a risk that causes injury that leads to death.

3 Death as a result of a minor injury caused intentionally or recklessly

This offence would carry a maximum sentence of between five and ten years and would be caused by someone who was reckless to whether an injury was caused but could not foresee death or serious injury.

Web activity

Further information on these proposals and updates on the legislation is available on the Internet. Go to www.heinemann.co.uk/hotlinks and click on this unit.

Quick revision questions

1 What is the key aspect to involuntary manslaughter?

2 Name the two main forms of involuntary manslaughter.

3 What is the *actus reus* and *mens rea* of gross negligence manslaughter?

4 Outline the key aspects to *R v Adomako (1994)*.

5 List some examples of relationships that show a duty of care.

6 What might be considered as examples of gross negligence?

7 What is the *actus reus* and *mens rea* of unlawful act/constructive manslaughter?

8 What are the main issues courts have to deal with in cases of corporate killing?

9 Why is the law in this area under reform?

10 What three new offences are being considered by government?

Exam question

Examine the key ways a defendant may be committed of manslaughter.
[50 marks]

Exam answer guide

Knowledge and understanding [20 marks]

✓ Define involuntary manslaughter and voluntary manslaughter

✓ Distinguish between gross negligence manslaughter and unlawful act manslaughter. State the *actus reus* and *mens rea* for both offences

✓ Define corporate manslaughter and give the *actus reus* and *mens rea*

Analysis and evaluation [25 marks]

✓ Comment on problems with the range of offences covered by involuntary manslaughter

✓ Evaluate the use of subjective and objective tests in cases of manslaughter

✓ Evaluate the role of the jury in gross negligence manslaughter cases. Should this be left to the jury to decide?

✓ Discuss the need to establish duty of care in gross negligence manslaughter

✓ Comment on corporate cases and the need to tighten legislation. Quote cases such as *R v P&O European Ferries (1991)* and *Tesco v Nattrass (1972)* and the *mens rea* required

✓ Comment on potential reform of manslaughter and Law Commission proposals

Presentation [5 marks]

✓ Structure your work in a logical and well-planned way. Employ good quality and clear English in your writing. Make use of punctuation and correct spelling in your answers.

Criminal law 2

General defences

Key points

1 Insanity
2 Automatism
3 Duress, necessity
4 Mistake
5 Intoxication

Why do I need to know about general defences?

In the interests of justice, defendants may be allowed to put forward defences that reduce the level of fault and therefore *mens rea* that they are associated with. If these pleas are successful, they may be charged with a less serious offence, have their sentence reduced, receive a conditional or even absolute

Automatism

discharge, or perhaps be asked to attend a designated treatment facility. The defences studied in this unit are general defences to all crimes and will affect the level of criminal liability, *mens rea* and sentencing.

1 Insanity

This defence was used when the punishment for murder was hanging and there was little else on offer to escape the grisly death.

The key test for insanity was laid out in the Macnaughton Rules in 1843. The test is still used today and states:

'It must be clearly proved that, at the time of the committing of the act the defendant:
1 did not know what he was doing
2 if he did know what he was doing, he did not consider it wrong.'

Macnaughton murdered Edward Drummond who was secretary to a famous politician called Robert Peel. He was trying to kill Peel but missed. The jury found Macnaughton insane and he was committed to a secure mental hospital for the rest of his life.

If the court is satisfied that the defendant fits into one or both of the two categories, they have a range of options available.

- **Treatment orders**

  The offender may be required to receive treatment from their doctor or from the out-patient department of a hospital as part of their release from the court.

- **Hospital orders**

  Ordering the offender to attend a hospital as an in-patient to receive appropriate treatment.

- **Secure hospitals**

  If the patient is believed to be dangerous to himself or others, he may be detained under Section 41 of the Mental Health Act 1983 and held in a secure hospital.

The rules in Macnaughton are not strictly binding on judges, but they have used it as a valuable guide in this difficult area.

The psychological state of the defendant's mind may be relevant in one of two ways:

1 The defendant may not be mentally alert enough to understand the trial proceedings. They may not be in a position to make a sensible plea of guilty or not guilty or understand the charges against them. There would be little point in a trial in these circumstances.

2 The defendant may have been insane when the offence was committed. Normal trial proceedings may take place but the defendant may be found not guilty by reason of insanity.

The *defendant* must prove that they are unfit to plead or were insane at the time of the offence. This must be proved on a balance of probabilities. The prosecution must normally prove beyond a reasonable doubt.

It is much easier to prove on the balance of probabilities. This means that the defence just tips the scales with 51 per cent of the argument. Proving beyond a reasonable doubt indicates a substantial level of proof required. The jury should only convict if they are certain the defendant is guilty.

2 Automatism

A person who commits a criminal act must have done it voluntarily. The *mens rea* assumes that this is the case, as without it there cannot have been a criminal act.

There are times when the defendant may plead that they were not responsible for their actions. The defendant may claim that they had no conscious power over their physical movements and that they were acting as an automaton. There are two main types of this mechanical behaviour.

1 Acts performed by uncontrolled muscular reactions. This could be due to spasms of the limbs, reflex actions or convulsions.

2 Acts performed while the defendant was unconscious.

The defence must prove that their client committed the offence while suffering from either of these two automatist states. The courts have decided this to stop the prosecuting authorities being overwhelmed by such defences.

Non-insane automatism

The cause of automatism must be external. Automatism is sometimes known as non-insane automatism to make clear that it is not a defence of insanity. Insanity has internal causes. The source of non-insane automatism must be external such as:

● a physical blow to the head

● medication which induces a blackout or uncontrollable muscular actions.

If the defence is able to prove automatism then the defendant will be found not guilty, as the necessary *mens rea* is not present.

Self-induced automatism

The defence is not always available to defendants who voluntarily take drugs or alcohol that induce a state of automatism. If the prosecution must prove intention and a state of voluntary automatism is proved, the defendant may use this defence. If the prosecution is trying to prove a lesser *mens rea*, such as recklessness, then the defendant may be found guilty if they knew that their consumption of drugs or alcohol, for example, might have brought about such a state. If their medication states a warning on the bottle or their doctor or pharmacist has warned them of the possible side effects if mixed with other substances or taken in unusual ways then their defence is weakened.

3 Duress, necessity

Duress by threat

Duress by threat involves a criminal ordering an innocent person to commit a criminal act by using the threat of violence against them. The threat has to be very serious, amounting to a threat of death or serious personal injury. If, for example, a gang of robbers attack an all-night petrol station and threaten to shoot the cashier if money is not passed over from the safe, can the cashier be charged with theft? Absolutely not! This would be ridiculous. The defence of duress is used in these circumstances so that the innocent are not punished and the police and the courts do not waste their time on those who in effect are victims not criminals.

There is a test for duress that came up in a case from 1982.

Legal case: *R v Graham (1982)*

Graham was married to a woman called Betty. The couple lived in the same house as Graham's jealous homosexual lover, whose name was King. Graham was threatened by King and agreed to strangle Betty with a piece of flex from the coffee percolator. Graham pleaded duress: he said that King had threatened him with violence. Two important questions came from the case:

1 Was the defendant acting out of fear of death or serious physical harm?

2 Would a reasonable person sharing the defendant's characteristics have acted in the same way?

There is a subjective element and an objective element to the test. Question 1 looks at what the defendant thought/believed and Question 2 looks at what the reasonable man would have thought/believed.

Graham was found guilty.

An important aspect to duress is that the offence committed by the victim of duress must be one that was ordered by the criminals. If not then duress is not available. The following case illustrates this point.

Legal case: *R v Cole (1994)*

The defendant owed money to some moneylenders who had made threats of violence to the defendant and also to the defendant's wife and child. The moneylenders had already attacked the defendant using a baseball bat. The defendant eventually robbed two building societies and pleaded duress when caught. The court did not accept the plea since the moneylenders had not told the defendant to 'go and rob two building societies'.

There are a number of important points that must be addressed if duress is to be used as a defence.

- The defendant or the defendant's close family must be the ones under threat.
- The defendant must have no safe means of escape from the aggressors.
- The crime committed must be one that the aggressors demand.
- Duress can be used as a defence against all offences except for murder.

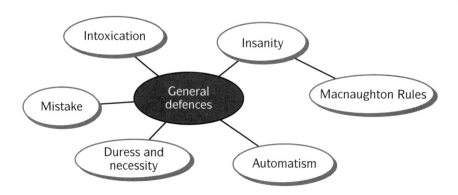

General defences

Duress of circumstances

The circumstances defendants find themselves in may at times be used as a defence. The first of such cases to be heard in front of the courts were driving offences.

Legal case: *R v Willer (1986)*

The defendant drove onto a pavement to escape from a group of boys who were threatening him. The police took him to court for reckless driving and the judge ruled that he had no defence. The Court of Appeal ruled otherwise. They said that it should have been left up to the jury to decide whether the defence was allowable or not.

Self-induced duress

If the defendant has put himself into the situation he finds himself, he may not be able to use duress as a defence. If he voluntarily joins a violent street gang who rob members of the public and is then put under pressure to continue even if he wants to leave, he must take the consequences.

4 Mistake

A defendant may make use of the defence of mistake. For this to happen two options are available:

1 There would have been no *mens rea* if the mistaken fact were true. If I was given the wrong coat by a cloakroom attendant and walked off with it, this would not be seen as theft. I would simply be collecting my coat from the cloakroom. There was a genuine mistake and no *mens rea*. There was no intention to permanently deprive the owner of the coat.

2 The defendant could have relied on another defence if the mistaken fact were true. If a policeman fires a weapon believing the victim is armed and about to shoot, then he could use the defence of mistake against the charge of manslaughter.

The mistake must take the form of mistake about facts and not of law: 'ignorance of the law is no defence.'

Quality of the evidence for mistake

Even if the defendant using the defence of mistake has made a very poor decision, the defence can still be used. The jury will take the circumstances into account in deciding whether mistake was genuine. The issue was clarified further in the following case.

Legal case: *DPP v Morgan (1975)*

The defendant was charged with rape. The House of Lords ruled that it was the state of mind of the defendant (subjective) rather than the reasonable man (objective) that was relevant to the *mens rea* of the case. There was no onus to prove reasonable grounds to support the mistake. The jury in this case thought that the possibility that the defendant believed he had consent from the victim was not possible in light of the circumstances of the case and he was found guilty.

Mistake and intoxication

Alcohol affects the central nervous system and one's ability to think rationally. Actions that are carried out whilst under the influence of alcohol may be done with the best possible of intentions and may well be honest, but the court may not see them as reasonable. Clearly, there is an important policy issue here. If the court dismissed all drunken mistakes then the implications could be terrifying.

The law does make a distinction between crimes of basic intent and those of specific intent. Crimes of specific intent (such as grievous bodily harm with intent and murder) require a much higher level of *mens rea* to be proved and mistake, intoxicated or not, might favour the defendant. Crimes of basic intent (such as assault and battery, actual bodily harm and rape), with the lower level of *mens rea*, can be committed through *mens rea* of recklessness alone and the defendant cannot use the defence of intoxication to support the plea of mistake.

The law is complicated in this area. The following case has *obiter* that states intoxicated mistakes should not be allowed.

Legal case: *R v O'Grady (1987)*

O'Grady and his friend had been drinking heavily. When O'Grady woke up he found his friend hitting him and responded by hitting him back with a nearby heavy ashtray. O'Grady then fell asleep. When he woke he found that the blow from the ashtray had killed his drinking partner. The court found him guilty of manslaughter. At his appeal Lord Lane stated (*obiter*) that for policy reasons intoxicated mistakes should not be available even for crimes of specific intent.

The Law Commission and the Criminal Law Revision Committee however, believe that intoxicated mistake may be seen as a relevant defence in murder cases.

5 Intoxication

Intoxication not only covers alcohol but also illegal drugs such as cannabis and solvents. Whether a person can use intoxication as a defence depends on the level of *mens rea* required for the offence.

Crimes of basic intent

The general principle in English law is that getting drunk is no excuse for criminal behaviour. Clearly, alcohol affects people's judgement and makes behaviour that is out of character more likely. For public policy reasons, however, the courts have decided not to accept voluntary intoxication as a defence particularly for cases where basic intent is required.

If the charge is rape then intoxication cannot be used as a defence since the crime is one of basic intent. This means that the defendant can be convicted if they recklessly got drunk. The *mens rea* component of the charge is met because of the reckless element.

Crimes of specific intent

The courts have a more difficult time when considering offences that require the highest level of *mens rea*. Crimes of specific intent such as grievous bodily harm with intent and murder fall into this category. The courts are more likely to accept pleas of intoxication. Offences under Section 18 of the Offences Against the Person Act (1861), require intent and this is much more difficult to prove since the defendant must have intention and not just be reckless.

Involuntary intoxication

If a person's drink is spiked with drugs or more alcohol than they realize, they may be able to use this as a defence. The key legal point is whether *mens rea* was formed. If it was the defendant may be found guilty. If not the defendant must be found innocent. A recent case involved a woman who ate too much brandy-based Christmas cake. The court felt that on this occasion the quantities in the cake would have been insufficient to show up on a breathalyser and that voluntarily consumed alcohol was the more likely culprit.

Group activity

The Guardian archive contains hundreds of reports on crime and sentences and legal reports. Go to www.heinemann.co.uk/hotlinks and click on this unit. Comment on the defences used in the cases. Do they correspond to ones studied in this unit?

Quick revision questions

1 Outline the Macnaughton Rules.

2 Why might the psychological state of mind of the defendant be relevant?

3 What might be classified as automatist acts?

4 What is the difference between insane and non-insane automatism?

5 List some causes of non-insane automatism.

6 How does intoxication work as a defence with crimes of specific intent and basic intent?

7 Distinguish duress by threat from duress by circumstance.

8 What conditions are required if duress is to be used as a defence?

9 What two possibilities are open for mistake to be an effective defence?

10 Where do the Law Commission and Criminal Law Revision Committee and Lord Lane disagree?

Why have courts had to limit the availability of defences available to defendants? [50 marks]

Exam answer guide

Knowledge and understanding [20 marks]
- ✓ Identify the main defences available
- ✓ Define insanity and how it is proved. Consider the consequences of such a plea
- ✓ Define automatism and illustrate the difference between non-insane and self induced automatism
- ✓ Define duress and necessity and identify when it can be used
- ✓ Define mistake and illustrate the two options
- ✓ Define intoxication paying particular attention to voluntary and involuntary

Analysis and evaluation [25 marks]
- ✓ Consider possible public policy issues of defences
- ✓ Consider each defence individually and comment on the key problems that might arise for example why are courts keen to limit the defence of intoxication?
- ✓ Why are courts careful about the use of duress and necessity?
- ✓ Discuss the public policy issues that arise from each defence and its possible misuse

Presentation [5 marks]
- ✓ Structure your work in a logical and well planned way. Employ good quality and clear English in your writing. Make use of punctuation and correct spelling in your answers.

UNIT 2

Assaults

Key points

1 Assault
2 Battery
3 Actual bodily harm (ABH)
4 Wounding and grievous bodily harm (GBH)
5 Law Commission proposals and response

Why do I need to know about assaults?

The difference between some non-fatal offences and murder may only rest on the outcome. Another important point to note is that the *actus reus* for offences may be very similar in some cases. The difference you must look out for is the *mens rea*. The government is currently changing legislation in the whole area of non-fatal offences against the person since the key legislation used to this point has become very out of date in terms of language and flexibility. The website where you can look at the proposals in more detail is given towards the end of this unit. It is well worth a read.

Actual bodily harm

1 Assault

Assault means putting someone in fear of immediate unlawful personal violence. There are some complications, however, since assault is both a common law offence and a statutory offence.

Another complication is that assault is so often used with the word battery that the general public use them as if they were the same. Judges have noted the fact.

Legal case: *Fagan v Metropolitan Police Commissioner (1968)*

The judge in this case stated during the trial that:

'assault is an independent crime, but for practical purposes today is generally synonymous with the term "battery".'

- The *actus reus* of assault is apprehension of immediate unlawful personal violence.

- The *mens rea* of assault is intention to put the victim in fear of immediate unlawful physical harm, **or** subjective recklessness as to whether they would fear immediate unlawful physical harm.

Sentence for assault

- Up to six months in prison (Section 39 of the Criminal Justice Act 1988)

Assault is covered in Section 39 of the Criminal Justice Act 1988. Section 39 refers to two separate offences – assault and battery. This upheld the common law distinction between the two crimes. Section 40, however, only refers to common assault and not assault and battery as two separate offences. In reality, attackers may commit both offences so close together that they are referred to as 'assault and battery'.

Elements of assault

The key to assault is putting someone in apprehension of immediate physical violence. This may involve the following.

- **Physical threat**

  A person may be put in fear when someone approaches them in a threatening manner armed with a weapon. This would be assault if the person believed that the threat was real and immediate.

- **Indirect threat**

  A telephone call, a text message or even e-mail may put a person in fear of immediate violence. In fact, even silent phone calls can be considered assault, as can be seen in the following case.

Legal case: *R v Ireland (1997)*

The defendant had made a series of silent phone calls to women. The women had no idea of where he was calling from and suffered fear that they were about to be attacked. The House of Lords felt that there was sufficient evidence, even though the calls were silent, that the calls themselves amounted to assault occasioning actual bodily harm.

Immediate and apprehend

Immediate does not have to be instantaneous. If someone makes a threatening telephone call from an unknown number or waves a fist from a passing car it can be classified as immediate. It depends on whether the victim perceives the violence to be immediate.

Although fear may well go along with an assault it is not necessarily the case. The word 'apprehend' is often used. Apprehend does not mean that you are necessarily put into fear from the defendant. A tall, powerful person with a black belt in karate may still not want someone shaking their fist and threatening them with immediate unlawful violence. Apprehend means that the victim is conscious of the possible threat but does not have to be scared of that threat. This allows the court greater flexibility.

Legal case: *Tuberville v Savage (1669)*

The defendant put his hand on his sword and said to the victim, 'If it were not assize time I would run you through with my weapon.' During assize time the judges would have been visiting the town and swift justice would have been done. The court decided that there was no assault because the words spoken would have reassured the victim that nothing was going to happen to him immediately. After the judges had left might be another matter of course.

A case where the defendant was not so lucky was the following.

Legal case: *R v Light (1857)*

The defendant held a sword over his wife's head and said, 'If there wasn't a policeman outside I would split your head open.' The court felt that assault had happened here because the wife could not be sure what her husband would do next. She was put in immediate fear of unlawful physical harm.

2 Battery

Battery involves the application of unlawful force. This could include a physical kick or the setting of a trap, which causes the application of force. Theoretically, any touching might be classified as battery, but two fundamentals stop a flood of charges being brought to the Crown Prosecution Service.

1 Most everyday contact with other people in trains, buses, or at football matches, for example, involves an element of consent. Our social activities would be impossible if we went to the courts every time another human being made physical contact with us.

2 The intention. Most people in these crowded, social, transport or work situations do not have the intention of causing harm. Sometimes it happens: people have feet trampled upon or are pushed by impatient passengers, but the intention to inflict harm is not there. There is only an intention to get on a busy train at rush hour.

- The *actus reus* of battery is the application of unlawful force on another.

- The *mens rea* of battery is the intention to apply unlawful force, **or** subjective recklessness as to whether unlawful force is applied to another.

Sentence for battery

- Up to six months in prison (Section 39 of the Criminal Justice Act 1988)

Battery may occur without the groundwork of a threatening assault. If someone fires an airgun from a secret position, hitting a person on the back, it might be classified as battery but does not have the assault element.

Direct and indirect

The defendant applying direct physical force produces the vast bulk of batteries: punching, kicking, throwing an object or striking with a weapon. The force can also be indirect and still be called battery.

Legal case: *DPP v K (1990)*

A schoolboy set up a booby trap in the hot air dryer of the boys' toilet to spray acid onto the next person who used the dryer. He was found guilty of battery even though the force was indirect.

Legal case: *R v Haystead (2000)*

The defendant attacked a woman who was holding a baby and, as a result, the woman dropped the baby onto the ground. The defendant was convicted of battery on the baby even though he did not directly touch the child.

3 Actual bodily harm (ABH)

Actual bodily harm is covered in Section 47 of the Offences Against the Person Act 1861. The offence is triable either way.

Actual bodily harm covers a broad range of injuries. They include:

● minor bruises and grazes

● injuries which are not permanent

● injuries which interfere with the comfort of the victim

● injuries which are more than trivial but not really serious.

Clearly, many situations are covered by such criteria. The harm caused may also include psychological injury and this does include the ordinary emotions one would feel if one was attacked. The wide definition of actual bodily harm suits the Crown Prosecution Service and the courts. It allows them a wide buffer zone to make criminal charges work.

● The *actus reus* of actual bodily harm is common assault that caused actual bodily harm.

● The *mens rea* of actual bodily harm is intention to cause actual bodily harm, **or** subjective recklessness as to the causing of actual bodily harm.

Sentence for actual bodily harm

● Up to five years in prison (Section 47 of the Offences Against the Person Act 1861)

● Up to seven years if actual bodily harm was racially motivated (Section 29 of the Crime and Disorder Act 1998)

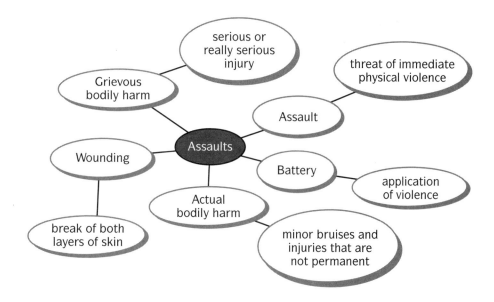

Assaults

4 Wounding and grievous bodily harm (GBH)

● Unlawful and malicious wounding or infliction of grievous bodily harm

Sections 18 and 20 of the Offences Against the Person Act 1861 cover the two most serious offences of wounding and grievous bodily harm. Both offences appear in both sections. The law is complex in this area since there are a number of overlapping offences, which have similar *actus reus* but very different *mens rea*. Take some time to read the following sections from the Offences Against the Person Act 1861 to understand how they interrelate and quoting small relevant references to this Act is likely to impress examiners.

Legislation

Section 20 Offences Against the Person Act 1861

20 Whosoever shall unlawfully and maliciously wound or inflict any grievous bodily harm upon any other person either with or without any weapon or instrument shall be guilty of an offence triable either way and being convicted thereof shall be liable to imprisonment for five years.

Section 18 Offences Against the Person Act 1861

18 Whosoever shall unlawfully and maliciously by any means whatsoever wound or cause any grievous bodily harm to any person with **intent** to do some grievous bodily harm to any person or with **intent** to resist or prevent the lawful apprehension or detaining of any person shall be guilty of an offence and being convicted thereof shall be liable to imprisonment for life.

The key difference between the two offences is the *mens rea*. In Section 18 the defendant must have had **intent**. This makes it the most serious offence of the non-fatal offences. This is an absolutely crucial point to understand. The difference between the two can also be seen in the sentences available to the judge. Crimes with intent carry life imprisonment whilst others vary between six months and five years.

Wounding

Wounding means a break of the inner **and** outer skin. A scratch of the outer skin, the epidermis, is not enough. The wound must include a puncture of the inner skin, the dermis.

Legal case: *JJC v Einsenhower (1984)*

A boy was shot by an air gun, which hit his eye and there was an internal rupture of the blood vessels but no external bleeding. As there was no break of both skin layers the charge did not succeed.

- The *actus reus* of wounding is unlawful wounding.

- The *mens rea* of wounding is the intention to inflict some harm even though it might not be serious harm.

- The *actus reus* of grievous bodily harm is unlawful infliction of grievous bodily harm.

- The *mens rea* of grievous bodily harm is intention to inflict grievous bodily harm, **or** intention to resist lawful arrest.

Sentence for wounding and grievous bodily harm

- Section 18 = up to life imprisonment

- Section 20 = up to five years imprisonment

Cause and inflict

In Section 18 the word 'cause' is used when referring to grievous bodily harm: Section 20 uses the word 'inflict'. The courts have decided that the words are effectively interchangeable.

Serious and really serious

In some cases judges have referred to grievous bodily harm as 'really serious bodily harm'. In others the judge has referred to grievous bodily harm as 'serious bodily harm'. The defendant may wish a direction from the judge of really serious bodily harm since this may make the jury think this case has not reached the higher level. It might be seen by some that the prosecution has a more difficult job in proving 'really serious bodily harm'. The following case clarified the position.

Legal case: *R v Saunders (1985)*

Saunders broke a stranger's nose by punching him. He was convicted when the judge directed the jury to believe that grievous bodily harm meant 'serious bodily harm' and not 'really serious bodily harm'. Saunders felt disadvantaged by the omission of the word 'really'. On appeal the Court of Appeal said that the omission of 'really' was not important and has since stated that the judge has discretion when using the word 'really' or not.

Group activity

Do you think that the words omitted such as 'really' in court cases such as *R v Saunders (1985)* make any difference to the decision that the jury makes?

What other factors other than the evidence brought before them might change the verdict of the jury?

Examples of grievous bodily harm

As the offence moves from wounding to 'really serious bodily harm' we can perhaps look at some examples of what this might mean.

- An injury that leads to a permanent disability. This could include loss of sight or paralysis.
- Permanent visible scarring.
- Broken limbs or bones.
- Injuries that led to a significant healing period.
- Injuries that led to the need for a blood transfusion.

Wounding might be fairly trivial – a small cut or a graze that penetrated both layers of skin would classify as wounding but not grievous bodily harm. A stab wound to the internal organs that led to a blood transfusion and six months off work would almost certainly be grievous bodily harm.

5 Law Commission proposals and response

The Law Commission, the only full-time law reform agency, has suggested change in this area. A report called *Offences Against the Person and General Principles* contained a draft bill on criminal law, which it hoped would update provision in this important area. According to the Law Commission the reasons for this necessary reform included:

- Old-fashioned language, which confused all who used it. The Offences Against the Person Act 1861 was itself a codifying Act, which brought even older pieces of legislation together in one place.
- The structure of existing legislation is unhelpful to easy access and cross-referencing of sections.
- Ordinary members of the public do not understand the existing legislation and even professionals find room for confusion and loopholes within the existing law.

The Labour government produced its own report in February 1998 called *Violence: Reforming the Offences Against the Person Act 1861* along with a draft bill.

Web activity

The full text of the proposed legislation from the government is available from the Home Office website, go to www.heinemann.co.uk/hotlinks and click on this unit.

The draft bill sweeps away existing law in this area and gives birth to four new offences:

- Assault
- Intentional or reckless injury

- Reckless serious injury (replaces Section 20)
- Intentional serious injury (replaces Section 18).

Words often found in the Offences Against the Person Act 1861, such as 'maliciously' and 'wounding', are not seen at all in the new bill. Section 18 is replaced with intentionally causing serious injury and Section 20 is replaced by recklessly causing serious injury. Grievous bodily harm is replaced by the term 'serious injury'. The issue of assault is still not entirely satisfactory. It possibly should have been separated into assault and battery, although to all intents and purposes the public sees assault and battery as one offence rather than two.

Under the Offences Against the Person Act 1861 there were sometimes problems over the precise meaning of bodily harm in terms of physical and mental harm. Cases mounting up seemed to suggest that this would become more and more of an issue. The proposed legislation clarifies the issue. Section 15 of the new bill states that injury can be both physical and mental harm.

The proposed legislation was not intended to toughen the government's response to crime. It was merely intended to clarify and illuminate legislation that had become antiquated and open to misunderstandings. It is a good example of where statutory interpretation by judges had reached the outer limits of credibility and where reform is well overdue.

Summary of offences

Common assault

Up to six months. Statutory offence. Section 29 of the Criminal Justice Act 1988.

Assault

Up to six months. Was common law offence/statutory offence. Section 39 of the Criminal Justice Act 1988.

Battery

Up to six months. Was common law offence/statutory offence. Section 39 of the Criminal Justice Act 1988.

Actual bodily harm

Up to five years. Statutory offence. Section 47 of the Offences Against the Person Act 1861.

Malicious wounding or inflicting grievous bodily harm

Up to five years. Section 20 of the Offences Against the Person Act 1861.

Wounding with intent or causing grievous bodily harm with intent or intent to resist arrest

Up to life imprisonment. Statutory offence. Section 18 of the Offences Against the Person Act 1861. This is the most serious non-fatal offence.

Quick revision questions

1 Define assault and state the *actus reus* and *mens rea* of the offence.

2 Why was *R v Ireland (1997)* an important case?

3 Define battery and state the *actus reus* and *mens rea* of the offence.

4 Give examples of what would constitute actual bodily harm.

5 Define wounding and show how it varies from Sections 18 and 20 of the Offences Against the Person Act 1861.

6 What is the *actus reus* and *mens rea* of grievous bodily harm?

7 Distinguish between cause and inflict in Sections 18 and 20.

8 Is there a difference between serious and really serious? Which one would a defendant choose?

9 Give a list of injuries that could be classified as grievous bodily harm.

10 Summarize the reforms suggested by the government's bill on non-fatal offences.

Exam question

Outline the key non-fatal offences against the person. Why is reform thought necessary in this area of the law? [50 marks]

Exam answer guide

Knowledge and understanding [20 marks]

✓ Outline assault. Quote *Fagan v Metropolitan Police Commissioner (1968), R v Ireland (1997), Tuberville v Savage (1669)* and *R v Light (1857)*
✓ Outline battery. Quote *DPP v K (1990)* and *R v Haystead (2000)*
✓ Outline actual bodily harm and give some examples
✓ Outline wounding and grievous bodily harm – break of both skins for wounding
✓ Comment on the seriousness of grievous bodily harm and the differences between Section 18 and Section 20. Quote *R v Saunders (1985)*
✓ Highlight the intent issue. How does this make offence more serious?

Analysis and evaluation [25 marks]

✓ Outline reasons for current problems with these offences
✓ Analyse and give your view on the Law Commission proposals
✓ Comment on the offences of assault, intentional or reckless injury, reckless serious injury and intentional serious injury. Are these clearer than the old 1861 offences?

Presentation [5 marks]

✓ Structure your work in a logical and well-planned way. Employ good quality and clear English in your writing. Make use of punctuation and correct spelling in your answers.

UNIT 3

Defences

Key points

1 Self-defence, defence of another
2 Prevention of crime
3 Justification of self-defence/prevention
4 Consent and limitations

Why do I need to know about defences?

Defences either reduce fault completely or reduce it to a certain extent so that sentencing is more lenient. The courts are very careful, however, not to send the wrong signals out to the general public about their rights to self-defence, prevention of crime or issues of consent. Within decisions made by courts are issues of public policy and signals about what is acceptable or unacceptable behaviour.

Prevention of crime is a defence

1 Self-defence, defence of another

Self-defence

Self-defence is allowed for crimes against the person and can be used in defending oneself or others. Section 3 of the Criminal Law Act 1967 outlines the rules that apply for this defence to be possible.

- The amount of force used to defend oneself must be reasonable.
- The danger must be present and immediate and not passed.
- If force is used as revenge or retaliation then there is no defence.

Legal case: *R v Clegg (1995)*

Private Clegg was positioned on a checkpoint in Northern Ireland monitoring the movements of people and cars. A vehicle driven by 'joy riders' went through the barrier despite warnings shouted by the soldiers. Private Clegg fired and killed eighteen year old Karen Reilly. Evidence later showed that the car was at least ten yards beyond Clegg's position when he fired the shot. The immediate danger seemed to have passed when the weapon was fired. The courts found that excessive force was used and Private Clegg was convicted of murder. His conviction was upheld on appeal in 1995.

2 Prevention of crime

Section 3 of the Criminal Law Act 1967 also allows two further defences:

1 Preventing a crime

If an heroic bystander wants to get involved in dangerous actions, such as foiling a robbery, and commits criminal damage as part of that crime prevention, they may put up a defence under Section 3. The damage might, for example, involve taking a nearby vehicle and ramming a getaway car. The Crown Prosecution Service would be unlikely to press charges of taking without owner's consent, dangerous driving and criminal damage in such a situation.

2 Arresting an offender

Arresting an offender may require using reasonable force to subdue them. Citizen's arrest is fraught with danger – not only physical danger to the 'hero' but also legal danger. Arresting the offender does not mean beating them up, but it may involve wrestling them to the ground and pinning them down. In normal circumstances this might involve assault and battery and possibly even actual bodily harm. If the defendant himself has just been involved in an armed robbery then the authorities would probably regard this as reasonable force. If the person had simply parked their car in a no parking zone and the 'hero' tackles them to the pavement, the courts might take another view.

Defence of property

The law makes allowances for self-defence and defence of others, but is less sympathetic to defence of possessions and property. A famous case that has caused much controversy is the following.

Legal case: *R v Martin (1999)*

Tony Martin shot dead a sixteen year old boy in defence of his property. Martin lived in an isolated farm called 'Bleak House', which had been burgled on a number of previous occasions. Martin was found guilty of murder and of wounding the second burglar. On appeal Martin's lawyers focused on self-defence and diminished responsibility as defences to both charges. The Lord Chief Justice sitting in the Court of Appeal reduced the murder conviction to one of manslaughter. The sentence for murder was reduced from life to five years and the ten year sentence for wounding was reduced to three years.

The courts hoped to send out a clear signal in this case to others who felt the need to use lethal force to protect goods and possessions.

3 Justification of self-defence/prevention

The courts are very sensitive to the issue of self-defence and the degree of force to be used. In situations of stress, some 'heroes' may overreact and deliver what might be regarded by some as 'kangaroo court justice' with full punishment meted out by the hands of the 'victim'. Feelings of concern over the level of street violence, robbery and burglary may tempt some to take the law into their own hands and juries are sometimes sympathetic to those who are put into these difficult and dangerous situations. The rule of law and due process are important

Defences

concepts here and cases such as Tony Martin's and Private Clegg's mentioned earlier should cause much concern. Lord Lloyd in Clegg's case stated that excessive force should not reduce liability from murder to manslaughter – in other words, excessive self-defence is no defence.

4 Consent and limitations

Consent raises fascinating legal and moral problems. There are two cases that go to the heart of the debate.

Legal case: *R v Brown and others (1993)*

Brown and friends were involved in a variety of violent sexual activities including the nailing of their genitals to pieces of wood and being beaten with whips. All consented, but the police found out about their extreme hobbies via a video recording and they were all prosecuted. The Court of Appeal and the House of Lords dismissed their appeals against conviction.

Legal case: *R v Wilson (1997)*

Mr Wilson decided to go along with his wife's wish to have his initials branded onto her buttocks. Her doctor saw these 'fashion accessories' and reported the matter to the police. Wilson was convicted of actual bodily harm but won the case at the appeal court.

Group activity

Do you think prosecution was the right course of events, given the individuals involved in the cases of Brown and Wilson were all adults and all gave consent of their own free will?

Consent occurs in a number of other settings.

- **Surgery**

  Clearly, doctors need legal permission to cut into flesh without being charged with wounding or even manslaughter if things go wrong on the operating table. They can, however, be brought under legal challenge if they perform unnecessary or intrusive work.

- **Sports**

  This obviously applies to boxing, judo and fencing, but also, to a certain extent, football, rugby and other sports which involve physical contact. Some sports have questioned the legal position of deliberate and dangerous fouling, which can cause serious injury.

- **Tattooing**

  Again, this might theoretically come under actual bodily harm or wounding if both skin layers are penetrated. The customer gives their consent for this permanent decoration and the tatooist is free to pursue their noble but bloody art.

- **Sex**

  Sex can sometimes involve dangerous practices for which consent is normally given. *R v Brown (1993)* and *R v Wilson (1997)* highlights legal risks in this area even if consent is given.

- **Rough and tumble**

  Young people in particular enjoy 'rough and tumble' type games that can sometimes end in serious injury. Consent is given by the context of these activities, although when they get out of hand one party or another can withdraw consent.

Quick revision questions

1 Section 3 of the Criminal Law Act 1967 allows what defences for crimes against the person?

2 The amount of force must be reasonable and the danger must not be passed already. If force is used for retaliation or revenge the defence fails. How is reasonable force measured?

3 What other two defences are allowed by Section 3 of the Criminal Law Act 1967?

4 What is the courts view of force used to defend property?

5 What is a well-known case involving force used to defend property heard in 1999?

6 How do the courts view self-defence issues? Consider Lord Lloyd's judgement.

7 What issues were raised in *R v Brown and others (1993)*?

8 Under what circumstances would consent break down in sporting events?

9 What other areas of life is consent normally given when physical danger may be present?

10 Should consent remain a valid defence to offences that might otherwise be considered illegal?

Evaluate the use and limitations of the following defences

a self defence

b prevention of a crime

c consent.

[50 marks]

Exam answer guide

Knowledge and understanding [20 marks]

a ✓ Define self-defence. Outline rules when self defence can be used. Quote *R v Clegg (1995)*

b ✓ Outline the two possibilities when using prevention of crime. Comment on defence of property and the *R v Martin (1999)* case

c ✓ Define consent and illustrate with *R v Brown (1993)* and *R v Wilson (1997)*

  ✓ Outline other situations which involve consent in more normal circumstances. Surgery, sports tattooing, sex and rough and tumble

Analysis and evaluation [25 marks]

✓ Consider the problem courts have with issues of self-defence. Possibility of overreaction, introduction of vigilante culture. Underline the need for care when danger has passed and point out that revenge is not self-defence

✓ Consider public policy issues that might arise from ordinary citizens taking on an active role in the prevention of crime

✓ Consider *R v Martin (1999)* in terms of damage caused and public reaction to the courts seeming to favour such actions

✓ Consider moral issues involved in *R v Brown (1993)* and *R v Wilson (1997)*. Should police and courts interfere in private sexual matters?

Presentation [5 marks]

✓ Structure your work in a logical and well-planned way. Employ good quality and clear English in your writing. Make use of punctuation and correct spelling in your answers.

UNIT 4

Theft

Key points

1 *Actus reus* and *mens rea*
2 Appropriation -7 - 3
3 Property- 8 - 4
4 Belonging to another - 5
5 Intention permanently to deprive 6
6 Dishonesty - 2

Why do I need to know about theft?

Theft is one of the most common crimes the courts have to deal with. It also provides the basis for other more serious crimes such as robbery. Questions on theft will be in the form of a short case study involving potential offences where you will be required to apply your understanding of the law. The key issues to look out for in this unit are appropriation, property, belonging to another, dishonesty, and

Theft

intention permanently to deprive. The key pieces of legislation are the Theft Act 1968 and the Theft Act 1978. The 1968 Act covers theft and two other offences that you will look at in the next unit, robbery and burglary. The 1978 Act covers offences such as making off without payment.

1 *Actus reus* and *mens rea*

Actus reus of theft has three elements which will be looked at in detail. They are:

- appropriation 3
- property 4
- belonging to another. 5

These terms are explained in detail in Sections 3, 4 and 5 of the Theft Act 1968.

There are two elements to the *mens rea* of theft:

1 dishonesty 2
2 intention permanently to deprive. 6

Both elements must be proved. For it to be theft.

2 Appropriation

Section 3 of the Theft Act 1968 states that appropriation is 'assumption of the rights of the owner'. Appropriation means taking something for your own use and it is normally used when describing something illegal. Appropriation of property may come in a variety of ways: using in push del. Sell in dest.

- taking property away
- treating property as your own possession
- destroying property
- selling property.

The scope of this definition is very broad. The following important case widens it even further.

Legal case: *R v Gomez (1992)*

Gomez was charged with theft after persuading the manager of a shop he was working in to sell goods worth £17,000 to an accomplice with a cheque known to be worthless. This widened the scope of theft considerably.

The timing of when the goods were appropriated is also important in proving whether an offence took place, as the following case illustrates.

Legal case: *R v Morris (1984)*

The defendant went into a supermarket and changed the prices of the goods he was buying by tampering with the price labels. He went to the checkout where the assistant recognized the fiddle. The defendant argued that he had not left the shop and therefore had not stolen the goods. The House of Lords rejected the appeal saying the offence happened at the moment of appropriation.

3 Property

The legal definition of property can be found in the Theft Act 1968 Section 4(1):

'Property includes money and all other property, real or personal, including things in action and other intangible property.'

cannot be seen or touched.

Money

Obviously money in the form of coins and notes are included in this definition. The use of credit cards, debit cards and cheques to dishonestly pay for goods is covered by Section 15(4) of the Theft Act 1968. The latter comes under the heading of deception. This section relates to the deception of human beings. The use of a debit card in cash-dispensing machines or a foreign coin to get chocolate from a machine would be classified as theft.

A further Theft Act was passed in 1978 to deal with the rise in deception cases. This was caused by the increased use of credit and debit cards and the move away from money as a way of paying for goods and services.

All other property, real and personal

Real

Real refers to land. In the US land and houses are referred to as 'real estate'. There are some complications in the Theft Act 1968 with regard to land. At one point it states that land cannot be stolen but then goes on to make a number of exceptions including:

- soil
- shrubs
- plants
- structures sitting on the land.

These can be stolen, but whether a person would regard them as land is another question. One could say that the geographical position on the map cannot be stolen.

Personal

This is the vast bulk of theft cases. These include video recorders, televisions, jewellery, paintings, cars and anything else that is held near and dear.

Things in action and other intangible property cannot be touched or seen, but are still held to be very important to most who possess them. Examples include:

● bank and building society accounts

● shares in companies

● intellectual property, such as copyrights, product designs and commercial logos.

The word 'intangible' refers to things that cannot be seen or touched and yet exist and have some value.

_ Oxford v Moss

Certain things cannot be stolen, including electricity, examination questions, wild animals and parts of dead human bodies. The court can often find a way around these exceptions, however, if it so chooses.

In theory, the work of a poacher is not theft if wild animals cannot be regarded as property. They may, however, be trespassing and tort may be used against them.

The human body will not be property unless it has been altered in some way for medical or scientific research.

Legal case: *R v Kelly (1998)*

An artist and a junior technician at the Royal College of Surgeons stole 35 body parts from the College so that the artist could use them for professional anatomical drawings. They were both convicted of theft since the body parts had undergone a variety of processes as part of their use in the College and had gained a financial status.

Information

Information can be sold and has value but it is not regarded as property. Two cases of 'stolen information' show different results.

Legal case: *Oxford v Moss (1979)*

A student at Liverpool University obtained a draft copy of his civil engineering paper, noted the contents and then returned the item from where it was taken. He was taken to court and charged with theft. The magistrates dismissed the case as there had been no intention permanently to deprive, even if the cheating student had actually got all he needed by seeing the draft. → what?

Legal case: *R v Akbar (2002)*

Mrs Akbar was a teacher at a secondary school in Croydon. Her husband ran a tutorial college where she also taught private students. She managed to steal five GCSE maths examination papers from the school where she had worked for thirteen years. The court found her guilty of theft and sentenced her to three months in prison.

In the first case the student had returned the paper that the information was written on – the schoolteacher in the second did not. She was found guilty of stealing paper the value of which was nominal. More importantly for the court were breach of trust and the undermining of the examination board by such an action.

The law is certainly weak in this area and the Law Commission is looking at creating a separate offence that would have dealt with the case of *Oxford v Moss (1979)* and others who steal information from employers, schools and universities.

4 Belonging to another

Most cases of theft involve the defendant stealing from a person who has ownership of the property stolen. Section 5(1) of the Theft Act 1968 states:

'Property shall be regarded as belonging to any person having possession or control of it.'

A thief who steals from a shop or steals from a handbag is clearly stealing from an organization or a person. The shop has possession of their stock and the person has possession of their purse.

There are, however, cases where the thief can steal their own property, particularly when they pass control of it to another person.

Legal case: *R v Turner (1971)*

The defendant had taken his car to a garage for repair. When most of the repairs were completed he used a duplicate key and took the car back into his possession. He had taken the vehicle out of the control of the garage and as a result was guilty of theft.

A case of particular interest to students planning to live away from home is the following.

Legal case: *Davidge v Bunnett (1984)*

The defendant shared his flat with some other flatmates and was given money to pay the household bills but spent it on Christmas presents instead. The defendant was guilty under Section 5(3) of the Theft Act 1968, which says that when money is given for a particular purpose it must be spent in that way or the money goes back to the original owners.

Mistake

Property acquired by another's mistake generally has to be returned.

Section 5(4) Theft Act 1968

Where a person gets property by another's mistake and is under an obligation to make restoration (in whole or in part) of the property or its proceeds or of the value thereof, then to the extent of that obligation the property or proceeds shall be regarded (as against him) as belonging to the person entitled in restoration, and an intention not to make restoration shall be regarded accordingly as an intention to deprive that person of the property or proceeds.

Therefore, if an employer overpays an employee, or a social security office overpays a claimant, or a housing benefit office overpays a tenant, these organizations have a lawful right to claim these monies back, although they may at times have policies that decide not to in certain circumstances that they see fit.

Legal case: *R v Gilks (1972)*

A gambler called Gilks laid several bets including one on a horse called Fighting Scot that lost. The temporary manager of the Ladbrokes betting shop believed that Gilks had laid a bet on the winning horse called Fighting Taffy and paid out £106 to him. Gilks was charged with theft but complained that since there was no obligation for the betting shop to pay him under contract law, there was no obligation for him to repay them under these circumstances. Gambling contracts are not enforceable under English law. The Court of Appeal held that the obligation to repay had to be a legal one and no such obligation existed in this case. Gilks therefore kept his windfall.

Lost property and abandoned property

Lost property is still owned until it is abandoned. Until it is ownerless a person cannot legally claim it as their own. Property is only abandoned when the owner does not care if another appropriates it. If property is not being used or the owner has no further use for it, it does not mean that another person may appropriate it. If a person owns a broken lawnmower that sits in a garage at the end of the garden, they may have no further use for it but that does not give the next-door neighbour the legal right to take it. If the person has lost a diamond ring in the garden, then the likelihood that they have abandoned the object will be very unlikely and if found will welcome its return and assert their ownership rights over it.

Property with no owner

There are a number of possibilities.

- If property is not owned by someone, a person cannot be charged with stealing it.

- If property was once owned but has been abandoned, then a person cannot be charged with stealing it.

- If property is capable of being owned but is not at present owned, then a person cannot be charged with stealing it.

There are a number of things that we have seen that cannot be stolen including land, wild creatures, mushrooms, fruit and flowers and knowledge.

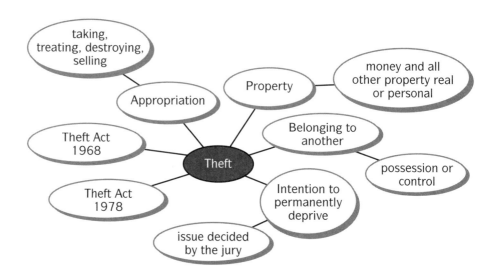

Theft

5 Intention permanently to deprive

It is the function of the jury to decide whether there was intent permanently to deprive or not. In other words, whether the defendant stole the property and had no plan to give it back to the owner. The jury will look at the evidence and decide whether intent was present. There are four main conclusions the jury might come to.

- If there is intention to deprive and deprivation does take place: verdict is theft.

- If there is intention to deprive and deprivation does not actually take place: verdict is theft.

- If there is no intention and permanent deprivation does take place: verdict is no theft.

- If there is no intention and no permanent deprivation does take place: verdict is no theft.

Intent must be present at the time the property was appropriated.

The importance of the jury is underlined in the following case.

Legal case: *R v Feely (1973)*

The manager of a betting shop 'borrowed' £30 from the till without the owner's permission. He intended to replace the amount within a few days. The judge, when directing the jury, stated that the defendant's behaviour was 'clearly dishonest'. The Court of Appeal quashed the conviction on the grounds that it was the jury's role to decide dishonesty not the judge's.

Theft of money

If money is taken from an employer, a friend, or a relative without their permission but with the aim of putting a similar amount back at a later date, theft has still technically taken place. The defendant would be unable to return the precise notes or coins, therefore they have substituted without permission one set of property with another.

Legal case: *R v Velumyl (1989)*

The defendant was a manager of a company who borrowed money without the owner's permission. He intended to repay it when a friend of his repaid money he owed. The Court of Appeal upheld the conviction arguing that he had no right to take property (money) and replace it with other property (money) without the permission of the owner.

Group activity

Do you think the verdict in *R v Velumyl (1989)* was fair given that one amount of money does essentially the same thing as another equal amount of money?

Regardless of other's rights

The defendant may appropriate the property but not intend to permanently deprive the owner or may not care whether they see it again. Section 6(1) of the 1968 Act, covers this situation: 'If the defendant's behaviour amounts to treating the property as his own to dispose of regardless of the other's rights' then sufficient *mens rea* is present for permanent deprivation to have taken place. This often applies to situations where the defendant pawns the possession of another.

Borrowing and lending

Section 6(1) of the 1968 Act, continues on to cover the situation of borrowing or lending. Here the issue of permanent deprivation is also in a grey area of human conduct.

'A borrowing or lending of a thing may amount to permanent deprivation if the borrowing or lending is for a period and in circumstances making it equivalent to an outright taking or disposal.'

Legal case: *R v Lloyd and others (1985)*

A projectionist working for an Odeon cinema borrowed tapes and allowed two others to tape them onto a master video for subsequent pirate videoing. The tapes were out of the cinema for only a few hours before being taped and returned. The gang were eventually caught and convicted of conspiracy to steal. Lord Lane, however, overturned these convictions stating:

'The second half of Section 6(1) of the 1968 Act is intended to make clear that a mere borrowing is never enough to constitute the necessary guilty mind unless the intention is to return the "thing" in such a changed state that it can truly be said that all its goodness or virtue has gone.'

The court felt that there was still virtue and goodness contained in the films, in a legal sense.

What amounts to theft or not depends on the circumstances. If someone borrows a hammer from a neighbour and it is eventually returned in the same condition as it was when it was lent, then theft has not taken place. The 'goodness or virtue' of the hammer has not gone.

If a neighbour borrows a saw and it is returned in a state where it is blunted and incapable of being sharpened, then it is not fit for its purpose and the 'goodness and virtue' has gone from it.

The 'thing' may be in a state where some virtue and goodness has gone but not all. If you lend your car to a neighbour while you are away on holiday and they manage to clock up 50,000 miles in two weeks, it could be said that the wear and tear would amount to a diminished goodness of the vehicle. Section 6(1) of the 1968 Act seems to suggest that unless it is disposed of without consideration of the owner's rights or all the goodness and virtue has gone, then theft has not taken place. Be careful whom you lend to!

6 Dishonesty

Dishonesty is not defined in the Theft Act 1968 but the case of *R v Ghosh (1982)* produced a two-part test.

Legal case: *R v Ghosh (1982)*

A surgeon claimed fees that were not owed to him. The Court of Appeal considered the case and applied a two-part test to explore the idea of dishonesty.

1 Would an ordinary, reasonable and honest person regard the act as dishonest?

2 Did the defendant realize that an ordinary, reasonable and honest person would think it was dishonest?

It does not matter what the defendant thought was honest: he may be able to convince himself of the merits of his actions. The key issue is whether he would know that others would think it wrong.

There are three situations where the defendant may argue he is not guilty of dishonesty.

- The defendant has the legal right to deprive a person of property to take for himself or a third party.
- The defendant would have been given consent if the owner knew about the circumstances in which he had taken the property.
- It would be impossible to find the rightful owner by taking reasonable steps.

Legal right to deprive

If a person believed that they had a legal right to take property, they should not be found guilty no matter how unreasonable that belief was. The *mens rea* for theft does not exist and so the person cannot be found guilty. If a young barman sees others helping themselves to drinks whilst on duty, he may believe that this is current practice and permitted by the owner. In reality, it may be theft and a sackable offence if the owner finds out.

Legal case: *R v Holden (1991)*

A temporary worker in a garage was charged with theft after taking some scrap tyres. He believed that the supervisor had given permission as he had seen others taking tyres in the past. The manager's view, however, was that this was theft and a sackable offence. The Court of Appeal quashed the conviction taking the view that if the defendant honestly believed it was a legitimate practice then he should not be found guilty of theft.

Belief that consent would have been given

If the defendant honestly believed that consent would have been given to take property, they cannot be found guilty. If a young member of the family regularly uses the family car but on one particular night cannot reach their parents and takes the vehicle without formal permission, this would not be theft. The youngster would have a reasonable belief that one of the parents would have given permission if they had been available.

Impossible to find the right owner

If a person finds £10 on Oxford Street on a busy Saturday afternoon, do they commit theft if they put it in their pocket? Section 2(1)(c) of the Theft Act 1968 would allow them a defence, in that it would be impossible to find the owner. If the £10 was in a purse that also contained the name, address and telephone number of the owner, then the legal and moral course of action would be to contact the owner (and hope for a reward).

Legal case: *R v Small (1987)*

The defendant believed that a car had been abandoned and took possession of it. The car had been parked on the same corner for two weeks. Its battery was flat, there was no petrol in the tank, one tyre was flat, the doors were open and the keys were in the ignition. The defendant was convicted but the Court of Appeal quashed the conviction. The court used the two-part test. By these standards the defendant was not guilty although what he thought was another matter.

Quick revision questions

1 What is the *actus reus* of theft?

2 How can appropriation take place?

3 Why is *R v Gomez (1992)* important?

4 Define property.

5 Can information be stolen? Illustrate your answer with a case.

6 What does Section 5(1) of the Theft Act 1968 state?

7 What is the legal position with mistake?

8 What is the *mens rea* of theft?

9 How is dishonesty proved?

10 Outline when a jury can establish theft.

Exam question

Outline the ways a theft can be committed. Comment on the cases you use.
[50 marks]

Exam answer guide

Knowledge and understanding [20 marks]

✓ *Actus reus* of theft, appropriation, property and belonging to another. Illustrate understanding of each of these concepts

✓ The following cases illustrate the key ways that theft can occur:

Appropriation: *R v Gomez (1992)*, *R v Morris (1994)*, and *R v Kelly (1998)*

Information theft: *Oxford v Moss (1979)* and *R v Akbar (2002)*

Belonging to another: *R v Turner (1971)* and *R v Davidge v Bunnett (1984)*

Mistake: *R v Gilks (1972)*

Intention to deprive: *R v Feeley (1973)*

Theft of money: *R v Velumyl (1989)*

Borrowing and lending: *R v Lloyd and others (1985)*

Dishonesty: *R v Ghosh (1982)*

Legal right to deprive: *R v Holden (1991)*

Impossible to find the owner: *R v Small (1987)*

Analysis and evaluation [25 marks]

✓ For each of the above comment on the cases involved and give your view on whether they are fair or not to the defendant

Presentation [5 marks]

✓ Structure your work in a logical and well-planned way. Employ good quality and clear English in your writing. Make use of punctuation and correct spelling in your answers.

UNIT 5

Other offences

Key points

1 Elements of Section 9(1)(a) of the Theft Act 1968 – burglary
2 Elements of Section 9(1)(b) of the Theft Act 1968 – burglary
3 Robbery – theft with use or threat of use of force
4 Making off without payment

Why do I need to know about other offences?

The three offences covered in this unit are burglary, robbery and making off without payment. They all involve theft but each offence is carried out in a very different way. Burglary and robbery are covered by the Theft Act 1968 and making off without payment is covered by the Theft Act 1978. Examine the legislation that goes with each offence carefully, particularly Section 9 on burglary, which can be difficult to grasp at first.

Burglary

1 Elements of Section 9(1)(a) of the Theft Act 1968

Burglary involves issues around entering premises and theft, and law relating to burglary is contained in the Theft Act 1968. To get the most from this unit you will need to know the law surrounding theft and trespass and apply the principles to burglary. The key sections of the Theft Act 1968 you will be expected to know are Sections 9(1)(a) and 9(1)(b). You need to use established cases to illustrate the concepts of burglary. The law can be quite complicated in this area so put key points down on index cards and take things step by step.

The difference between the two types of burglary is the different intentions of the defendant involved at various stages of the offence. Both types of burglary involve trespass, which is part of civil law and is a tort.

The first type of burglary involves an intention from the beginning to commit theft, rape, criminal damage or grievous bodily harm. It is covered by Section 9(1)(a) of the Theft Act 1968. The offender must have entered the premises with the listed offences on their mind.

> **Legislation**
>
> **Section 9(1) Theft Act 1968**
>
> A person is guilty of burglary if:
>
> **a** he enters any building or part of a building as a trespasser and with intent to commit any such offence as mentioned in Subsection 2.

Subsection 2 lists the further offences that support the charge of burglary.

> **Legislation**
>
> **Subsection 2 Theft Act 1968**
>
> **2** Stealing anything in the building or part of a building in question, of inflicting on any person therein any grievous bodily harm or raping any person therein and of doing any unlawful damage to the building or anything therein.

The only difference between the two offences in Sections 9 (1)(a) and 9 (1)(b) relates to the *mens rea*. The *actus reus* is the same for both:

- the defendant entered,
- a building or part of a building,
- as a trespasser.

The *mens rea* for Section 9(1)(a) is:

- intention or recklessness as to trespass
- intention to commit the following offences: theft, criminal damage, grievous bodily harm, rape.

Entered

Whether the defendant entered the building or not is explored in the following, unusual, cases.

Legal case: *R v Collins (1973)*

The defendant who was virtually naked (only his socks were on) went up a ladder to a young girl's bedroom window. In her drunken state, the girl thought that the defendant was her boyfriend. She invited him in and they began to have sex. She realized her mistake after a short time, slapped his face and asked him to leave her room. The defendant was charged under Section 9(1)(a) – entry with intent to rape. The defence argued that he was not a trespasser since he was not fully in the room before being invited in by the girl. He was convicted. On appeal the conviction was quashed with the Appeal Court saying that he had not made an 'effective and substantial entry'.

Legal case: *R v Ryan (1996)*

The defendant was found with his head and arm stuck in the window of an elderly man's house. He denied that he was a burglar since he would have been unable to steal anything in his predicament. He was charged under Section 9(1)(a) – burglary with intent to steal.

The physical position of the defendant in *R v Ryan (1996)* poses some interesting questions for the list of offences that the defendant might commit to become a burglar. Ryan may have been in a position to swipe something of value from his uncomfortable position stuck in the window of the elderly man's house. He would, however, have been almost incapable of inflicting grievous bodily harm on the sleeping senior citizen.

Time

The defendant must be a trespasser during the time of his entry into the building. A college student on college premises may not be a trespasser at 9am on a Monday morning but may be at 9pm.

Legal case: *R v Laing (1995)*

The defendant was found in the stockroom of a department store after it had closed. He was convicted of burglary but appealed. The prosecution was unable to prove that he had been a trespasser when he entered the store and his conviction was quashed.

Building or part of a building

A building is something quite substantial. It could include a house, an inhabited caravan or houseboat but not a tent. The word is not strictly defined in the Theft Act 1968, but an important aspect is whether the 'building' is inhabited or not.

Subsection 4 Theft Act 1968

4 References in Subsections 1 and 2 to a building shall also apply to an inhabited vehicle or vessel and shall apply to any such vehicle or vessel at times when the person having a habitation in it is not there as well as at times when he is.

In other words, the defendant can be charged with burglary even if the person who owns the building is at home or out.

Legal case: *R v Walkington (1979)*

The defendant entered Debenhams in Oxford Street shortly before they closed. Since the shop was open he was not entering as a trespasser. If it could have been proved that he intended to steal or commit any other prohibited act, he may have been seen as a trespasser under Section 9(1) (a). He went behind the till into an area where customers would not normally go. He was, therefore, trespassing into an area where he had been given no permission to be and he was liable for a charge of burglary.

Domestic and commercial premises

The type of building the defendant burgles is very important in terms of the maximum allowed sentence.

- Domestic household – fourteen years maximum imprisonment.
- Commercial premises – ten years maximum imprisonment.

Group activity

Comment on the maximum terms for each type of premises burgled. Should there be a difference? Are the sentences too short or too long? What effects do each of the types of burglary have on the victim?

Mens rea

There are two elements of *mens rea* with regards to premises, trespass and offence.

1 Intention or recklessness to being a trespasser.

2 Intention to commit an ulterior offence.

Trespass

Whether the defendant is charged under Section 9(1)(a) or 9(1)(b), they must have trespassed. The *mens rea* of trespass in the context of burglary is:

- intention to trespass
- being reckless as to whether trespassing or not.

If you visit a friend for dinner and leave your house keys behind, you have no right to come back later that evening when your hosts are asleep and let yourself back into their home. The first visit was given under the occupier's permission, the second was not and you would be a trespasser.

Legal case: *R v Jones and Smith (1976)*

The defendant had left the parental home but still had the keys to the house and permission to visit whenever he wanted. One night he entered his father's house and stole two television sets with the help of another defendant. Although the son had permission to enter the house, he came as a thief that night and was therefore a trespasser. He was convicted of burglary.

In terms of trespass, the prosecution must prove *mens rea* for the criminal offence of burglary.

Ulterior offence

The intention to commit one of the prohibited offences must be in the mind of the burglar at the time they enter the building as a trespasser. The prohibited offences mentioned under Section 2 of the Theft Act 1968 are:

- stealing
- grievous bodily harm
- rape
- criminal damage.

2 Elements of Section 9(1)(b) of the Theft Act 1968

The second type of burglary offence involves the defendant entering the premises without the permission of the owner and then *going on to commit* additional offences. The defendant does not plan the offences he is about to commit after trespassing and may not commit any – they will see what they find.

Legislation

Section 9(1)(b) Theft Act 1968

b Having entered any building or part of a building as a trespasser he steals or attempts to steal anything in the building or that part of it or inflicts or attempts to inflict on any person therein any grievous bodily harm.

Actus reus and *mens rea*

The *actus reus* is the same as for Section 9(1)(a), but in addition, the defendant has gone on to commit one of the prohibited offences. The *mens rea* is:

- intention or recklessness as to trespass

- dishonesty and an intention to steal

- intention or subjective recklessness with regard to causing harm.

The *mens rea* for these prohibited offences do not have to be committed at the time of entry into the building but must be present when the prohibited but unplanned offences are committed.

The key difference with Section 9(1)(b) offences is that the defendant breaks into the building but is not sure what he will do. He goes on to commit the offences of stealing or attempting to steal and/or inflicting or attempting to inflict grievous bodily harm.

Key points for burglary offences

Sections 9(1)(a) and 9(1)(b) of the Theft Act 1968 cover the offence of burglary.

Section 9(1)(a)

Section 9(1)(a) covers burglary where the defendant has the intention to commit a specified offence after they have trespassed.

For burglary under Section 9(1)(a), the specified offences are: theft, grievous bodily harm, rape, or doing any unlawful damage to the building.

The *actus reus* of Section 9(1)(a) is the defendant entered, a building or part of a building, as a trespasser. The *mens rea* for Section 9(1)(a) is intention or recklessness as to trespass **and** intention to commit the following offences: theft, criminal damage, grievous bodily harm or rape.

Section 9(1)(b)

Section 9(1)(b) covers burglary where the defendant has committed trespass and then *goes on to commit* specified offences.

The specified offences under Section 9(1)(b) are: 'he steals or attempts to steal or inflicts or attempts to inflict on any person therein any grievous bodily harm.'

The *actus reus* for Section 9(1)(b) is the defendant entered a building or part of a building as a trespasser (this is the same as Section 9(1)(a)). The *mens rea* for Section 9(1)(b) is intention or recklessness as to trespass, dishonesty and an intention to steal, intention or subjective recklessness with regard to causing harm.

Words used in Sections 9(1)(a) and 9(1)(b)

The issue of 'entered' is explored in *R v Collins (1973)* and quotes 'effective and substantial entry' as a criteria.

A 'building' is something quite substantial – house, caravan, houseboat or vehicle but not tent.

Domestic premises are inhabited by people as their homes and carry a sentence of fourteen years maximum imprisonment for burglary. Commercial premises used by businesses have ten years maximum imprisonment for burglary.

3 Robbery – theft with use or threat of use of force

Robbery involves the use of force to steal. It includes the use or threat of use of force. Knowledge and understanding of the principles around theft are essential for understanding and application in this unit. Robbery ranges from bag snatches to armed bank and post office robberies. Robbery has always grabbed the headlines and causes great concern amongst the public. The government, concerned about the political implications of rising street crime in particular, has put huge resources into its control. The introduction of mobile phones has allowed violent offenders a valuable new source of income. Lord Woolf, the Chief Justice, has recommended severe penalties for this offence – eighteen months in prison on conviction and three years if violence has been used.

Actus reus

The *actus reus* of robbery is closely connected with the *actus reus* of theft but has the additional component that force has been used. The *actus reus* of robbery is where:

- property belonging to another person has been appropriated
- force has been used on a person to appropriate the property, or
- a person has been put in fear of immediate force being used upon them.

The force must be used in the course of the theft. If it is done significantly before or after then this cannot be classified as robbery: theft and assault may have happened instead. Another important point is that the force may be directed against a third party and still be robbery. If a street robber threatens someone's child in order to steal property, this would be robbery and not separate theft and assault charges.

Group activity

Get some local newspapers and select some articles on crimes where robbery has been involved. Apply the principles you learn in this unit to examine them.

Two important cases illustrate the timing issue with robbery.

Legal case: *R v Hale (1979)*

Two defendants had tied up the victim while the property was carried off the premises. The theft was an ongoing act and force took place during this period and so the offence was one of robbery.

Legal case: *R v Lockley (1995)*

The defendant, along with others, took beer from an off-licence. The shopkeeper challenged them after the goods had been appropriated. The defendants argued that the violence took place after the theft and therefore robbery was not an issue. The Court of Appeal applied *R v Hale (1979)* and stated that the theft was an ongoing act and the defendants were guilty of robbery.

In both of the above cases it was the role of the jury to decide whether theft was ongoing when force was applied.

Mens rea

The *mens rea* of robbery is a combination of the *mens rea* of theft with the force element added in.

- Dishonesty and the intention permanently to deprive the owner of the property.

- The intention to use force or the threat of use of force on a person.

Section 8 of the Theft Act 1968 covers the offence of robbery and gives a sentence of up to a maximum of life imprisonment. Robbery can cover incidents from the theft of a purse from a shopper to a full-scale armed robbery on a bank with firearms. For robbery to be proved there must have been theft. This does not mean that the robbers need to be successful in their act of theft, only that they appropriated the property.

Legal case: *Corcoran v Anderton (1980)*

Corcoran had attempted to steal a bag from a woman, Mrs Hall, walking in the street. A friend called 'P' helped him. 'P' hit Mrs Hall in the back knocking her to the ground. The victim screamed and released the bag and the pair ran off with nothing. Corcoran appealed on the grounds that he did not have sole possession of the handbag. The court ruled that this did not matter for robbery to be proved since appropriation was enough.

Actual force need not have been used during the robbery for robbery to be committed. The threat of use of force is enough. If a six foot, heavily built robber threatens a pensioner with force to obtain their pension money, this will be classified as robbery. The pensioner would have been put into fear that immediate force was going to be used.

The force used does not have to be on the actual body of the victim. If a handbag is wrenched from the control of the victim, force is being used. This was established in *R v Clouden (1987)* where the robber attempted to pull a shopping bag from the hands of the victim.

4 Making off without payment

There are two main pieces of legislation in this area: the Theft Act 1968 and the Theft Act 1978. The latter is a classic example of Parliament updating the law to cope with new types of offences. The Theft Act 1978 was the direct result of an explosion in growth of financial services and products including the rise of the almost universal credit and debit card. Always think about the type of offence in terms of goods or services. Different legislation generally applies for each. For the OCR syllabus the key offence you will need to know about is making off without payment. Other offences are included for the sake of comparison and to show the development of the law.

A person who realizes that payment is expected there and then for a service provided or a good supplied is committing an offence under Section 3 of the Theft Act 1978 if they have the intention to permanently avoid payment. The sentence is imprisonment for up to two years.

The *actus reus* is:

- making off

  This means leaving the place where you have enjoyed a service or been sold a good, for example:

Legal case: *R v Brooks and Brooks (1982)*

A father and daughter had enjoyed a meal in a restaurant. The father attempted to avoid payment and had gone past the point where payment would normally have been made. The father was still on the premises but was near the back door. He was convicted.

- without payment for services supplied or goods provided

  These payments must be legally enforceable and ones where payment is expected 'on the spot'.

The *mens rea* is:

- dishonesty

  The two-part test is used to establish dishonesty (see *R v Ghosh (1982)*, page 109).

- knowledge that payment is normally required or expected on the spot

  Custom and practice establish when payment is required on the spot and when not. Buying a house is rarely a cash transaction but buying a newspaper almost always is.

Legal case: *Troughton v Metropolitan Police (1987)*

The defendant who was drunk ordered a taxi home but refused to give the taxi driver his address. The driver drove him to a police station where the defendant took the opportunity of running off. The defendant was charged with making off without payment, but since the driver had not driven him to his destination the defendant was under no legal obligation to pay. Under Section 3 of the Theft Act 1968 there must be a legally enforceable liability. The defendant was found not guilty.

- intention to permanently avoid payment

  If a person dining in a restaurant received a mobile phone call telling them a member of their family was in a burning building, the court would probably be sympathetic to a charge of avoiding payment: a person running from a restaurant owing the price of a dinner under other circumstances would have a more difficult time in court.

Legal case: *R v Allen (1985)*

Allen had a temporary money problem and left the hotel he was staying in. He told the court that he had intended to return later to pay his bills once he received money from a business venture he was involved in. The court found him guilty, but on appeal the House of Lords stated that the prosecution would have to prove that he had intended to deprive the hotel 'permanently' and this issue had to be left to the jury to decide. The House of Lords quashed the conviction.

Group activity

Do you think decisions in the cases of *Troughton v Metropolitan Police (1987)* and *R v Allen (1985)* were fair? How might the law be changed to improve the rights of the victims in these evasions of payment?

Obtaining property by deception

The offence of obtaining property by deception is covered by Section 15(4) of the Theft Act 1968. The offence involves the handing over of property to the defendant that they are not legally entitled to. The person transferring the property does not necessarily have to be the owner of the property. This offence may be:

- deception by words relating to fact, law or intention of the defendant or another person
- deception by actions relating to fact, law or intention of the defendant or another person.

The deception can be intentional or with recklessness.

In reality, these two types of deception relate to offences such as:

- using another person's credit or debit card to falsely pay for goods. This is relatively easy if the defendant is in a position of trust and can make notes of credit card or debit card numbers and later order goods over the telephone for themselves.
- using false or meaningless cheques to pay for goods and take them away. The defendant may have stolen a chequebook and signed the cheques themselves. They may also be using bank accounts that have no money in them to pay for goods. The cheque then 'bounces'.

For there to be an offence, the defendant must be successful in obtaining the goods and a *person* must have been the victim of the deception. Using a foreign coin in a chocolate machine would not be deception but theft.

The *actus reus* of obtaining property by deception is:

- obtaining property belonging to another by deception.

Obtaining

This involves the defendant securing ownership, possession or control of the property.

Property

Unlike Section 1 of the Theft Act 1968, offences under Section 15 relating to deception include land as property.

Belonging to another

The victim has control ownership or a right or interest in the property in question.

By deception

This involves false statements or actions that influence the decisions of the victim in giving the property to the defendant.

The *mens rea* of the offence is:

● intention or recklessness for deception

● dishonesty

● intention to permanently deprive.

The defendant may face up to ten years in prison for this offence.

Obtaining services by deception

Section 1 of the Theft Act 1978 covers obtaining services by deception. A service might include:

● massage and facials

● hotel accommodation

● taxi rides

● medical or legal advice.

The *actus reus* of this offence is:

● obtaining by deception,

● services.

The *mens rea* of this offence is:

● dishonesty

● deliberate or reckless behaviour in committing the deception.

Evasion of liability

Section 2 of the Theft Act 1978 covers this offence. A liability is a debt that a person owes to a person, a company or an organization. Evasion of liability means that they try to avoid paying what they owe. The *actus reus* of the offence is:

- a person by deception,
- produces an evasion,
- of a liability.

Deception

The same as for obtaining property and services. Misrepresentations are made to deceive a person about the facts.

Evasion

This is the crucial part of the offence. It consists of three possibilities:

- Remission of debt

  The cancellation of a debt is known as remission. This may happen through deception. The offender may claim that they have been made homeless, lost their job or suffered some major family disaster that makes it impossible for them to pay their debts.

- Waiting or forgoing a payment

  If an offender persuades a creditor to wait indefinitely for payment with the intention of not paying, or pretends that the debt does not exist (forgoing), they have committed an offence.

Legal case: *R v Holt (1981)*

The defendant dined in a restaurant and when asked for payment told the waiter that he had already paid someone else. The restaurant was persuaded to forgo the debt as a result of the deception since the waiter did not initially realize that the liability was still outstanding. An off-duty police officer overheard the defendant planning the deception and informed the manager.

- Exemption or abatement

  If the defendant dishonestly secures an exemption (does not have to pay anything) or an abatement (a reduction), such as using someone else's Family Rail Card, they have committed an offence.

Legal case: *R v Sibartie (1983)*

The defendant bought a season ticket for the first and last leg of his journey on the London underground, avoiding payment for the middle section of his passage. He was asked to produce his ticket by an inspector whilst travelling on the middle unpaid section of his journey. He was convicted of 'abatement of liability to make a payment'.

Liability

A liability under Section 2 of the Theft Act 1978 must be one that is legally enforceable in a court.

The *mens rea* of evasion of liability is:

● dishonesty

● deliberate or reckless deception

● intention to default permanently.

Dishonesty

Use of the two-part test from *R v Ghosh (1982)* (see page 109) is used to establish dishonesty.

Quick revision questions

1 Define robbery.

2 What is the *actus reus* and *mens rea* of robbery?

3 What key point did *Corcoran v Anderton (1980)* show?

4 What is the *actus reus* and *mens rea* for Section 9(1)(a) and for Section 9(1)(b) offences?

5 Outline *R v Collins (1973)* and the concept of entry.

6 Which section of the Theft Act 1968 covers obtaining property by deception?

7 What is the *actus reus* and *mens rea* of obtaining property by deception?

8 Which law covers obtaining services by deception?

9 What is the *actus reus* and *mens rea* of evasion of liability?

10 How is dishonesty tested?

Analyse the differences between a charge of burglary under Section 9(1)(a) and Section 9(1)(b). [50 marks]

Exam answer guide

Knowledge and understanding [20 marks]
- ✓ Define burglary using Section 9(1)(a) and Section 9(1)(b)
- ✓ Distinguish between *mens rea* in Section 9(1)(a) and Section 9(1)(b)
- ✓ Quote *R v Collins (1973)* and *R v Ryan (1996)*
- ✓ Consider the time factor in burglary quote *R v Laing (1995)* and *R v Walkington (1979)*
- ✓ Define issues of trespass using *R v Jones and Smith (1976)*

Analysis and evaluation [25 marks]
- ✓ Comment on effectiveness of legislation in separating Section 9(1)(a) and Section 9(1)(b) offences
- ✓ Evaluate any problems that might arise in assessing whether offence was Section 9(1)(a) or Section 9(1)(b) offence

Presentation [5 marks]
- ✓ Structure your work in a logical and well-planned way. Employ good quality and clear English in your writing. Make use of punctuation and correct spelling in your answers.

Criminal damage

Key points

1 Simple criminal damage
2 Aggravated criminal damage
3 Fire and criminal damage

Why do I need to know about criminal damage?

Offences in the area of criminal damage are covered by Section 1 of the Criminal Damage Act 1971. There are three main types of criminal damage that you need to study: Section 1(1) – simple criminal damage, Section 1(2) – aggravated criminal damage, and Section 1(3) – arson. You need to know issues around what is considered damage, property, and when life is endangered. There are lawful defences contained in the key act that covers these offences.

Simple criminal damage

1 Simple criminal damage

Simple criminal damage (also known as basic criminal damage) involves the destruction of property; no one's life is endangered by the damage created. Section 1(1) of the Criminal Damage Act 1971 covers this and other related offences explored in this unit.

Legislation

Section 1(1) Criminal Damage Act 1971

A person who without lawful excuse destroys or damages any property belonging to another, intending to destroy or damage such property or being reckless as to whether any such property would be destroyed or damaged, shall be guilty of an offence.

The maximum sentence for this crime is ten years imprisonment.

The *actus reus* of the offence is:

- destroys or damages property belonging to another.

Each case would have to be looked at separately using the following questions.

- How permanent or temporary was the damage?
- How was the usefulness of the property affected?
- What was the extent of the cleaning or repair needed?

A series of classic cases illustrates what is meant by simple criminal damage.

Legal case: *A v R (1978)*

A juvenile spat on a policeman's raincoat and was taken to court charged with criminal damage. The damage to the coat was considered insufficient for the charge to lead to a conviction: any spittle could easily have been wiped away using a damp cloth. If the coat had required dry cleaning, the offence may have been proved. Presumably a raincoat would have been made with the intention of repelling most ordinary liquids.

Legal case: *Hardman v Chief Constable of Avon and Somerset Constabulary (1986)*

A similar case to *A v R (1978)* is one where the issue of cleaning led to a conviction. The defendant produced a work of art on the pavement drawn in water-soluble chalks. If the rain had come it would have wiped out the masterpiece, but the local council washed it away before this happened. As expense had been incurred in cleaning the pavement, the defendant was found guilty of criminal damage.

Property

Section 10(1) of the Criminal Damage Act 1971 gives a definition of property.

Legislation

Section 10(1) Criminal Damage Act 1971

In this Act 'property' means property of a tangible nature, whether real or personal, including money and –

a including wild creatures which have been tamed or which are ordinarily kept in captivity, and any other wild creatures or their carcasses if, but only if, they have been reduced into possession which has not been lost or abandoned or are in the course of being reduced into possession, but

b not including mushrooms growing wild on any land, or flowers, fruit or foliage of a plant growing wild on any land.

Property is confined to tangible items in the Criminal Damage Act 1971. Section 4 of the Theft Act 1968 includes intangible items such as trusts and bank accounts.

Belonging to another

Section 10 of the Criminal Damage Act 1971 refers to those who have custody, control, or propriety rights (ownership rights) or interest. Having an interest means 'rights, titles, advantages, duties, liabilities connected with it'.

The *mens rea* of basic criminal damage is:

● intention or recklessness

This is objective recklessness (Caldwell): what would the ordinary, prudent person believe?

Legal case: *MPC v Caldwell (1982)*

Caldwell was unhappy with his employer and to pay him back he decided to start a fire in a ground-floor room of the hotel where he had worked. Ten guests were in the hotel at the time, but fortunately the fire was quickly brought under control. Caldwell was charged with criminal damage (arson), as he was reckless as to whether life would be endangered by his actions.

Lord Diplock, a lawlord, stated during the case that:

'A person is reckless if he does an act which in fact creates an obvious risk and when he does the act he has either not given any thought to the possibility of there being any risk or has recognized that there was some risk involved and has nonetheless gone on to do it.'

This case created an important principle known as objective 'Caldwell recklessness'. The Caldwell test means that the courts are applying an external test. They are not simply looking at what the defendant thought to be the case but what an ordinary, prudent person might believe also. This extended the scope of recklessness. Before this the court would only consider what the defendant believed to be the case.

Objective recklessness is nearly always used when considering cases of criminal damage.

- without lawful excuse

Obviously, criminal damage would not be criminal damage if a person was trying to save their own or someone else's life and had to break down a door or smash a window or damage a car.

Group activity

Get some local newspapers and identify some criminal damage cases. Which category of criminal damage is used and what punishments are issued?

2 Aggravated criminal damage

The key difference between criminal damage and aggravated criminal damage is that the latter may endanger life. Aggravated criminal damage is a peculiar offence since it mixes offences against property with offences against people. What might start out as a simple bit of criminal damage might end up with a charge of endangering life and a prison sentence of up to life.

Section 1(2) of the Criminal Damage Act 1971 covers the offence. The *actus reus* is the same as for Section 1:

- destroys or damages property belonging to himself or another.

The *mens rea*, however, is:

- intention to damage property and thereby endanger the life of another
- intention to damage property and recklessness as to whether the life of another is endangered
- recklessness as to whether property is damaged and reckless as to whether life is endangered.

Life endangered

Legal case: *R v Sangha (1988)*

The defendant had been drinking all day and decided to set a fire in his neighbour's unoccupied flat. He used a mattress and two chairs to start the blaze. Fortunately the design of the building meant that the fire endangered no one else. He was found guilty and his appeal failed. It did not matter that no one was in actual danger. The court felt that the ordinary bystander would have felt there to be a risk of danger to others by such an action.

For the purposes of aggravated criminal damage it does not matter whether life was in fact endangered. As long as the defendant intended or was reckless as to whether it was endangered is enough.

Defences against criminal damage

The law states that 'a person without lawful excuse. . .shall be guilty of an offence'. There are, therefore, lawful excuses that can be used as a defence against a conviction of criminal damage.

Consent

If the defendant honestly believes that the owner of the property has given their consent, then the criminal damage has not taken place.

An interesting but futile attempt to use this defence appears in *Blake v DPP (1993)*.

Legal case: *Blake v DPP (1993)*

A vicar protesting against the Gulf War wrote a biblical quotation on a pillar of the House of Commons. He claimed that he was acting with the consent of the owner – in this case God. The court felt that his defence fell outside the provisions of Section 5(2)(a) of the Criminal Damage Act 1971 and he was convicted of criminal damage.

Other property was in need of immediate protection

During the 1980s a long-running protest against US air bases located in the UK was waged by women around the country including the famous air base at Greenham Common. Another such base was the US naval base at Brawdy.

Legal case: *R v Hill (1988)*

Hill cut fences around the naval base at Brawdy and claimed that she was doing so to protect her house against Russian nuclear attack since the base would be a priority target in the event of a nuclear exchange. Her reasoning was that if enough damage was caused then the US would locate the offending base somewhere else. The court decided that the real intention of Hill was not to protect her property but to encourage the US to move its base. She was convicted of criminal damage..

Criminal damage

3 Fire and criminal damage

Criminal damage using fire is regarded as one of the most serious offences in the criminal code. It is also known as arson. Section 1(3) of the Criminal Damage Act 1971 covers the offence. Fire quickly gets out of control and defendants who start fires for various petty reasons often end up with long prison sentences. The maximum penalty for aggravated criminal damage using fire is life imprisonment.

Legislation

Section 1(3) Criminal Damage Act 1971

An offence committed under this section by destroying or damaging property by fire shall be charged as arson.

- The *actus reus* is that there must be damage by fire.
- The *mens rea* is that the defendant must intend to destroy or damage property by fire, **or** the defendant must be reckless as to whether property was destroyed or damaged by fire.

Aggravated arson

The defendant must have intended, or be reckless, as to whether life was endangered by fire. The maximum sentence for this offence is life imprisonment.

What is fire?

This may seem obvious, but there are different scenarios possible. The burning or singeing of materials capable of combustion will be considered as fire. The damage caused by smoke from a careless neighbour will not be considered as fire and there is no charge of arson even if damage was intended by creating the smoke.

The classic case in this area is *R v Miller (1983)*.

Legal case: *R v Miller (1983)*

Miller started a fire by his recklessness. He dropped a cigarette that set light to a mattress. Instead of trying to put the fire out, he simply moved to another room and went back to sleep. The fire caused £800 of damage. He was found guilty of arson through his omission in not putting out the fire that he had started.

Exam question

Discuss how simple criminal damage differs from aggravated criminal damage.
[50 marks]

Exam answer guide

Knowledge and understanding [20 marks]
- ✓ Define simple criminal damage using Section 1(1) legislation
- ✓ Consider the type of damage, usefulness of property damaged and the extent of cleaning needed. Quote *A v R (1978)* and *Hardman v Chief Constable of Avon and Somerset Constabulary (1986)*
- ✓ Define property and belonging to another. Use *R v Caldwell (1982)*
- ✓ Define aggravated criminal damage using Section 1(2) legislation
- ✓ Highlight aggravating feature which is endangering life. Quote *R v Sangha (1988)*

Analysis and evaluation [25 marks]
- ✓ Comment on the key differences and assess the fairness of aggravated criminal damage when clearly no life was in fact endangered. Is it fair to convict in these circumstances? Illustrate using *R v Sangha (1988)*

Presentation [5 marks]
- ✓ Structure your work in a logical and well-planned way. Employ good quality and clear English in your writing. Make use of punctuation and correct spelling in your answers.

Criminal law examination

Examination questions for OCR

What do I need to know about the criminal law exam?

The examination board produces a guide which examiners use when they mark your essays and case studies. This section shows you what examiners are told to look out for in students work. There are three main stages to securing a good grade.

Knowledge and understanding

Recall, select, deploy and develop knowledge and understanding of legal principles accurately and by means of example and citation.

What do I need to know about knowledge and understanding?

When examiners are marking your script they look out for certain things. The first is your level of knowledge of law and how well you understand that knowledge. Law is a difficult but interesting subject where you are required to make sense of some very difficult ideas. This knowledge and understanding is the first step on the road towards getting a good grade.

It is important that you have a good understanding of the basic ideas of law, this will help you to find the modules easier to handle. If you do not understand something it is important to ask your teacher, another student or read another book, which might be able to explain the idea in a way you might understand more easily. Remember it will be difficult at first, but keep on trying it will click into place!

There are three ways you can show the examiner that you have covered the course and have understood some of the key points.

- **Quote relevant legal cases**

The use of cases to back up your arguments is crucial to examination success. All law made by judges is made by using cases and law made by Parliament is tested in the courts which also produces cases. Use index cards (small pieces of card to carry around with you and read whenever you can) and build up a library of cases. It is best to do this gradually and look at them often. For example you would need to know key cases such as *R v Gibbins (1918)*, *R v Pittwood (1902)* and *R v Miller (1983)* if you want to illustrate that you understand the concept of *actus reus* and omission. If you were illustrating oblique intention you would need to quote *R v Nedrick (1986)* and *R v Woolin (1998)*. Examiners will give you credit for using these types of cases to show your knowledge.

- **Quote statutory legislation**

Use important pieces of law passed by Parliament that you know; in most topics there will be one. The government is keen to make laws that reflect its interests and the job of Parliament is to look carefully at the ideas suggested by the government to make sure they are fair. Index cards with key pieces of Parliamentary law will help with this.

- **Quote key legal ideas**

Concepts such as *actus reus* and *mens rea* need to be defined and explained. Again you can make a set of index cards, which hold these key ideas. Eventually you will find that the more you know the more links you will see between cases, Parliamentary law and legal ideas.

Display analysis, evaluation and application

Analyse legal material, issues, and situations, and evaluate and apply the appropriate legal rules and principles.

What do I need to know about analysis, evaluation and application?

There are a lot of marks to be gained in this section. The first skill you must display is analysis. This is something you do all the time in other areas of your life, when you look at the pros and cons of buying something such as choosing a holiday or which college to go to. There are two main ways you can look at analysis in your law work.

Analysis

1 Break a complicated idea down to help understanding

For example *actus reus* can be a positive voluntary act or it can be an omission. This can lead to discussion of duty of care and a breach of duty of care and finally the need for the event to cause the consequence might be referred to. Breaking this complicated idea down into little chunks is analysis.

2 Develop a flow of ideas

To do this you must see connections between different ideas and put them altogether. You might look at murder for example and consider what the *actus reus* and *mens rea* are and then go on to talk about the defences available and the punishment that can be expected. Putting all these pieces together into a flow of ideas is analysis.

Evaluation

The examiner is interested in your views on legal issues. Giving your view is also known as evaluation; other words for evaluation are opinion, conclusion, recommendation or judgement. Evaluating legal issues or cases will help you to get marks.

An example of evaluation

Student evaluation

The cases of R v Duffy (1949) and R v Ahluwalia (1992) looked at issues of provocation when used against a charge of murder. R v Duffy (1949) might seem more relevant to men and the case of R v Ahluwalia (1992) might seem to be more relevant to women. Overall however I feel that the court system still seems very unfair to women particularly given the fact that Ahluwalia was not released by the Court of Appeal even when they admitted that battered wives syndrome might be an important factor in 'slow burn fuse' cases.

This gives some information about the issue, points out some issues and then gives an opinion. Never forget to include an evaluation and practice forming a view about everything you hear!

Application

This involves thinking about which law or cases you would use in a particular situation.

For example if you were considering the issue of assault, some possible cases you would apply to the situation might be *Fagan v MPC (1968)*, *R v Ireland (1997)* and *Tuberville v Savage (1669)*. Legislation you might consider might be the Criminal Justice Act 1988. You would use these as tools to examine the case in front of you as if you were a barrister for the prosecution or defence.

Applying points of law will give you credit with the examiner.

The OCR A2 examinations are currently marked using five levels of response covering three key assessment objectives. Typically, assessment objectives are given the following potential marks in a question that has 50 marks available.

Assessment objective 1: Knowledge and understanding
42%   25 marks

Assessment objective 2: Analysis, evaluation and application
48%   20 marks

Assessment objective 3: Communication and presentation
10%   5 marks

Examples of criminal law questions

1 Assess the meaning of recklessness as is it applied to offences in English law.

[50 marks]

Answer guide for Question 1

- Distinguish between subjective and objective recklessness.
- Use relevant cases such as *R v Cunningham (1957)* and *R v Caldwell (1982)*.
- Explore relevant cases such as *R v Adomako (1994)*.
- Explore relationship with Offences Against the Person Act 1861.
- Refer to Law Commission's work in the area of involuntary manslaughter.
- Analyse the moral dimensions to the various offences.
- Consider the effectiveness of such offences on deterrence.
- Consider the issues of punishment around these offences.
- Cite all relevant cases to support your argument.

2 Unlike some countries, there is no general duty to act to save others in English law. How true is this statement and do you think the law should be changed in this area? [50 marks]

Answer guide for Question 2

- Most crimes are prohibited conduct crimes.
- Duty situations may impose a specific duty that must be followed. Omission can be a crime. See *R v Pittwood (1902)* and *R v Gibbins and Proctor (1918)*.
- Situations caused by the defendant as in *R v Miller (1983)*.
- Duty may also come from statutory law and common law.
- Examine the difficulties in creating such duties if decided upon.
- Evaluate whether English law should be changed to impose such a duty.

3 Tommy and Ian were out on a stag night in town and drinking very heavily. Tommy was particularly intoxicated and eventually knocked into another person called Stephen who became angry at Tommy. Stephen challenged Tommy to a fight, but Tommy hit Stephen before he was ready and Stephen injured his back on the kerb as he fell.

Jack, a friend of Stephen's, who was watching the brawl, ran after Ian who tried to escape up an alley. Jack caught up with Ian put his arm around Ian's neck and strangled him slowly. Ian punched Jack in the stomach as they struggled and Jack fell to the ground in great pain begging for help. Ian left the scene without helping Jack. Jack was found dead from a ruptured spleen.

Discuss the areas of liability produced by the night's events and consider any defences that might be available. [50 marks]

Answer guide for Question 3

- Explain unlawful and malicious inflicting/causing of grievous bodily harm. Refer to Sections 18 and 20 of the Offences Against the Person Act 1861.

- Also consider assault occasioning actual bodily harm, referring to Section 47 of the Offences Against the Person Act 1861.

- Explain possible defences. Intoxication and reference to basic and specific crimes and their *mens rea*. Consider automatism, self-induced automatism through intoxication. Remember that consent to fighting is no defence.

- Explain unlawful act manslaughter and self-defence. Also consider the response by Ian. Was his reaction disproportionate to the attack on him? If this is the case then the use of force by Ian was unlawful.

- Explain gross negligence manslaughter and liability for omissions. Consider Ian's liability in not helping Jack.

- Consider the huge breadth of offences covered by this offence.

- Consider problems with interpreting the act itself as a crime with the necessary *mens rea*.

- With gross negligence manslaughter, consider duty issues, risks to be foreseen and the test of gross negligence.

- With regard to subjective recklessness, consider degree of harm that needs to be foreseen.

4 Examine the issue of 'appropriating property belonging to another'. What difficulties have arisen in practical use of this phrase in the court? [50 marks]

Answer guide for Question 4

- Definition of theft.

- Outline legislation contained in Section 3 of the Theft Act 1968 in relation to appropriation.

- Outline legislation contained in Section 4 of the Theft Act 1968 in relation to property.

- Outline legislation contained in Section 5 of the Theft Act 1968 in relation to belonging to another.

- Outline legislation contained in Section 2 of the Theft Act 1968 in relation to dishonesty.

- Outline legislation contained in Section 6 of the Theft Act 1968 in relation to permanently deprive. Note this is not part of *actus reus* but is an intention. The thief does not have to actually permanently deprive.

- Discuss methods of appropriation.

- Analyse what is and is not property, in particular land.

- Refer to *R v Gomez (1992)*.

5 What are the problems when using intoxication as a defence to criminal charges? [50 marks]

Answer guide for Question 5

- Explain intoxication and the effect on formation of *mens rea*.

- Distinguish crimes of specific intent such as murder, theft and grievous bodily harm with intent from crimes of basic intent such as rape and criminal damage.

- Distinguish between voluntary and involuntary intoxication. See *R v Tandy (1989)*.

- Outline relationship of intoxication with other defences such as mistake. See *R v O'Grady (1987)*.

- Law Commission and the Criminal Law Revision Committee and intoxicated mistake as a relevant defence in murder cases.

- Consider public policy reasons for judgements in intoxication.

6 Dawn and Catherine were friends but had recently not been speaking to each other because of a bad debt. Dawn owed Catherine £1000 and had not paid the money because of a boyfriend Eddy who was a violent alcoholic. Dawn was frightened of Eddy and what he might do to her and her two small children, Joshua and Connor. Dawn had also violently attacked an old man in the street and stolen his wallet.

Catherine found out that Dawn was telling lies over the money owed but did not know the exact cause of the non-payment. She let herself into Dawn's ground floor flat and searched for money. While she was there she threw a glass at the fireplace that damaged the gas fire allowing gas to escape. She left the flat without repairing the damage or leaving a warning note for Dawn.

Outline the criminal offences carried out by Catherine. [50 marks]

Answer guide for Question 6

- Explain offences in relation to robbery and dishonesty.

- Explain the defence of duress in relation to Eddy.

- Explain possibility of burglary under Sections 9 (1)(a) and 9 (1)(b) of the Theft Act 1968. Weigh up dishonesty with Catherine's reasons for going to Dawn's.

- Explain offences of criminal damage and criminal damage in relation to being reckless to endanger life.

- Analyse *actus reus* and *mens rea* of offences selected.

Law of contract 1

Formation of a contract

1 Offer and acceptance

2 Consideration

3 Legal intent

4 Capacity to form a contract

5 Contractual terms

6 Types of terms

7 Exemption clauses

Offer and acceptance

Key points

1 General principles of a contract
2 Offer and invitation to treat
3 Counter offer, request for information, termination
4 Acceptance
5 Auctions, tenders and collateral agreements
6 Multipartite agreements
7 Dealing with machines

Why do I need to know about offer and acceptance?

Offer and acceptance are the beginning of the process of contracting with another party. If these building blocks are not sound, the whole contract will fall to pieces. It is important that the rules in this area are followed. Freedom to

Felthouse v Brindley (1862)

contract is an important part of contract law, but it must be based on mutual understanding of what is being offered and what is being accepted. This is a fascinating area of law, which has had to develop in relation to new technology such as the Internet and telephone sales.

1 General principles of a contract

A contract is an agreement between two parties normally involving the exchange of goods, services or money. The party putting forward the offer is known as the 'offeror' and the person who the offer is made to is known as the 'offeree'.

A contract has the force of the legal system backing the agreement. The courts may be used if one of the parties withdraws from the contract or if there are disagreements when the matter may end up in the civil court for a solution. This unit looks at the four main elements in producing a successful contract:

- offer

- acceptance

- consideration

- intention.

The elements above may lead many to think that a contract is a complex and difficult legal issue involving solicitors, barristers and courts. This is one aspect when dealing with important commercial matters, but all of us play our part in the world of contracts almost everyday of our lives. Every time you buy an item from a shop or get on a bus a contract has been created. You may have a part-time job that involves a contract between you and an employer, you may have a mobile telephone, which often involves a contract between you and the provider. There are countless other examples of contracts in our consumer society today.

A contract can be made in many ways. Sometimes the contract involves virtually no evidence at all.

- Buying a newspaper from outside a railway station involves little more than 'please' and 'thank you' and a newspaper and money changing hands.

- Some contracts may be made verbally through a quick conversation. Your gardener may cut your lawn on simple verbal instructions. Minor building work or the use of a window cleaner may involve a brief exchange of words and money.

- Some may involve written documents drawn up by professionals. For instance, in the purchase of a house or how you want your assets given out on your death.

- Some may occur via computer systems, Internet, e-mail or even phone calls to specified numbers. Mail-order goods and Internet services may also be sold in this way.

- In the London stock market when shares were being traded, 'My word is my bond' was a principle used. No written documents were drawn up and a person's reputation or word was put on the line. The stock market now often uses computers to automatically sell or buy shares at pre-determined prices.

The nature of the contract relates to the nature of the goods or services being exchanged and their value. The main aim of contract law is to ensure that agreements are carried forward in a fair and efficient manner. Judges using judicial precedent develop some contract law and some is developed by Parliament passing statutory law.

Legal case: *Mariah Carey v EMI (2001)*

EMI, the music group, recently withdrew from a long-term contract it had made with singer Mariah Carey. It had to pay many millions of dollars to release itself from the contract with the star whose album sales had not matched up to the early expectations of the music group. A more recent contract with Robbie Williams for four albums, worth £80 million, was more carefully written with sales figures featuring as a more important part of the deal.

2 Offer and invitation to treat

An offer is an indication that you are willing to enter into a contract on certain terms. This offer becomes binding when it is accepted by the other party.

Offers can be one of two types.

1 Specific: the offer is targeted towards individuals or individual groups, such as direct mail shots made to specific types of people.

2 General: the offer is made to all via public advertisements, such as TV adverts.

The classic legal case in the general area is *Carlill v Carbolic Smoke Ball Company (1893)*.

Legal case: *Carlill v Carbolic Smoke Ball Company (1893)*

This case involved a general offer to the whole world via an advert in a newspaper. It was claimed that a device they were selling would stop the user and anyone in the house from getting influenza. Mrs Carlill took the company to court when the product failed in its claim. The company tried several defences to get out of its responsibility but lost the case and eventually went bankrupt. The court decided that the company had made a binding offer that was not upheld.

Invitation to treat allows some flexibility in these arrangements, particularly from the side of the seller. It allows the seller not to do business if they choose. An invitation to treat is an invitation to make an offer, not an offer itself. The wording of the invitation should make this clear. The following case illustrates this point.

Legal case: *Fisher v Bell (1961)*

The owner of a shop was accused of offering for sale offensive weapons contrary to the Restriction of Offensive Weapons Act 1959 as a flick knife was on display in the shop's window. The court decided, however, that this was not an offer, only an invitation to treat. The owner would have been within his legal rights not to sell the knife to a customer. It would have been up to the customer to make an offer.

This case illustrates the fact that a shop is a place where bargaining takes place with both buyer and seller having the freedom not to enter into contract.

Legal case: *Pharmaceutical Society of Great Britain v Boots the Chemist (1953)*

Under the Pharmacy and Poisons Act 1933 a registered pharmacist (chemist) had to be present when certain medical goods were sold. Boots did not have a pharmacist at the display of medical goods itself but they did have a pharmacist at the till. The displays did not amount to an offer made by Boots at the display therefore they did not break the law, they were to be considered an invitation to treat.

Legal case: *Partridge and Crittenden (1968)*

A magazine advert seemed to be offering a bramble finch for sale. The Protection of Birds Act 1954 made such a sale illegal as the bird was an endangered species. The court decided that the advertisement was not an offer but an invitation to treat.

The invitation to treat is only a starting point for discussions on a contract.

Group activity

Do you think the ruling in *Partridge and Crittenden (1968)* was right? Can you think of similar situations where invitation to treat might be used to avoid liability or guilt?

3 Counter offer, request for information, termination

Counter offer

If a party accepts a contract it must be unconditional. The following case shows the problems that can exist when a counter offer is made by one party and the way that courts can assist.

Legal case: *Brogden v Metropolitan Rail Company (1877)*

Brogden was a coal merchant who supplied fuel for the rail company's steam engines. There had been no written contract between them. The company eventually formalised their arrangement by producing a written contract, which Brogden amended, signed and returned. A dispute later arose between the two and Brogden declared that no contract existed between them. The court decided that their mutual conduct had formed a contract: Brogden by supplying coal after the written document had been returned and the Metropolitan Rail Company by ordering it from him.

In the normal course of events, a counter offer cancels the original offer and becomes a new offer, which the other party may accept or decline. Offers and acceptances can change between parties depending on when they are made.

Request for information

A request for information is not a counter offer.

Legal case: *Stevenson v Mclean (1880)*

An offer to sell iron was made on a Saturday and the offer was to remain open until the following Monday morning. Stevenson responded by asking if the iron could be bought on credit terms but he received no reply to this request for information. On Monday he contacted the seller to accept the offer but was told it had been sold. The courts decided that the request for information was not a counter offer and a contract was formed on the acceptance since the defendants had held the offer open until the Monday.

If the claimants in the above case had argued about the price or the quantity of the iron, this would have amounted to a counter offer. The request by Stevenson did not amount to a change in the terms of the offer.

Termination of an offer

The only way an offer can be accepted is by unconditional acceptance of the terms of the offer. An offer, however, can be terminated in a number of ways.

- Acceptance

  This forms a contract and effectively stops the offer being made to anyone else.

- Refusal

  The offeree can refuse what they are presented with. If refusal takes place, the offeree cannot change their mind later and attempt to accept the original offer.

- Death

  If the offer is one involving a personal service, such as singing or playing the piano, then the offer lapses with the death of the offeror. If the offer is something that may be of benefit to the offeror's estate and is capable of completion, then the offer may stand even after death.

- Lapse of time limit

  If there is a clear indication of when the offer will be withdrawn, such as that in *Stevenson v Mclean (1880)*, then time will automatically cancel the offer. If there is no clearly expressed limit then the courts will decide what is a 'reasonable' time limit.

- Counter offer

  If a genuine counter offer is made and not merely a request for information, then the offer will cease. The counter offer implies that the offeree is not happy with some of the terms in the original offer and wants to make a counter offer that they prefer.

- Revocation

  The offeror can withdraw an offer at any time before the acceptance is made but the offeror must communicate this withdrawal to the offeree. The communication would normally come directly from the offeror but can come from another party.

- Failure of pre-condition

  If an important term in the contract is substantially altered then the offer is no longer valid.

Legal case: *Financings Ltd v Stimson (1962)*

A car was offered for sale, but between the time of the offer and the acceptance, the car was stolen and damaged. The acceptance was made without knowledge of the car's damaged condition. The court decided that a pre-condition of the contract would be that the car was in a fit state and therefore the contract had failed.

4 Acceptance

If a person is happy with the terms contained in the offer they may accept. This means that they agree to all the terms in the offer. The acceptance can be made in three main ways:

- verbally
- in writing
- by completing some agreed action.

The actual agreement may be difficult to locate particularly if negotiations have been long and complex.

Silence is not considered enough for acceptance of an offer as the following case illustrates.

Legal case: *Felthouse v Brindley (1862)*

An uncle intended to buy a horse from his nephew. He said that unless he heard from the nephew the sale would go through at £30 and fifteen shillings. The uncle heard nothing else from the nephew. The horse was then mistakenly sold to another person and when the issue went to court it was decided that because of the silence from the nephew no contract was made.

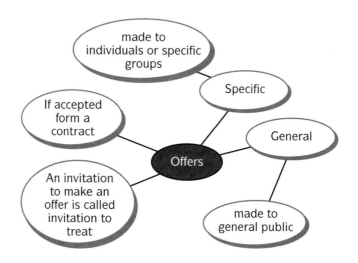

Offer and acceptance

5 Auctions, tenders and collateral agreements

Auctions

Each bid made in an auction by a potential buyer is considered an offer. Each offer is cancelled by any higher offer by another bidder. When the auction has come to an end, the fall of the auctioneer's hammer is the acceptance of the highest bid (offer). The auctioneer is not party to the contract itself: the contract is between the bidder and the seller. The auctioneer is just providing a service to the bidder and seller of the goods. The proceedings of auctions are regulated by Section 57(2) of the Sale of Goods Act 1979.

Tenders

A tender is an invitation to treat often made by large public organizations such as councils, hospitals and government departments. The tender is often related to fairly large contracts that need to be filled, such as the building of a hospital or the supply of a local service such as refuse collection.

Any response made as a result of the advertisement to tender is considered an offer. It is then up to the buyer of the goods or services to accept whichever tender is most suitable. At this point only does a contract form. There is one main exception to this: when the invitation to treat is framed in such a way that it becomes an offer rather than an invitation to treat. In this case, any response that fulfils the set criteria will become the acceptance rather than the offer.

Legal case: *Harvela Investments v Royal Trust Co of Canada Ltd (1985)*

The defendants communicated with two parties by telex inviting them to make tenders for shares, stating in the communication 'we bind ourselves to the highest offer'. The House of Lords decided that this was an offer rather than an invitation to treat and the highest bid formed the acceptance and therefore the contract was formed.

The invitation to treat is often made in local or national newspapers, and potential suppliers respond by specifying a price at which they can supply the goods or services. Tenders are similar in some respects to auctions, although at auctions the process is looking for the highest price from the bidder whilst the tender process is often looking for the lowest.

Collateral contracts

Collateral contracts are a device used by the courts to create a legal relationship between parties to escape the limitations of the privity rule. The following case illustrates this device.

Legal case: *Shanklin Piers Ltd v Detel Products Ltd (1951)*

Shanklin Piers Ltd employed some painters to paint one of their piers. They were concerned that the best quality and most appropriate paint be used on the pier in order to protect the fabric of the structure. Shanklin Piers contacted Detel Products Ltd who stated that the paint used would last for between seven and ten years. When the painters were employed, they were expressly instructed to use Detel paint. Detel paint was used but started to peel and deteriorate after three months. The courts decided that a collateral contract existed between Shanklin and Detel even though it was the painters who purchased the paint from Detel.

If the collateral contract device had not been used in the above case, Detel would have failed to acknowledge any contractual obligation towards Shanklin and probably have escaped liability. The painters would have had little incentive to take Detel to court but would have blamed them rather than their own poor workmanship for the state of affairs. The device in this case successfully brought the two relevant parties together into a contractual relationship where the wronged party could seek damages.

6 Multipartite agreements

Multipartite agreements arise when a number of individual people make an agreement with one person. The courts have decided that this process may bind them to each other even if they have no direct contact. The key case that decided this issue was *Clarke v Earl Dunraven (1897)*.

Legal case: *Clarke v Earl Dunraven (1897)*

Clarke and Earl Dunraven were yacht owners who entered a race organized by a yacht club. During some movements at the start of the competition, the *Satanita* fouled the *Valkyrie*, which led to its sinking. The owner of the *Valkyrie* sued the owner of the *Satanita*. The defendant argued that he should only pay the statutory minimum for this type of accident, which was £8 per tonne of ship, which amounted to considerably less than the market value of the sunken yacht. All parties to the race had signed an agreement with the yacht club that required full damages to be paid in the event of a foul. The House of Lords stated that full cost of the yacht had to paid in these circumstances since a multipartite agreement had been made that bound one racer to the other.

Group activity

Does the *Clarke v Earl Dunraven (1897)* case go against the principles of contract law? Consider offer, acceptance, consideration, intention and privity.

7 Dealing with machines

Machines have become more accepted in the business world and offer an interesting area for consideration of contract law. Shopping by the Internet, paying a mobile phone account by debit card, buying a soft drink or food from a vending machine are all examples where human beings deal directly with machines. The question arises whether these transactions are different from those in traditional shops.

Legal case: *Thornton v Shoe Lane Parking (1971)*

Mr Thornton parked his car in a car park that had an automatic ticket machine and barrier. He took the ticket from the machine on entry to the car park and then parked his car. On his return there was an accident in which he was injured and the car was damaged. The owners of the car park tried to use an exemption clause to evade liability. The court decided that having the car park ready for use was the offer and Mr Thornton's purchase of the ticket was the acceptance. Therefore, there was a contract in existence at the point the ticket was taken from the machine.

To apply this case more generally, if a machine is filled with cans of drink and switched on ready for use, it is effectively making an offer. When the customer presses the button that activates the machine to deliver the can of drink, this is the acceptance. The money is given to the machine before the button is pressed in most cases.

Quick revision questions

1 What is the difference between an offeror and offeree?

2 What are the four main elements to forming a contract?

3 What is the difference between an offer and an invitation to treat?

4 What are the two main types of offer?

5 Outline the case of *Pharmaceutical Society of Great Britain v Boots the Chemist (1953)*.

6 What does a request for information do?

7 How can an offer be terminated?

8 How can acceptance be made?

9 Describe the process of auctions, tenders and collateral agreements.

10 Outline multipartite agreements and dealings with machines.

Exam question

Evaluate the key differences between offer and invitation to treat. [50 marks]

Exam answer guide

Knowledge and understanding [20 marks]

✓ Define offer. Show differences between specific and general offer. Quote *Carlill v Carbolic Smoke Ball Company (1893)*

✓ Define invitation to treat

✓ Use *Fisher v Bell (1961)* and *Pharmaceutical Society of Great Britain v Boot the Chemist (1953)* to illustrate differences

Analysis and evaluation [25 marks]

✓ Examine the effects of counter offer, request for information on offer and invitation to treat position. Quote *Brogden v Metropolitan Rail Company (1877)* and *Stevenson v McLean (1880)*

Presentation [5 marks]

✓ Structure your work in a logical and well-planned way. Employ good quality and clear English in your writing. Make use of punctuation and correct spelling in your answers.

Consideration

Why do I need to know about consideration?

Consideration is the thing that goes between the two parties when they have formed a bargain. It is the price each party pays. You will see that the courts do not normally intervene on issues of consideration and declare them to be unfair. It is up to the two parties in normal circumstances to decide what they want their contract to contain and what it should concern. On one side possibly 'some right, interest, profit or benefit' and on the other 'some forbearance, detriment, loss or responsibility given, suffered, or undertaken by the other'. You will look at the rules concerning consideration and you must be able to apply them to the cases you study.

Tweddle v Atkinson

1 Nature of consideration

When both parties agree to exchange certain goods, services or money, what passes between them is known as consideration. The consideration may be of value or may be worthless. It is the 'price' that each party pays for the bargain they enter into: it might be money or it might be a promise. This is a vital element in the formation of a contract. Both sides will gain something and lose something from the transaction. The key definition was produced in the following case.

Legal case: *Currie v Misa (1875)*

Consideration existed when 'some right, interest, profit or benefit accruing to the one party, or some forbearance, detriment, loss or responsibility given, suffered, or undertaken by the other'. In simple terms, it is what is given by each side to the other to enter a contract.

2 The rules of consideration

Consideration involves the following five rules.

1 Promissee/promisor and consideration

Up until recently only the two parties involved in the contract must have made the consideration. The two parties are called 'promissee' and 'promisor'. If both have not made the consideration, the contract could not be enforced. Therefore, if I had agreed with a parent to tutor a Law student, the student could not have sued if I failed to turn up. The consideration was between the parent and myself.

Legal case: *Tweddle v Atkinson (1861)*

A soon-to-be married couple were promised a sum of money by their fathers. The agreement was between the proud fathers and not between the two fiancés. Tweddle senior gave the money but then unfortunately died. Atkinson did not part with his promised share and was sued by his son-in-law. The court decided that consideration was between the two fathers and no one else. The contract was therefore not enforceable.

The law has moved on from this position to a certain extent. The Contract (Rights of a Third Party) Act 1999 allows some enforcement if the contract clearly states that the benefit is for a third party even if that third party provides no consideration.

2 Consideration cannot be past (past consideration)

A person cannot go to court to enforce a contract when the consideration occurred after the offer. If an elderly friend promises me £25 after I have painted their bathroom and then fails to pay, I cannot legally obtain the fee. In essence, I had voluntarily painted the bathroom and as courts do not normally enforce one-sided bargains that is my 'loss'.

Legal case: *Roscorla v Thomas (1842)*

A horse had been sold. The previous owner then informed the new owner that the horse was good tempered and obedient but this proved not to be the case. The new owner had already paid the price and the court decided that the new promise about the horses temperament was not therefore consideration.

Legal case: *Re: McArdle (1951)*

A granny flat was built for an elderly relative and members of the family volunteered to pay for the flat after they had seen the work, but the cash was not forthcoming. Eventually the builders sued the well intentioned but slow to pay relatives for the money. The judge decided that it was past consideration. The work had been completed before payment was promised and the relatives were under no legal obligation to pay for the renovations.

3 Must be sufficient but does not need to be adequate

The courts are not interested in the justice of the consideration, only whether it has happened. If I want to sell a new Jaguar XJ6 for £100, that it my business. The court will not force or advise me to sell it for more. Consideration may be formed even if it is clearly not a reflection of the real world economic situation.

Legal case: *Thomas v Thomas (1842)*

A man wished his wife to have the benefit of his house when he died. He formed a contract which charged her £1 a year. This was clearly not the market rent even in 1842. It was however sufficient for consideration.

4 Consideration must not be illegal

A consideration which is illegal cannot be held up in court. One party or another may end up in court possibly not aware of the illegality of their situation. They might not have kept up to date with changes brought about by statutory instruments or been unaware of statute or common law in certain areas. If this is the case the contract is not enforceable.

5 Existing duty

If there is an obligation as part of an existing duty then this cannot be taken as consideration. There are two aspects to this situation – existing public duty and existing contractual duty.

Existing public duty

The police have an existing public duty to maintain law and order and protect the ordinary citizen. Performing this task is not defined as consideration. If they fulfil their normal functions this is not consideration, but there are times when they do perform beyond these normal functions and create a situation that might be classified as consideration, as the following case illustrates.

Legal case: *Glasbrook Brothers v Glamorgan County Council (1925)*

In 1925 the local council was responsible for keeping the peace. During the 1920s there had been a number of strikes and problems within the coalfields of South Wales. The police believed that a mobile unit would be enough to protect the areas coal mines. Glasbrook Brothers disagreed and asked for a greater degree of police protection that they agreed to pay for. When the time came for payment the company refused saying that it was the duty of the police to protect property and they were doing nothing more than their job. The courts found that the company was liable for the debt since the local council had gone beyond their existing duty by agreeing to allocate a greater number of police than it thought necessary to protect the coal mine.

Legal case: *Harris v Sheffield United Football Club (1988)*

The football club blamed the poor behaviour of football crowds at the time for needing greater numbers of police to preserve law and order. They cited the case of *Glasbrook Brothers (1925)* and stated that they thought the police had a duty to preserve law and order and this was not an extra that they should pay for. The Court of Appeal felt that the club deliberately timed matches for the maximum number of people to attend and this made them partly responsible for the problem. In addition, the timing of matches for Saturday afternoon meant that officers were taken off of their rest days, therefore making the payment of overtime necessary. The Glasbrook case was different – here neither party went out of their way to encourage the potential breakdown of law and order.

Group activity

Comment on the rulings given in the *Glasbrook Brothers v Glamorgan County Council (1925)* and *Harris v Sheffield United (1988)* cases. Do the police owe a duty of care in these circumstances that should be paid for by the taxpayer?

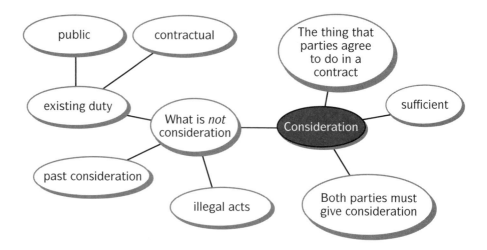

Consideration

Existing contractual duty

Performance of an existing contractual duty is not consideration for the same duty. The following case shows this.

> ## Legal case: *Stilk v Myrick (1809)*
>
> Two out of eight sailors deserted a ship and the captain, wanting to get home, promised the remaining crew a share of the deserter's wages. When the ship got back to port the captain refused to pay the extra money. The courts found that the sailors were under a contractual obligation to sail the ship home and were not entitled to extra pay.

The second similar case shows a very different outcome.

> ## Legal case: *Hartley v Ponsonby (1857)*
>
> A ship set sail with 36 members of crew. Seventeen members deserted and again, the captain, wanting to get home, promised the nineteen remaining crewmembers a share of the deserter's wages. On return to port the captain refused to pay, but in this case the court felt that the nineteen, experienced crewmembers had gone beyond their existing duty. The court ruled that the dramatic change in circumstances had discharged the old contract and formed a new one.

The courts are keen to allow the principle of freedom to contract and also show their willingness to make contracts work, particularly in hard commercial environments. A key case from 1990 shows the courts responding to financial difficulties – in this case caused by the severe economic recession of the early 1990s.

> **Group activity**
>
> Try to find a simple contract and see if the five rules of consideration apply.

3 Part payment of a debt and promissory estoppel

Looking at the end of the process, part payment of debts is not the same as paying of the whole debt. An important rule was produced in the following case, which, although very old, still holds true.

> **Legal case: _Pinnels case (1602)_**
>
> Pinnel was owed money by a man named Cole. Both came to an agreement that Pinnel would be paid part of the debt one month early and this would then be the end of the matter. This money was paid but Pinnel later tried to sue for the money 'owed'. The court decided that the payment had been made in full because of the new agreement between the two men.

There are other situations that may discharge the debt.

- Money paid early

  Money that is paid early by agreement is to the advantage of the person owed. They can put this in the bank or pay off debts that they might have. It may be agreed that if an early payment is made the debtor can pay a reduced amount.

- Payment method changed

  Businesses like to be paid by the easiest and most cost-effective method. Utility providers such as gas and electricity suppliers and telephone companies will normally offer a discount to customers who pay by direct debit. A creditor may also accept a reduction for changing the geographical location where a payment is made if it makes the creditor's life easier.

- Additional items

  A creditor may accept part payment as long as the debtor gives something else as well. For example, this might be including a gift in with the lesser payment or taking the creditor out to a dinner and drinking spree instead of full payment. The value of the addition does not have to equal the missing part of the payment. The key thing is that the creditor is happy with the arrangement.

● Third parties

If a third party kindly agrees to pay some of the debt of a debtor to clear the matter up, the creditor cannot later sue for the rest from the original debtor.

Promissory estoppel

Promissory estoppel is an important concept in equity law that was formulated by Lord Denning. Debtors may be able to protect themselves from the wish of the creditor to go back on a promise they may have made with regard to the cancellation of a debt.

Legal case: *Central London Property Trust Ltd v High Trees House Ltd (1947)*

The owners of a block of flats leased them to High Trees House Ltd who in turn rented them out to individual tenants. This arrangement started in 1937 and the rent payable to Central London Property was £2500 per year. During World War II tenants were hard to find and to keep the arrangement going the claimants agreed to halve the rent until things improved. By the end of the war in 1945 people were returning to London and the block of flats began to fill up with tenants. The claimants then sued for the full amount for the last six months of 1945 when the block was full. The court accepted this, but Denning used the case as an opportunity to develop the doctrine of promissory estoppel. The claimant would not have been allowed to sue for full payment for the period before mid-1945 since this would have meant them going back on their promise.

Quick revision questions

1 Define consideration.

2 Summarize the definition of consideration in *Currie v Misa (1875)*.

3 Define who the promissee and promisor are.

4 Outline the case of *Tweddle v Atkinson (1861)*.

5 What are the key points in *Roscorla v Thomas (1852)* and *Re: McArdle (1951)*?

6 What does 'must be sufficient but does not need to be adequate' mean?

7 Outline the impacts of existing duty issues.

8 Outline the case of *Glasbrook Brothers v Glamorgan County Council (1925)*.

9 What situations discharge an existing debt?

10 Define promissory estoppel and outline the *Central London Property Trust Ltd v High Trees House Ltd (1947)* case.

Exam question

Examine the five rules of consideration. [50 marks]

Exam answer guide

Knowledge and understanding [20 marks]

✓ Define consideration and illustrate the five rules

1 The need for consideration to pass between promissee and promissory. Quote *Tweddle and Atkinson (1861)*

2 Consideration must not be past. Quote *Roscorla v Thomas (1842)* and *Re: McArdle (1951)*

3 Consideration must be sufficient but does not have to be adequate

4 Consideration must not be illegal

5 Existing duty either public or contractual. Quote *Glasbrook v Glamorgan County Council (1925)*, *Stilk v Myrick (1809)*, *Hartley v Ponsonby (1857)* and *Williams v Roffey (1990)*

Analysis and evaluation [25 marks]

✓ Comment on the cases used above and the fairness of decisions made

✓ Evaluate the effect of the Contract (Rights of a Third Party) Act 1999

Presentation [5 marks]

✓ Structure your work in a logical and well-planned way. Employ good quality and clear English in your writing. Make use of punctuation and correct spelling in your answers.

Legal intent

Key points

1 Reason for the requirement
2 Social and domestic agreements
3 Commercial agreements

Why do I need to know about legal intent?

Freedom to contract is a fundamental right in our legal and economic system. Contracts form the basis of myriad human activities and allow protection for those who enter into agreements. Parties to contracts know that agreements can be enforced in the courts. These agreements must be freely and knowingly entered into and there must be an intention to form this legal relationship. If there is doubt on this then the contract may not be enforced. The parties must both be aware of their legal obligations and freely enter into these obligations fully aware of the consequences.

Commercial agreements normally involve intent

1 Reason for the requirement

People have the freedom to contract even if the contract may not be in their best interests. If two people make an agreement and one party has no idea that the agreement is legally binding then the courts will not enforce it. The courts use an objective assessment as to whether there was an intention to form a legal relationship. If they think there was intention then they will enforce the agreement.

Cases relating to this issue of intent to form legal relations fall into two categories:

- social and domestic agreements
- commercial agreements.

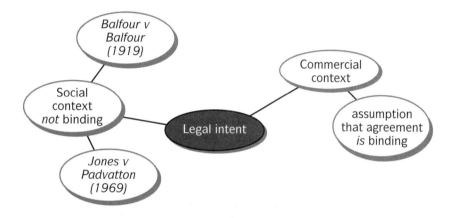

Legal intent

2 Social and domestic agreements

If I promise to give my two children chocolate for being good, could I end up in court if I do not? If I promise my wife a weekend in Paris for looking after the children whilst writing this book, could I end up in court if I let her down? The courts have come to the point of view that social and domestic arrangements are best kept out of the courts.

These decisions are sometimes quite complex, as we will see in the following cases. The method used by the courts is application of the objective test. The courts will consider what the 'ordinary prudent' person would have believed to be the arrangement when they are told the facts. It is irrelevant that one, or both, of the parties to the arrangement may have had secret misgivings about the relationship. The key thing is what the relationship looked like to an ordinary outsider.

Legal case: *Balfour v Balfour (1919)*

Mr Balfour was a civil servant who was working in Sri Lanka. His wife became ill while they were on holiday in England and Mr Balfour was forced to return to Sri Lanka alone. He promised Mrs Balfour a payment of £30 per month for living expenses while he was away. When the couple separated Mr Balfour stopped these payments and was sued by Mrs Balfour. The court decided that there had been no intention to form legal relations when the original promise had been made.

Legal case: *Merritt v Merritt (1970)*

Mr Merritt had already left his wife and was living with another woman. During a discussion with his estranged wife certain financial plans and promises were made with regard to maintenance and the mortgage on the house. These broke down and the judge decided that the provisions of *Balfour v Balfour (1919)* did not apply since the couple in this case were already separated. Any agreements made should be seen as creating legal relations.

Legal case: *Jones v Padvatton (1969)*

A mother persuaded her daughter to move to England to study for her Bar examinations. As a temptation she bought a house, which the daughter was allowed to live in. The pair argued after the daughter constantly failed her examinations and the issue of whose house it was went to court. It was decided by the Court of Appeal that this was a family dispute and no legal relations were intended.

Another family relationship involving the actual sharing of a house between the two parties and the difficulties that this often entails is *Parker v Clark (1960)*.

Legal case: *Parker v Clark (1960)*

Two elderly couples, the Parkers and the Clarks, who were related to each other decided that it would make better financial sense if they lived together in a large house owned by the Clarks. A careful list was compiled of which party should pay which bills. Unfortunately a dispute arose about what should happen to the house when the various people died. The court felt that the arrangement was a binding legal one. The fact that the Parkers had actually sold their own house to enter the relationship was used as evidence of the fact.

The following two cases illustrate close relationships other than family, which can lead to complexities particularly when there is money involved.

Legal case: *Simpkin v Pays (1955)*

Simpkin was a lodger who enjoyed competitions in Sunday newspapers which she completed with her landlady and her granddaughter. Each of the three would put a third of the entry fee into the pot and Simpkin filled out the form in the name of Pays. Pays promised to share the winnings if they were ever successful. Eventually the trio did win £750 but the defendant refused to pay the agreed third to the claimant, which would have totalled £250. The defendant claimed that she had never intended to be legally bound by the relationship even though the claimant had always paid a third of the entry fee. The court found in favour of Simpkin and she received her £250 stating that there was a clear expectation because they had all contributed financially so they should all share any potential winnings.

Legal case: *Peck v Lateu (1973)*

This case has similarities to the case of *Simpkin v Pays (1955)*. Two women friends enjoyed going to bingo together and often shared the cost of the bingo card. They had agreed that any winnings would be shared between them. A big win eventually came and Lateu tried to withdraw from the agreement. The court found that there was an intention to create legal relations and Peck was forced to share the win.

Finally two cases involving 'friends' where the relationship was taken to court over the issue of intent to form legal relations or not.

Legal case: *Buckpitt v Oates (1968)*

Buckpitt and Oates were seventeen year old friends who often shared each others cars. Buckpitt was injured in an accident caused by Oates' negligence. Buckpitt had paid a contribution of ten shillings (50p) toward the cost of the petrol but the relationship was seen as non-commercial by the court when Buckpitt tried to claim against insurance. There was no intent to form a legal relationship between the two according to the court.

Legal case: Taylor v Dickens (1997)

A woman had promised her gardener that he would have her house when she died. He was grateful for this promise and did all gardening and other work for free. When the woman died it was discovered that she did not leave the house to the faithful gardener. He sued the estate but the judge in the case declared that as there had been no formal offer and acceptance there was no binding contract and no intent to form a legal relationship.

Group activity

Outline three situations that occur in everyday life between friends or family which might be seen by the 'ordinary prudent person' as forming **and** not forming legal relations.

3 Commercial agreements

A plumber who carries out work in your house is not doing it because they like you or want to improve your bathroom – they are doing it for payment. We can, therefore, presume that in commercial situations legal intent exists; they intend a commercial and legal arrangement with you. Therefore, the customer is under obligation to pay and the plumber is under obligation to carry out the service.

Honourable pledge clauses

In certain circumstances one party or another may seek to rebut (deny) the presumption that there is a legal intent between them.

Legal case: *Rose and Frank Co v Crompton Bros (1925)*

Two businesses formed an agreement but put in writing that they did not intend the agreement to be a legally binding one. A dispute arose and when it went to the House of Lords it was decided that the written statement would hold. Despite the fact that they had spent time putting the issue into writing in a very formal way it was accepted that the agreement itself was in fact a very informal one.

Pools companies often put honourable pledges into their literature. Two cases that went to court were *Jones v Vernons Pools (1938)* and *Appleson v Littlewoods (1939)*. The courts refused to enforce the claims in both cases. A more recent case went to court in 2002 when the popular TV show *Who Wants to be a Millioniare?* refused to pay out the prize money. The show claimed that someone in the audience using well-timed coughs was helping the contestant. The honourable pledge clause often gives flexibility to companies on such payouts but may soon be obsolete due to a new piece of legislation called the Unfair Terms in Consumer Contract Regulations Act 1994 that came about from a European Directive.

Group activity

Find the terms and conditions of the National Lottery. What limitations are there on payouts?

Quick revision questions

1 What are the main reasons for the requirement to intend legal relations?

2 How do the courts test whether there is an intent to form a legal relationship?

3 What are the two categories of legal relationship?

4 What did *Balfour v Balfour (1919)* indicate?

5 What did *Merritt v Merritt (1970)* indicate?

6 Outline the facts in *Jones v Padvatton (1969)*.

7 Outline the issues with commercial agreements.

8 What did *Rose and Frank Co v Crompton Bros (1925)* show?

9 What does an honourable pledge clause do?

10 What effect does the Unfair Terms in Consumer Contract Regulations Act 1994 have on honourable pledge clauses?

Exam question

Comment on the differences between intent to create legal relations in:

a domestic situations

b commercial situations.

[50 marks]

Exam answer guide

Knowledge and understanding [20 marks]

✓ Define intent to form legal relations

✓ Outline how social and domestic have no presumption to create legal relationships quote *Balfour v Balfour (1919)*, *Merritt v Merritt (1970)* and *Jones v Padvatton (1969)*

✓ Outline how commercial agreements have presumption of a legal relationship. Quote *Rose and Frank Co v Crompton Bros (1925)*

Analysis and evaluation [25 marks]

✓ Analyse reasons why the courts presume legal relations in commercial transactions and no legal relation in domestic situations

Presentation [5 marks]

✓ Structure your work in a logical and well-planned way. Employ good quality and clear English in your writing. Make use of punctuation and correct spelling in your answers.

Capacity to form a contract

Key points

1 Reasons for limitation
2 Minors
3 Corporations
4 Persons of unsound mind and drunkards

Why do I need to know about capacity?

Capacity goes to the heart of contract making particular reference to the need to prove that legal relations were entered into knowingly and fairly. If this is not the case, courts will not enforce the agreement and there is then no enforceable contract between the parties. The key groups of people protected by capacity rules are minors, drunkards and those with mental impairment. This unit also deals with corporations, which are seen as separate legal entities in the eyes of the law.

Capacity to contract?

1 Reasons for limitation

We saw in the last unit that an important legal issue with regard to contracts is the intent to form legal relations. The courts allow freedom of contract but will not enforce agreements where they believe one of the parties had no intention of forming a legally binding agreement and do not understand the obligations of that agreement. This unit investigates those individuals and organizations that do or do not have the capacity to enter into such agreements.

2 Minors

Up to 1969, minors were considered anyone under the age of twenty-one as a result of the Infant's Relief Act 1874. At the age of twenty-one infants became adults and were traditionally given the 'key to the door' that you still see on some birthday cards today. In 1969, however, the 'age of majority' was lowered to eighteen by the Family Law Reform Act 1969 and finally in 1987, the Minor's Contracts Act was introduced, which repealed the 1874 Act completely and restored common law provisions that regulated contracts made by those under eighteen. The key part to the reintroduction of the common law in this crucial area was that minors are not generally bound by contract. However, we are now going to look at provisions that allow exceptions to this position.

Exceptions to the common law on contracts for minors

It would be most difficult if all those members of society under the age of eighteen were not allowed to form and be bound by contracts. Life for the typical twelve to seventeen year old would be much impoverished as the purchase of a cinema ticket, a bus ticket, a soft drink, a bag of chips, a pair of shoes or an item of clothing involves a contractual arrangement. Businesses and minors would not want to see problems in the purchase of these and countless other items essential to modern-day living. Minors are prohibited from buying certain products such as alcohol until the age of eighteen or cigarettes until the age of sixteen, but would find it unacceptable if they were asked to provide proof of age to purchase a CD or a bag of crisps. The law has compromised and has allowed the contractual possibility for goods and services that are regarded as necessary.

Necessary goods and services

Legislation

Section 3(2) Sale of Goods Act 1979

'Necessaries' means goods suitable to the condition in life of the minor or other person concerned and to his actual requirements at the time of sale and delivery.

The wording of the legislation allows a degree of leeway to the courts in deciding what is or what is not a 'necessary'. If your family has fallen on hard times, the purchase of an expensive handmade pair of shoes might not seem in keeping with your present lifestyle. If your family was wealthy and normally bought £200 pairs of shoes, then this might seem an acceptable, normal, although extravagant by some standards, use of money. The judge in *Chapple v Cooper (1844)* expressed it neatly by saying 'articles of mere luxury are always excluded, though luxurious articles of utility are in some cases allowed'.

Group activity

Collect some information from your local trading standards office or library on the rights that young people have in the area of consumer law.

Legal case: *Nash v Inman (1908)*

The son of a wealthy architect ordered eleven waistcoats from an expensive Savile Row tailor whilst studying at the University of Cambridge. The tailor was forced to sue for payment, but a defence was made that the son was a minor at the time and therefore not liable for payment. The Court of Appeal agreed that his position in life might make the waistcoats a necessary good, but as he had already been given clothing by his father, the goods ordered were not regarded as suitable to his actual requirements at the time.

The courts sometimes have a difficult time in considering what is and what is not necessary. Their work has been complicated by the rise in the consumer culture we live in and the amount of income some minors have at their disposal through part-time work and other sources. On the whole, courts take the line that the majority of consumer contracts are enforceable, whereas commercial contracts are not.

Services for the benefit of the minor

Some services may be set up expressly for the benefit of minors. A good example would be apprenticeship schemes where young people are trained in a skill or profession and may expect the main benefit in terms of reward at a later time. It would be in the interests of the minor to allow such contracts to exist.

Legal case: *Clements v London and North West (1894)*

A minor gave up his statutory rights to claim personal injury benefits. In return he was covered by a scheme set up and partially paid for by his employer. The benefits he would receive would be greater under the private arrangement. The courts felt that the contract was for the minor's benefit and therefore enforceable.

Other cases show otherwise.

Legal case: *De Francesco v Barnum (1890)*

A fourteen year old dancer entered an agreement that was more to the benefit of her employer than herself. She agreed not to marry for the seven years duration of the apprenticeship and her professional engagements were under the complete control of De Francesco. He could, however, end the agreement at any time. The court decided that the contract was more for the benefit of De Francesco than the girl and refused to enforce it.

Common law and voidable contracts for minors

Apart from arrangements that look at necessaries, such as in *Nash v Inman (1908)*, and services specifically designed for the benefit of a minor, such as in *Clements v London and North West (1894)*, the vast majority of minors contracts are voidable. This means that the courts have the choice in whether to honour them or not. Generally the minors obligations will not be enforced but the adults obligations will. In addition the minor normally has the power to cancel the contract without penalty to themselves, although if money has changed hands and goods and services have been supplied, there may be complications. The following three cases illustrate some of the possibilities.

Legal case: *Steinberg v Scala (Leeds) Ltd (1923)*

Steinberg, a minor, was the claimant in this case which involved the purchase of shares in Scala (Leeds) Ltd. The sale was in two parts totalling £350. Ms Steinberg requested her last instalment back, which had amounted to £250. Scala refused and when the case went to court it was decided that since she had received the shares from the company in return for her payment a contract had been properly formed which she now had to abide by.

Legal case: *Corpe v Overton (1833)*

Corpe was a minor who entered into a partnership that had not yet been put into place. He paid £100 deposit. When he sought to cancel the contract the courts backed his position on the grounds that he had not yet received any benefit from the transaction. His £100 would be returned.

Another case, which saw a contract not enforced by the courts, was *Mercantile Union Guarantee v Ball (1937)*.

Legal case: *Mercantile Union Guarantee v Ball (1937)*

A young businessman, who was a minor, entered into a hire purchase contract with Mercantile Union Guarantee. The contract was not enforced by the courts on the grounds that the courts were there to stop the exploitation of minors who perhaps did not enjoy the necessary level of experience which an adult might have.

The minor has one more option. If they repudiate the contract before they are eighteen, or shortly after this, then the courts will not enforce the contract. This is to allow those whose judgement may not be completely 100 per cent an escape route from a contract they may have entered into hastily. If, however, the contract involved continuing payments on a mobile phone for example, then unless the minor has repudiated the contract the court will generally enforce it.

Tort and voidable contracts

Judges are not keen on using one branch of the law to wriggle out of obligations in another branch of law. In tort damages may be charged against a minor but if a claimant is only using tort to enforce an obligation that might not be used in contract law then they are unlikely to be successful. The following case shows this very situation.

Legal case: *Leslie Ltd v Sheill (1914)*

A minor, Sheill, borrowed money from Leslie Ltd but lied about his age. When the company tried to use the tort of deceit to claim damages back from the minor the court refused to support them believing that the company was using tort as an alternative to enforcing the contract through the normal but unsuccessful means.

Statutory law and the protection of adults

On the whole the courts consider that contracts that concern minors can be voidable at any time. In other words they are not set in concrete and the courts can if they wish refuse to enforce them. This is a powerful signal to businesses and others to be careful when they are dealing with minors rather than adults. This was seen by many to be a bit one sided. In return the Minors Contracts Act 1987 allowed the return of goods purchased by minors to in some way compensate the adult who has perhaps entered into a contract without the knowledge that the other party is in fact a minor. If the minor does not have the goods however that is the end of the matter.

The Minor's Contracts Act 1987

It was felt by many that minors who contracted with an adult could often leave the adult in a very vulnerable position. Common law seemed to protect the minor by allowing them to escape from any contractual obligations whilst the adult was always bound to fulfil their part of the deal. The Minor's Contracts Act 1987 evened the situation up slightly. There are two key provisions of importance:

● Loans

An adult who guarantees repayment of a loan for a minor must pay the balance if the minor fails in their payments. If there is no guarantee by adult however the courts will not enforce repayment of a loan by a minor. The lender would therefore be wise to insist on an adult guarantor. Before the 1987 Act the courts could not insist that the adult repay the loan.

● Restitution

Goods that have been acquired unjustly may be handed back to the original owner. This is known as restitution. The wording of the act in this area however only says 'may' order restitution. It is up to the court to decide whether it thinks restitution is just. If the adult has put pressure on the minor then the court will have the power to avoid restitution.

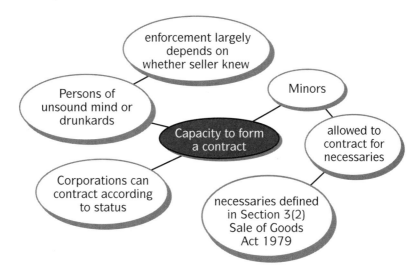

Capacity to form a contract

3 Corporations

A corporation is a legal entity that is designed to protect the owners from financial liability if things go wrong and the business ends up owing money. Without this legal immunity, investors would be less willing to put money into businesses in general since they might then become liable for the debts of the corporation and lose their own possessions. Not all businesses have this limited liability in law, but all companies registered with Companies House under the provisions of the Companies Act 1985 do. The word 'Limited', 'Ltd' or 'PLC' (Public Limited Company) must appear in their title to alert those who deal with these business organizations that their owners have limited financial liability.

The Companies Act 1989

Before 1989 a company that made a contract outside of its registered activities could not have that contract enforced against it. The actions in forming such an agreement were deemed *ultra vires*, that is, beyond their power. The Companies Act 1989 changed this and now all agreements made by a company may be enforced provided the other party has acted in good faith.

Statutory corporations

Statutory corporations such as the British Broadcasting Corporation (BBC) will be limited in the contracts they enter into by their statute. The BBC will not, for example, be allowed to enter into contracts for the provision of financial services unless the statute says so or is amended to allow for such an activity.

Chartered corporations

Examples of chartered corporations are universities and charitable bodies. They are allowed to enter into any contract that an adult person of full capacity can enter into. The charter comes from the Crown (the State) and can be reviewed if contracts entered into are of a dubious or unsuitable nature.

4 Persons of unsound mind and drunkards

Whether a contract is enforced by the courts depends on whether the person providing the services or goods realizes the customer is suffering from unsound mind or drunkeness.

A contract will be valid unless the customer is drunk or of unsound mind and is incapable of understanding the contract, **and** the provider of the goods or services does know it or ought to know it.

On the other hand, the contract is enforceable if the customer is drunk or of unsound mind and is incapable of understanding the contract, but the provider of the goods or services does **not** know it.

An interesting case, which shows the courts making decisions based on the circumstances of the case, is the following.

Legal case: *Barclays Bank v Schwartz (1995)*

Schwartz claimed that he did not understand the full contractual obligations of an agreement he entered into with Barclays Bank. It eventually left him owing £500,000. He argued that his illiteracy and his poor grasp of spoken English negated his capacity to form a contract. The court decided that it was his obligation to get the contract explained to him before he entered into it.

Very young minors

The last element to consider here is looking at very young children and their capacity to enter into contracts. The courts may take the view that they do not have the mental capacity to enter into a contract. There are two key issues that must be understood.

1 Does the minor understand the agreement itself?

2 Does the minor understand any ongoing financial responsibilities of the agreement?

The issue of the type of contract is crucial. Buying a bag of sweets from the local corner shop is a very different situation compared to entering into a mobile phone contract with ongoing costs to the user. The court might accept the former contractual arrangement as a normal state of affairs from a five year old, but probably not the latter.

Quick revision questions

1 What are the key reasons for the use of capacity in contracts?

2 What did the Infant's Relief Act 1874, the Family Law Reform Act 1969, and the Minor's Contracts Act 1987 do to the position of minors?

3 Why are exceptions allowed to capacity to form contracts with minors?

4 What are necessaries?

5 Outline the case of *Nash v Inman (1908)*.

6 How are services for the benefit of the minor viewed?

7 Outline the cases of *Clements v London and North West (1894)* and *De Francesco v Barnum (1890)*.

8 How does capacity affect corporations?

9 How are drunkards protected by the law with regard to contracts?

10 How are those of unsound mind protected by the law with regard to contracts?

Exam question

Discuss the need for capacity when forming contracts.
[50 marks]

Exam answer guide

Knowledge and understanding [20 marks]
✓ Define the principle of capacity
✓ Consider situations of minors using Sale of Goods Act 1979 and cases such as *Nash and Inman (1908)*, *Clements v London and North West (1894)* and *De Francesco v Barnum (1890)*
✓ Consider situations of corporations
✓ Consider situations of persons of unsound mind and drunkards. Quote *Barclays Bank v Schwartz (1995)*
✓ Consider situations of very young minors

Analysis and evaluation [25 marks]
✓ Comment on the fairness of each situation with regard to both parties to the contract

Presentation [5 marks]
✓ Structure your work in a logical and well-planned way. Employ good quality and clear English in your writing. Make use of punctuation and correct spelling in your answers.

Contractual terms

Key points

1 Express and implied terms
2 Sale of Goods Act 1979
3 Contract law protection for the consumer
4 Standard form contracts

Why do I need to know about contractual terms?

The terms in a contract are vital in establishing the legal relationship between the parties involved. Some terms are clearly stated in the contract, but others are also there by way of statute or common practice. One of the most important pieces of legislation in this area is the Sale of Goods Act 1979, which implied into the contract five key protections for the consumer. A raft of legislation now protects the consumer. Large businesses are prompted to be fair in the market place and not to use their considerable strength against the relatively weak position of the individual consumer.

Consumers are protected by legislation

1 Express and implied terms

There are times when the parties to a contract are supported by an agreement, which may be oral or may be written. These are the 'express terms' of the contract. There may, however, be other elements, which are taken for granted known as 'implied terms'. These terms may not have been discussed or included in the written documentation but are assumed to be present. This may be due to the nature of the business, the character of the parties involved in the deal, or because statutory provision plays a part in such agreements.

Express terms

Oral statements

Only the most naïve of customers would make a contract with a builder, for example, without something being written down. Sometimes a customer will get an estimate for the work being carried out or sometimes a quote. In addition, discussions may take place with your builder as work progresses although many a newcomer to the world of building and builders will get a surprise when the project is completed. Prices may have risen, work not commissioned may have been carried out, work desperately needed may have been forgotten and many other difficulties are waiting for the unwary. There may be times when statements *are* agreed upon but disagreement arises over whether the statements were part of a contract or simply 'I think this would work'.

Timing

Statements about what is required may be made some time before a contract is drawn up. These representations should then be verified or confirmed if one party wishes to have them in a contract.

Legal case: *Routeledge v McKay (1954)*

Discussions about the sale of a motorbike took place that included a debate on how old it was. The motorbike was bought a week later. The contract made no mention about the age of the machine. The bike turned out to be twelve years older than first thought. The court felt that the passage of a week between discussion and sale indicated the age of the bike was a representation rather than a term.

On the other hand –

Legal case: *Schawel v Reade (1913)*

A horse was being sold by Reade. Schawel was led to believe that the horse was 'perfectly sound'. This turned out not to be the case. The time between the statement made by Reade and the contract being formed was three weeks. The words were taken as a term of the contract. The court therefore found in favour of the claimant, Schawel.

Specialist knowledge

If one of the parties to a disagreement had specialist knowledge about the subject of the contract then the court is more likely to believe that this is a term of the contract. Two cases highlight this issue.

> ### Legal case: *Dick Bentley Productions v Harold Smith Motors (1965)*
>
> A prestigious Bentley car was purchased. The seller, Harold Smith Motors, claimed that the car had only travelled 20,000 miles since its last major overhaul. The car later developed problems and the truth came out – that the car had actually done 100,000 miles. The court decided that the claim that the car had only done 20,000 miles was a term and the claimant won the case.

> ### Legal case: *Oscar Chess v Williams (1957)*
>
> A private individual genuinely believed the second-hand car he sold to a professional car dealer was newer than it was. The court felt that the professional dealer should have known better and that the seller could not be expected to have such expert knowledge.

The statement itself

If one party would not have entered into the contract without the presence of a particular statement, it is often seen as a term. If an employee enters into a contract of employment but has been misled over pay and fundamental conditions of service then these statements would be seen as terms of the contract.

> ### Legal case: *Bannerman v White (1865)*
>
> The defendant bought some hops used in the making of beer on the understanding that they had not been treated with sulphur. However, a small proportion had been treated and the defendant refused to pay. The court agreed that the claim that sulphur had not been used was a term since White had specifically asked about the matter.

Agreements in writing

Agreements are often put into writing for a number of reasons.

- They give precision to any verbal representations made.
- They underline the significance of the obligations being entered into.
- During the course of negotiations hundreds of details may be discussed and these need to be written down so none are missed.
- Others who may have to implement the contract may need a written document.
- In case there are future disagreements, a written document may help if the case goes to court.

There are often disagreements even about what is put in black and white. A statement that appears in a written document is normally regarded as a term. Any statements discussed before the contract and which are not in the written contract are regarded as representations and not of great importance.

There are two important rules used in written contracts.

1 *L'Estrange v Graucob*

This comes from the case of the same name heard in 1934. Even if a person does not read the terms of the contract they are bound by them if they sign it. This does pose a problem for those who are not legally trained in reading the small print of some contracts, which can be deliberately complex.

2 The parol evidence rule

This rule came about from *Goss v Lord Nugent (1833)*. A written contract cannot be overturned by oral evidence as written evidence has more weight than oral evidence. There are, however, a number of exceptions to this rule. If a contract is clearly written *and* oral then the oral evidence will be allowed. There may also be a contract running alongside the main contract called a collateral contract. Evidence from this may be allowed.

Implied terms

Some terms in the contract may not be written down – they may be taken for granted or possibly left out by mistake. If there are problems, the courts can add them in formally. On the whole, the courts are happier to allow the parties to decide what should be in or not themselves. They will normally only involve themselves when they feel that their input will make commercial agreements smoother and workable. The implied term may be either a condition or a warranty.

There are four main groups of implied terms.

1 Law

There may be law covering certain legal situations. It might not be necessary to include this legislation in every contract but it will still have to be followed by the parties involved in the contract. The Sale of Goods Act 1979, for example, will take the place of any contract made by individual parties. Contracts must obey the law.

Legal case: *Liverpool City Council v Irwin (1977)*

The residents of a high-rise block of council flats had stopped paying their rent as a protest against the condition of the building they lived in. The rubbish chutes were in a poor state, which meant that rubbish often accumulated. The lifts were often unusable and human and animal urine and excrement was often found on the stairs. The tenants felt that there was an implied term in their housing contract for the council to keep the building in a good state of repair. The House of Lords decided that Liverpool City Council had taken reasonable steps to keep the building clean and in a good state of repair. They were under no obligation as landlords to *constantly* repair and clean up damage created by vandals and some of the tenants. The House of Lords felt that the implied term in the contract was to take reasonable care of the building.

2 Custom

If a local custom dictates the presence of a particular term the courts may uphold this. In the case of *Smith v Wilson (1832)* the local custom meant that the quantity 1000 actually meant 1200.

3 Trade usage

It may be common for businesses to use trade association contracts or keep to certain terms in their operations within a particular industry. Travel agents, for example, may follow guidelines issued by the Association of British Travel Agents (ABTA) on how contracts between holidaymakers and the company are put together.

Legal case: *British Crane Hire Corp Ltd v Ipswich Plant Hire Ltd (1975)*

An association represented the interests of those who hired out cranes and other building machines. The association had a standard contract, which was often used in the industry. The contract used meant that the person hiring the machine would take it back to where they had hired it. However, the crane got stuck in some mud and a disagreement erupted. The courts decided that previous trade practice should be observed and it was the responsibility of the company that hired the crane to return it to base.

4 Intentions

The aim of the courts is to make sure that contracts work in situations where items are forgotten or assumptions made have proved to be a problem. The courts may use two tests to ascertain what the contracts intended to do.

1 Officious bystander

If a busybody comments on the implied terms in a contract and the reply from both parties is an irritated 'Yes, we know that', it is known as 'the officious bystander test'. The comment relates to a point so glaringly obvious that it gets on the nerves of those who are asked it.

2 Business efficacy

The courts will not look for minor technicalities to destroy a contract. The parties have entered the contract freely and are hoping to bring benefit to one another. The courts will imply terms either to make obvious the intentions of the parties if necessary or to make the contract workable.

One of the classic cases in this area is the following.

Legal case: *The Moorcock case (1889)*

The claimants wanted to moor their boat on a jetty to unload goods. The boat was run aground due to the water being too shallow. The claimants argued that an implied term in the contract would be that the water was deep enough to bring the boat in safely. They won the case.

An implied term such as the one mentioned in *The Moorcock case (1889)* would clearly pass the officious bystander test. Obviously the water should be deep enough!

Terms only known to one side

It would be unfair if a relevant term known to one party and not the other were employed to the prejudice of the second party. A famous agreement used by trade unions called the Bridlington Agreement was the subject of the next case, which illustrates the point.

Legal case: *Spring v National Amalgamated Stevedores and Dockers Society (1956)*

Mr Spring joined the union without knowing anything about the Bridlington Agreement that allowed transfer and poaching of union members from one organization to another. The contract Mr Spring signed made no mention of this agreement. The officious bystander test was used. The trade union may have said, 'Yes of course', but Mr Spring may well have said, 'What's that?' The union lost. Spring was unaware of the supposed well-known and 'obvious' agreement.

If one of the parties may have been put at a disadvantage by one of the supposed implied terms then the court will be unlikely to imply it into the contract.

Cooper, the defendant, had asked an estate agent to sell two of his cinemas. The commission for the sale of the buildings would be paid on completion of the sale. The estate agent arranged for a buyer who was prepared to give the asking price. However, the cinema owner changed his mind, withdrew from the sale and the estate agent failed to get any money despite having done the work. The estate agent argued that there was an implied term that the seller should go through with the sale unless there was a very good reason for not doing so. The House of Lords rejected this saying that it might have been obvious to the estate agent but it might not have been so to the seller.

Parliamentary intervention

We have already seen that statute law will override terms of contract if those terms go against what Parliament has intended. The Sale of Goods Act 1979 and the various employment acts will come into play even if they are not expressly mentioned in the contract. The courts will imply these terms if it goes that far.

2 Sale of Goods Act 1979

The Sale of Goods Act (SGA) 1979 was one of the most important pieces of legislation passed for consumer protection in the UK. It was amended by the Sale and Supply of Goods Act 1994. It hoped to change the practices of retail businesses and give the ordinary consumer the power of legislation and the courts to back them up.

Although an incredibly useful piece of legislation, the SGA 1979 still suffers from what all legislation suffers from – a lack of knowledge by those who might benefit from it most. The average consumer often feels powerless against large well-organized and well-financed companies who use the law to their own advantage and often misquote or undermine law that is meant to protect the consumer's interests.

Ethical and positive looking companies not only observe statutory rights that the customer has, but even gives them extra through contractual obligations they place upon themselves. However, there will always be a minority of businesses in every industry who pay little respect to their customers and who may well exploit the market in the short run.

The Sale of Goods Act 1979 implied five key terms into consumer contracts. Even if the contract did not state these terms, the courts would imply them.

1 Title

The seller of the goods to the consumer must own those goods; he must have title to them. Section 12 also implies that the goods have no charge on them. A charge is a claim by someone else to the ownership of those goods in certain circumstances. Title is important criteria of the transaction since without it the buyer cannot become the owner even if they have paid the seller, as it was not the sellers to sell in the first place. The buyer may claim back the price of the goods from the seller.

2 Description

The goods must match their description. This is important when consumers are buying goods from catalogues such as Argos, cable channels such as QVC, or Internet sites. Descriptions often appear on boxes or promotional materials. The consumer is protected under Section 13 in these circumstances.

3 Quality

The goods must be of a satisfactory quality. This includes fit for purpose, appearance, free from minor defects, safety and durability. There is an exception to this. If the seller points out any defect or the defect is an obvious one then Section 14 is not relevant. The goods should be fit for their purpose, but second-hand goods may not be up to the standard of new goods and the act allows for this state of affairs.

The Sale of Goods Act 1979 referred to 'merchantable quality'. If merchantable quality was poor in general however, that was what the consumer could expect. The Sale and Supply of Goods Act 1994 updated that definition to 'satisfactory quality'. Satisfactory quality gives the consumer and their representatives more leverage when there is a dispute about the nature of quality. The move from merchantable quality to satisfactory quality was a step forward but the courts still would had faced difficulty if the legislation had not been as clear as it was. The term quality is given a great deal of description in the actual Act. There are a number of cases, which are currently going through the courts testing the scope of this latest legislation, the Sale and Supply of Goods Act 1994. An important point to remember is that the objective test is used to decide whether an article is satisfactory or not, that is what the reasonable person thinks is satisfactory.

Legislation

Sale of Goods and Services Act 1994

Section 14(2A) Goods are of satisfactory quality if they meet the standard that a reasonable person would regard as satisfactory, taking account of any description of the goods, the price (if relevant) and all the other relevant circumstances.

Section 14(2B) The quality of goods includes their state and condition and the following (among others) are, in appropriate cases, aspects of the quality of the goods: (a) fitness for all the purposes for which goods of the kind in question are commonly supplied; (b) appearance and finish; (c) freedom from minor defects; (d) safety; and (e) durability.

The implied term 'satisfactory quality' is an extremely important one in the consumers armoury against rogue traders. This term only however applies to transactions, which are in 'the course of business'. This means that is does not apply to private sales such as those from the local paper or from car boot sales. Here the buyer must have in their mind the warning *caveat emptor* a Latin phrase that means 'let the buyer beware'.

The following cases show the range of situations where consumer legislation and intervention by the courts have been used to support the consumer.

Legal case: *Bernstein v Pamsons Motors (1987)*

A three week old car seized up on the motorway due to a faulty sealant. The courts considered that the consumer was entitled to a car, which did not fail within such a short period of time. The car was deemed to be not of 'merchantable quality'.

Legal case: *Shine v General Guarantee (1988)*

The claimant had purchased a car from General Guarantee who stated that the car was in 'good condition'. It was later found out that the car had been immersed in water and had been written off by the insurance company. Although the car was fit to be on the road its monetary value would have been much less if the purchaser had been aware of its history. It was therefore decided that the car was not of 'merchantable quality' and the buyer should be entitled to damages, which amounted to the sum between the purchase price and the true market price.

Legal case: *Rogers v Parish (1987)*

A brand new Range Rover vehicle had caused its owner numerous problems. There were problems with its bodywork, engine and gears. The claimant constantly complained and the car was constantly being repaired. Eventually the court decided the issue and declared the vehicle not to be of 'merchantable quality'.

Group activity

If it had been available, what sections of the above legislation from the Sale of Goods and Services Act 1994 would have helped the claimant in the case of *Rogers v Parish (1987)*?

A case where the quality issue was responsible for a serious accident was the case of *Godley v Perry (1960)*.

Legal case: *Godley v Perry (1960)*

A six year old boy lost one of his eyes when a poorly constructed catapult misfired. The court decided that in this case the 'toy' was not of 'merchantable quality' and the child was entitled to damages.

Finally a very old case from the turn of the last century illustrates the perils of going for a quiet drink in your local public house.

Legal case: *Wren v Holt (1903)*

A customer who consumed a large quantity of beer became ill. It was discovered that the beer contained a small quantity of arsenic, a highly dangerous poison. The defendant was found guilty of supplying beer to the public, which was not of a 'merchantable quality'.

4 Fit for purpose

If the buyer makes known that they want the goods for a specific purpose then there is an implied condition that the goods will be fit for that purpose if sold. If the buyer does not take the advice of the seller in this respect then this condition cannot be implied.

Legal case: *Priest v Last (1903)*

The buyer bought a hot water bottle. The specific purpose was to fill it with hot liquid and place it in his bed to keep warm on cold nights. The water bottle split and was considered not fit for the purpose.

5 Sale by sample

A sample provided by the seller must match the actual goods purchased. The sample must not mislead or hide any defect. Samples are covered by Section 15.

Acceptance of goods

Acceptance of the goods occurs when the following happens.

- The buyer tells the seller he wants the goods, provided the buyer has had a reasonable chance to inspect the goods.

- The buyer alters the goods in some way.

- The buyer accepts the goods after a reasonable length of time has passed and the buyer has not rejected the goods.

- If there are defects that need repair by the seller, acceptance has not occurred until these defects are rectified.

Passing of ownership

The passing of ownership also means the passing of certain liabilities for the goods. Unless otherwise agreed, the passing of ownership (also known as passing of goods) occurs in the following way under Section 18 of the Act.

- If the goods can be delivered, the ownership passes on signing of the contract.

- If the goods are not yet deliverable, the ownership passes when they are ready and the buyer tells the seller.

- If goods are given on approval, the lapse of time will transfer ownership or if the buyer states he wants the goods.

Group activity

Try to watch or tape some episodes of *Watchdog* or a similar consumer programme. What laws are used in the cases featured?

---

3 Contract law protection for the consumer

An offer is a promise to do something, which, if accepted, becomes an agreement that is legally enforceable – a contract is formed. It is important to realize that the business or the consumer may make the offer and there are times when it is difficult to tell without looking closely at the words used in advertisements or contracts.

To form a consumer contract the first step in the process is making an offer. A person may make an offer to an individual person, a group of people or even the general public.

Unilateral contract

If a company makes an offer to the general public it is called a unilateral contract. When the offer is made, it is taken up by the offeree (the party to whom the contract is offered) and they then let the offeror (the party that makes the contract) know. A classic case that explored the relationship between the two parties in a contract offered to the general public is the following.

Legal case: *Carlill v Carbolic Smoke Ball Company (1893)*

Mrs Carlill purchased a product from the Carbolic Smoke Ball Company, which promised to protect against flu. After using the device Mrs Carlill still contracted flu and asked the company for the £100 it had promised if its product failed. They claimed that a contract had not been made since it would have been impossible to make a contract with everybody in the world. The court thought otherwise. An advertisement promising the £100 was seen as part of the offer and the acceptance was the purchase and use of the product by Mrs Carlill.

This case meant that companies would now be seen as making contracts with their individual customers when the customer accepted the offer made.

Pre-contract discussions

The offer by one party may be preceded by exploratory moves. The offer is not set in stone at this point and prices and conditions may change after haggling. These movements are steps on the way to a fully-fledged contract and the tentative offers are known as invitations to treat. They are designed to sound out the other side before something more binding is arranged.

Legal case: *Gibson v Manchester City Council (1979)*

Mr Gibson was thinking about buying his council house so he filled in an application form and the council sent a letter that said it 'may consider selling for £2180'. Discussions took place about the poor state of repair of a footpath to Mr Gibson's house. By the time this issue had been sorted out there had been an election and the new political party in control refused to sell the house. Mr Gibson took the council to court but it was decided that the letter from the council was only an invitation to treat and not an offer, which would form part of a binding contract along with his acceptance.

This is a complex area where decisions by the courts may be seen as very unpopular by the losing party since the difference between an invitation to treat compared to an offer may seem quite trivial. Other places where invitations to treat might be seen are the following.

- **Shops**

  Goods marked up with prices in windows or on shelves in a shop are invitations to treat rather than offers. A customer has no right to insist on buying a good at the price on the ticket or even the right to buy the good at all. There is no contract until offer has been made at the checkout and the customer has made an acceptance. The legal case *Pharmaceutical Society of Great Britain v Boots the Chemist (1953)* on page 143 is another example of this.

- **Advertisements**

  If a seller advertises goods showing a specific price, this is normally seen as an invitation to treat. The customer may negotiate about price or other conditions. If a customer was buying a DVD player, they might ask for a better deal on price or to have something extra included such as DVD discs or an extended warranty. There is room for manoeuvre.

  If an advertisement is like the Carbolic Smoke Ball Company's then the promise of £100 if it does not work is seen as an offer. There is nothing to negotiate. A promise has been made and the customer wants to see this honoured. The same situation arises if a person responds to a leaflet stuck on a tree about a lost puppy. If they find the dog and respond directly to the advertisement, they will expect to be paid the reward. An offer has been tendered and acceptance made.

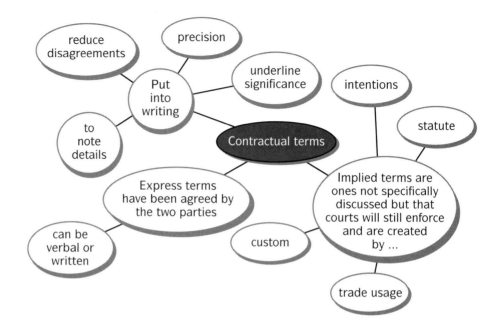

Contractual terms

Failure or withdrawal of an offer

An offer made by a party is subject to time constraints known as the life span of the offer. There are two principal methods of dealing with the issue.

1 Time limits formally stated

If an offer is made to fumigate a house, the offer may only remain open for six months or so and after this a new price may have to be fixed. Costs change and inflation erodes the value of money. Businesses cannot be bound by offers they make for years on end. This may be stated in the quotes offered by the business or in other literature. The Argos shops have a number of catalogues each year changing what goods they provide and the prices. The front cover often states when the catalogue expires. This is an example of a time limit.

2 Reasonable time limits if none mentioned

Some prices may change much more rapidly than others. The price of garden lawnmowers are probably much more stable than shares in certain high-risk businesses or house prices in many areas of the country. Each case needs to be looked at in turn.

Legal case: *Ramsgate Victoria Hotel v Montefiore (1866)*

Montefiore applied for shares in the Ramsgate Victoria Hotel and paid a deposit. Nothing was heard from the hotel for five months. Eventually they asked for the balance of payment stating that the shares had at last been allocated. Montefiore refused due to the significant time delay. The courts backed his argument and stated that the contract had failed due to the five month delay.

Shares fluctuate in price and such a contract would have to be completed fairly speedily. If a customer had ordered a large piece of furniture such as a sofa, they may well be told that delivery may not happen for four or five months. This case would be treated very differently and a customer putting down a deposit might be deemed to have agreed to a binding contract.

If there is a set time within which the offer may be accepted, the offeror is still able to revoke the offer before the time period is up. The one exception to this is if a consideration has been made, which keeps the offer open. We will look at the full meaning of consideration later in this unit.

Group activity

Look at some adverts and 'offers' in a local newspaper. Determine if they are invitations to treat or offers.

Pre-conditions

Some contracts may be subject to pre-conditions, which, if they are not met, will lead to the repudiation (rejection) of the contract.

Counter offers

Counter offers may bounce backwards and forwards between the parties until there is a satisfactory agreement. If one party makes a counter offer that is considered but rejected by the other party, this cancels the original 'agreement' and they are back to square one. A legal case clarifies this issue.

Legal case: *Hyde v Wrench (1840)*

Wrench was going to sell his farm for £1000. Hyde offered £950. This was known as the counter offer. Wrench refused the lower offer and Hyde then attempted to accept the offer at the original level of £1000. The court decided that the offeror was not compelled to offer at this price.

Death

Death is not as bad as it seems, at least when dealing with contracts. If an offer has been made by the offeror and they die soon afterwards, the offeree will be able to claim enforcement of the contract. This is particularly so if they have accepted in ignorance of the death of the offeror. *Bradbury v Morgan (1862)* illustrated that the death of an offeror did not cancel the contract. The offeree may be unaware of the death of the offeror and events start to take place, which discharge the contract. If it is a personal service, the situation is different. The contract in this case would cease to be. The death of the offeree is still unclear in many contract terms.

Revocation by the offeror

The offeror can cancel an offer up to the point of acceptance by the offeree. Cancellation is known as revocation. The offeror must inform the offeree that this is their intention before the other party makes the acceptance. The following case explores this important issue and raises the idea of postal rule, which will be looked at later in this unit.

Legal case: *Byrne v Van Tienhoven (1880)*

One company in Cardiff was dealing with another in New York. The Cardiff company, Van Tienhoven, had offered to sell 1000 tinplates (thin steel or iron sheets covered with tin) by letter on 1 October to the New York company, Byrne. Byrne received the letter on 11 October and accepted the offer by telegram that day, which meant that the offer was accepted immediately. Van Tienhoven sent another letter on 8 October revoking the offer but this did not get to New York until 20 October – nine days after the offer was accepted via telegram by Byrne. The contract had been formed the day the telegram was sent.

Revocation by a third party

The revocation of the offer must be communicated to the offeree but it does not have to be by the offeror. A third party can do this as in the case of *Dickinson v Dodds (1876)*, which related to the sale of a house.

Revocation by publicity

If a unilateral contract has been made to 'the whole world', it may be withdrawn using the same level of publicity as the original offer enjoyed.

Legal case: *Shuey v US (1875)*

A person claimed a reward for the capture of a criminal. The reward had been withdrawn, however, by the same level of publicity that the original reward offer received. Whether all who read the first advertisement read the second is questionable.

Mail

One of the problems that often arises with communication of acceptance or revocation is time. When did one party or another receive the information? We saw in *Byrne v Van Tienhoven (1880)* a letter and a telegram crossing mid-Atlantic. There may also be a problem in big companies where the post is sorted in a central area and then distributed throughout the building. It may go to senior people first and then down through a hierarchy. This may delay the information considerably. The question arises of when does the information go live? Is it on receipt from the post van or when the relevant person opens the letter? The issue is unclear although e-mail may force some clarification on this issue soon.

Acceptance

If the offeree accepts an offer, they are agreeing to all the terms of the offer. An acceptance must take place whilst the offer is still on the table. If they attempt to change any of the terms of the offer, it might be seen as a counter offer, which will revoke the original. If this happens, the counter offer will now be an offer, which the other party must accept, that is, the roles are reversed. The offer can be accepted in three main ways:

- verbally
- in writing
- by conduct.

If the offeror lays down the method of acceptance, this must be obeyed. If written acceptance is called for then an answer phone message will not be enough. If no method is laid down then any reasonable method will do.

The case of *Brogden v Metropolitan Rail Company (1877)* illustrates the offer and acceptance issue and the way courts can assume contracts from the behaviour of the parties.

Legal case: *Brogden v Metropolitan Rail Company (1877)*

Brogden had supplied coal for a number of years to the Metropolitan Rail Company. They decided to formalize their arrangements and the Metropolitan Rail Company sent a draft agreement to Brogden asking for signature and the name of an arbitrator if there were future problems. Brogden signed the document but also made some amendments. The document was filed at the company. A dispute arose two years later and Brogden denied any binding contract. The courts decided that there was a contract. The continued business relationship between the two acted as an acceptance of Brogden's counter offer.

Brogden v Metropolitan Rail Company (1877)

Offer by Metropolitan Rail Company

⇓

Counter offer by amendments by Brogden

⇓

Order of coal by Metropolitan Rail Company seen as acceptance by conduct

⇓

Contract formed

Silence as acceptance

Silence is not regarded as an acceptable method of acceptance of an offer. This has been underlined in a number of important pieces of statute law including the Unsolicited Goods and Services Act 1971. A company cannot send goods or supply services without request and then attempt to insist on payment in the courts. Some book and music clubs will send items through the post every month unless the customer writes to them and tells them not to. A contract with written permission from the customer will have been drawn up first, however, so the goods are not completely unsolicited. The Unsolicited Goods and Services Act 1971 has got some power because the customer can keep the unsolicited goods as a gift after 28 days (if they have let the seller know they have the goods) or after six months (if they do not let the seller know that they have the goods).

Legal case: *Felthouse v Brindley (1862)*

An uncle and nephew had discussed the purchase of a horse. The uncle wrote to the nephew with an offer and stated that if he heard nothing more he would take this as an acceptance of his offer. The courts felt that silence even if invited could not be seen as an acceptance.

Reward cases and ignorance of offer

These cases highlight issues of acceptance. If a person reads a national newspaper that offers a reward for kidnapped children, in the full knowledge of that offer, they can legitimately receive the money rewarded providing theirs was the information that led to the desired outcome and they have met any other conditions of the offer. If the person had no knowledge of that offer and provided information to the police on a case that led to a successful outcome, there is no legal duty on the offeree to pay the reward. There has been no acceptance of the offer since there had been no knowledge of the offer. There might be a moral duty but no court could intervene in these circumstances.

Acceptance by the post – the postal rule

The date a letter was sent that included an acceptance is seen as the date of acceptance of the offer. The case of *Adams v Lindsell (1818)* illustrates this point.

Legal case: *Adams v Lindsell (1818)*

Lindsell offered Adams some wool and asked for a reply by post. The letter was late to arrive but Adams posted an immediate reply accepting the offer. As the letter was late, the defendant sold the wool. They were held to be in breach of contract since the contract was formed when the acceptance was posted back.

This legal principle is known as the postal rule and is still valid today although companies would be foolish to rely only on the post in an age of e-mails, faxes and other information technology.

Group activity

Should a rule such as the postal rule still be held valid today?

Consideration

Consideration is the thing that is of benefit to one party and possibly of detriment, initially at least, to the other. If someone pays for a cleaner to come in for three hours on a Tuesday morning to tidy up then the consideration is the £15 and the three hours of labour.

Executory consideration

This is what one of the parties promises *to do* to turn the agreement into a reality in exchange for the promise of the other.

Executed consideration

This is what one of the parties *does* to turn the agreement into reality in exchange for the promise of the other.

There are a number of key points to consider with consideration.

- The consideration must only be sufficient; it does not have to be adequate. I have the freedom to strike a bad bargain if I choose to. The law will not necessarily intervene to prevent this.

- The consideration must have occurred by moving from offeree to offeror. A third party who has provided no consideration cannot normally enforce the contract.

- Consideration must not be past. If the thing that is to be done has already been done then it cannot legally be seen as consideration. If I paint my mother-in-law's house and then go to seek a contract by offering to paint the already painted house, this is not consideration.

- Performance of an existing legal or contractual obligation is not seen as consideration.

Intention

There must be a genuine intention to create a legal relationship between the two parties. If they slip into it without awareness then this does not produce a consumer contract. There has to be a meeting of minds. There are two presumptions that the courts make in this area.

1 Social and domestic agreements do not give rise to legal relations. See *Balfour v Balfour (1919) (page 160)*.

2 Business arrangements and legal relations are assumed unless clearly indicated otherwise.

Most consumers purchase goods or essential services without ever reading the contract before them. This also happened in a huge contract between ITV Digital and the Football League over television rights to football games.

Legal case: *Football League v Carlton and Granada (2002)*

The Football League and ITV Digital had drawn up an unsigned contract between themselves, which promised £315,000,000 to the Football League for rights to broadcast certain important games. The contract did not contain a term which said that the parent companies would carry responsibility for the child in the event of financial problems. In the end there were financial problems and ITV Digital went bust. The Football League took ITV Digital and the owners, Carlton and Granada, to the High Court to seek payment of £178,500,000 that was still outstanding. The High Court felt that ITV Digital was a separate company and the owners did not have to pay the outstanding debt.

Privity

Only those actually involved in a contract can have obligations or rights under it. Third parties, even if benefiting from the contract, do not have rights. There have been a number of exceptions made to this rule over time.

There are two key points to the rule of privity.

1 Obligations cannot be enforced on a third party

This is relatively uncontroversial. No one would like to find out that they were legally obligated to perform terms in a contract without voluntarily doing so. If a friend hired you out for odd jobs without your knowledge or consent, it would not be long before you both had a fairly direct conversation.

2 Benefits cannot be claimed by a third party

This is more troublesome. If the contract has been made to benefit a third party, they have no right to enforce it if it goes wrong. Only the person who signed the contract has this right.

Legal case: *Tweddle v Atkinson (1861)*

Two fathers made a contract to give money to their newly married son and daughter. Mr Tweddle senior had given the money but then died. Mr Atkinson did not come forth with his share and was taken to court by his son-in-law. The court ruled that the son-in-law was a third party and could not enforce the contract even if it was to his benefit.

There has been a major change in the whole area of privity brought about by some major statutory legislation, the Contracts (Rights of Third Parties) Act 1999. This piece of legislation protects those who are beneficiaries of a contract that has been specially made for them. This third party may now enforce the contract even though they did not play a part in making it. The enforcement is possible providing:

- the contract states that the third party may enforce it
- a term gives a benefit to the third party.

4 Standard form contracts

Many contracts may involve negotiations before and during the formation of the contract and possibly even rectification after the contract has been signed as both sides attempt to get the best deal for themselves. The world of business has moved on significantly during the last 150 years. Large corporations dominate the market and exert huge influence over other businesses as well as their consumers. The world of consumer sovereignty, where the consumer was in theory all-powerful, seems to have disappeared from most markets.

Large businesses such as Dixons, Currys, AOL, BT, NTL, and the massive car producers, dominate the market and often provide consumers with a standard contract that is on their terms. Corporate lawyers carefully draw up contracts, which are then offered to millions of consumers. Individual negotiation is gone. The consumer either purchases on the terms of the giant business or does not purchase at all.

Group activity

Get a credit card contract or the terms and conditions of a bank account from your local bank. What problems might the typical customer have in understanding it?

Quick revision questions

1 What is the difference between express and implied terms?

2 What are the key issues surrounding express terms?

3 Why are agreements put into writing?

4 What are the two rules for written contracts?

5 What are the four types of implied terms?

6 What is an officious bystander?

7 What are the five implied terms in the Sale of Goods Act 1979?

8 How does contract law protect consumers?

9 What important point does *Byrne v Van Tienhoven (1880)* illustrate?

10 What are standard form contracts?

Examine the differences between express and implied terms.
[50 marks]

Exam answer guide

Knowledge and understanding [20 marks]
- ✓ Define express terms, can be oral can be written
- ✓ Quote cases such as *Routeledge v McKay (1954)*
- ✓ Mention the *L'Estrange v Graucob (1934)* rule and *Goss v Lord Nugent (1833)* (parol evidence)
- ✓ Define implied terms. Include legal, custom, trade usage and intentions
- ✓ Illustrate the effect of the Sale of Goods Act 1979 for an example of implied terms

Analysis and evaluation [25 marks]
- ✓ Evaluate the position of each type of term
- ✓ Comment on the need for implied terms
- ✓ Evaluate the impact of legislation on implied terms

Presentation [5 marks]
- ✓ Structure your work in a logical and well-planned way. Employ good quality and clear English in your writing. Make use of punctuation and correct spelling in your answers.

UNIT 6

Types of terms

Key points

1 Conditions and warranties
2 Innominate terms and effects of breach

Why do I need to know about types of terms?

The courts are keen to allow contracts to work – but not at all costs. If there are major problems with agreements, the courts will use their power to cancel them and award the innocent party some sort of compensation. Life is not always perfect and the same can be said for the performance of contracts. Sometimes small things will be disregarded, but there are times when such an important part of the contract has not been carried out satisfactorily that urgent action needs to be taken. There are two types of terms in a contract, conditions and warranties, one being more important than the other. This unit looks at them and what consequences follow in each case.

Conditions and warranties

1 Conditions and warranties

A 'condition' is a term in a contract that is of significant importance. If you were to buy a house and found out upon investigation that the foundations were just about to collapse then this would be a condition. The innocent buyer of the house may have been put into a very serious position if a condition was defective. If you were about to buy a house and found that the seller had removed all the light bulbs despite the fact they had been in the contract, it would not be the end of the world. The light bulbs would not be a condition, they would be known as a 'warranty'. A warranty can be broken without serious consequences. A contract is made up of terms that form part of the core to the agreement – the warranties in a contract are less important.

Legal case: *Bunge Corporation v Tradex (1981)*

A ship was given thirteen days notice to load its cargo rather than the fifteen days notice agreed in the contract. The House of Lords felt that although two days might seem a small amount to ordinary people in the world of shipping, it was significant enough to be a condition of the contract.

Legal case: *Lombard North Central v Butterworth (1987)*

The claimant leased a computer to the defendant and stressed in the contract that punctual and regular payments were an essential part of the agreement. The defendant was late with the majority of the payments including the last one that was six weeks late. The claimant terminated the contract and damages were claimed. The Court of Appeal supported the claimant on the grounds that the importance of punctuality of payments was crystal clear to the defendant.

If a warranty is broken, the claimant can seek damages but cannot terminate the agreed contract. If a condition is broken, the claimant has a choice: they can end, or repudiate, the contract or they can continue with the contract but sue for damages.

Obviously, the claimant and defendant may disagree about what is a condition and what is a warranty. There are a number of options available to the courts in deciding which is which.

- **The traditional approach**

  The judge will look to see whether a condition or a warranty has been breached. This approach was highlighted in the following case.

Legal case: *Poussard v Spiers and Pond (1876)*

An opera singer had missed final dress rehearsals and the first four performances of the opera. The opera producer dismissed the singer saying that there had been a breach of conditions. The judge stated that the failure of the singer went to the 'root of the matter'. The defendant was entitled to repudiate the contract and the singer lost the case.

- **Terms specified by the parties involved**

  Although agreements may have been voluntarily entered into, the courts sometimes put them aside if they believe they have been unfairly used.

  > **Legal case: *Schuler v Wickman Machine Tool Sales Ltd (1973)***
  >
  > A visit was agreed as part of a contract's conditions. The visits never actually happened and the courts decided that this was not a condition despite the two parties agreeing to it from the outset. The courts felt that Schuler were using it as an excuse to get out of the contract.

- **Statutory provision**

  Statutes such as the Sale of Goods Act 1979 override terms that are made in contracts if they conflict with the law. These are often terms that provide consumer protection against unfair activities of powerful businesses. Even if businesses issue standard contracts and put in exclusions, consumer interests are protected by the Unfair Terms in Consumer Contracts Regulations 1994.

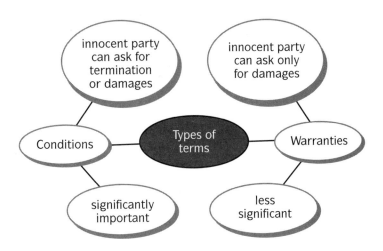

Types of terms

2 Innominate terms and effects of breach

Innominate terms, also known as the Hong Kong Fir Approach, considers the consequences of the breach before considering whether a term is a condition or a warranty. The word 'innominate' means 'without a name or anonymous'. An innominate term in a contract is neither a condition nor a warranty until we see the consequences of that breach. If the breach leads to a serious consequence, it is a condition; if it leads to a trivial consequence, it is a warranty. This differs from the traditional approach since it considers the consequences before establishing whether the terms were a condition or a warranty.

Legal case: *Hong Kong Fir Shipping Company v Kawasaki Ltd (1962)*

Kawasaki had rented a ship from the Hong Kong Fir Company which kept on breaking down. The rental lasted two years during which the ship was broken or being repaired for twenty weeks. The Kawasaki company repudiated the contract. Hong Kong Fir argued that since Kawasaki had the use of the ship for 84 weeks out of the possible 104 this was not a breach of condition, only warranty. The court agreed that the Kawasaki company was only entitled to claim damages and not to terminate the contract.

Group activity

Collect some examples of contracts possibly from hire companies, the back of a credit agreement or other businesses. Attempt to identify conditions and warranties.

Quick revision questions

1 What is the difference between a condition and a warranty?

2 Outline the case of *Bunge Corporation v Tradex (1981)*.

3 What happens if a warranty is broken?

4 What does repudiating mean?

5 Outline the traditional approach via *Poussard v Spiers and Pond (1876)*.

6 What approach did *Schuler v Wickman Machine Tool Sales Ltd (1973)* illustrate?

7 How does the Sale of Goods Act 1979 help in this area?

8 Outline the innominate terms situation.

9 Describe the case of *Hong Kong Fir Shipping Company v Kawasaki Ltd (1962)*.

10 Name four key pieces of vocabulary in this area of types of terms.

Exam question

Discuss the consequences of a breach of:

a a condition

b a warranty

c an innominate term.

[50 marks]

Exam answer guide

Knowledge and understanding [20 marks]

✓ Define the nature of a condition

✓ Define the nature of a warranty

✓ Define innominate terms

✓ Use the following cases to illustrate differences between conditions and warranties: *Bunge v Tradex (1981)*, *Lombard North Central v Butterworth (1987)*, *Poussard v Spiers and Pond (1876)* and *Schuler v Wickman Machine Tool Sales Ltd (1973)*. Quote *Hong Kong Fir Shipping Company v Kawasaki Ltd (1962)* for innominate terms

✓ Show effects of breach for each

✓ Define innominate terms and the effects of a breach

Analysis and evaluation [25 marks]

✓ Assess the value of each type of term in the functioning of a contract

✓ Discuss the reasons and benefits of innominate terms.

Presentation [5 marks]

✓ Structure your work in a logical and well-planned way. Employ good quality and clear English in your writing. Make use of punctuation and correct spelling in your answers.

Exemption clauses

Key points

1 UK legislation on exemption clauses
2 European legislation on exemption clauses
3 Common law on exemption clauses

Why do I need to know about exemption clauses?

The power of businesses to gain unfair advantage over consumers is seen in the area of exemption clauses, which means the avoidance of liability. The courts and Parliament, both UK and European, have involved themselves with this important issue. You should note that there are three main recent acts covering exemption clauses. The first was produced by the UK Parliament, the Unfair Contract Terms Act (UCTA) 1977, and the next two as the result of European Directives, the Unfair Terms in Consumer Contracts Regulations 1994 and the Unfair Terms in Consumer Contracts Regulations 1999. Knowledge of the first and the last is essential for strong answers in this unit.

Exemption clauses are limited

1 UK legislation on exemption clauses

Contracts impose liabilities and responsibilities and there are times when businesses attempt to reduce their exposure to these liabilities and responsibilities. They come in two main forms.

1 The exemption clause

This attempts to avoid any liability whatsoever. A sign saying 'customers leave their belongings in this cloakroom at their own risk' would be an example of an exemption clause.

2 The limitation clause

This attempts to reduce the liability to a fixed amount. Photo processors may state that even if valuable photographs are lost, the firm will only replace it with another blank film and processing credit. Truprint, for example, state:

'Our liability shall be limited to a replacement film and processing charges.'

Statutory UK legislation on exemption clauses is fairly recent but very effective. It puts the power in the hands of the court to decide whether the consumer has been unfairly treated by terms that appear in the contract. There are three significant pieces of legislation: the Unfair Contract Terms Act (UCTA)1977, the Unfair Terms in Consumer Contracts Regulations 1994 (to meet the European Directive on Unfair Terms), and the Unfair Terms in Consumer Contracts Regulations 1999 (to meet the European Directive on Unfair Terms in Consumer Contracts).

The Unfair Contract Terms Act (UCTA) 1977

The Act primarily covers transactions between consumers and businesses, and focuses on exemption clauses. The key provisions of this Act are:

- negligence for death or personal injury cannot be excluded by a term in a contract
- other liability can only be excluded or limited if there are reasonable grounds for doing so
- non-performance or performance which is substantially different from that agreed cannot be excluded or limited by a term in the contract unless it is reasonable to do so.

The first point is very clear but the other two rest on what is reasonable. The courts will take a number of factors into consideration when determining what is reasonable, including the following:

- what the parties understood to be the agreement
- resources available to meet the contractual liabilities
- the power of the business and whether the customer could have gone elsewhere
- previous practice between the parties or within the industry
- whether goods were made specifically for that customer.

This case highlights a number of additional but related factors that the courts take into consideration when deciding if an exemption clause was fair.

Legal case: *George Mitchell (Chesterhall) Ltd v Finney Lock Seeds (1983)*

A supplier of cabbage seed inserted an exemption clause into his contract limiting liability to the purchase price of the seed sold to the buyer. George Mitchell bought £192 worth but sustained £60,000 of damage when the crop failed. It was designed for spring not summer and was also defective. The courts decided that the clause inserted by the seed business was unreasonable because of:

- the size of the loss to George Mitchell
- the lack of care of the supplier
- the evidence of payments made to others by the business when similar circumstances arose
- insurance the supplier could have taken out to cover such situations.

Legal case: *Phillips Products v Hyland (1987)*

A business hired a digging machine along with a driver. Damage was caused during the work to the claimant's property but the firm hiring the machine out denied liability using an exemption clause in their standard contract. The court found the clause unreasonable. Reasons included hiring was at short notice, unfamiliarity with hiring such machines, the associated terms, and no control over the competency of the driver.

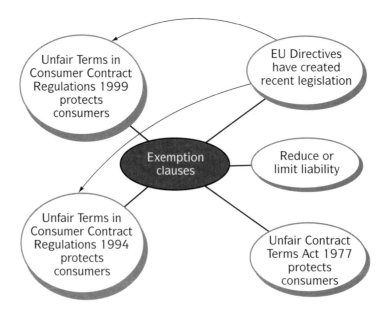

Exemption clauses

Reasonable and unreasonable exemptions

If an exemption clause is to be successful it must be reasonable and it must be incorporated in the contract in a fair way giving the customer reasonable notice. There may be good reasons why a company or organization attempts to limit its liability to customers and clearly not all exemption clauses are unfair. The court will consider a number of issues when it has to make judgement on these cases.

● The strength of each party

If an ordinary consumer is up against a powerful business or a monopoly supplier the courts may give consideration to the consumers relatively weak position. If the consumer has a choice they may go to a competitor although there are of course times when businesses collaborate or take notice of what each of their rivals is doing that produces an environment which is not in the consumers interest. The courts may take a much more robust line if they realise this is happening.

● Specialist or difficult orders

If the consumer has very particular requirements the supplier may have to insist on protection for their own business. This may involve penalty payments for cancellation and other arrangements that ensure they are not put in a vulnerable position. The supplier would not be able to sell the specialist order to another customer in order to defray costs. A difficult order may also fall into this category. It might be risky for the supplier to produce a particularly difficult order and easy to get certain details wrong. They may again feel the need to limit their exposure.

● Current practice

It may be that particular industries of businesses have built up a history of doing business in a particular way, which all are aware of and all agree on.

An example of a case that shows an unreasonable term is the following.

Legal case: *Green v Cade (1978)*

Seed potatoes were supplied to a farmer, which contained an exemption that if there were complaints they had to be made within three days of the delivery. It was impossible to tell from inspecting the potatoes whether there was a defect or not. The farmer would have to wait until the potatoes were due to appear in the fields. When a defect was finally recognised it was too late. The three day deadline had long passed. The court felt that this was an unreasonable exemption.

Another example of unreasonable exemption involves two powerful players in a very complex market. The claimants used the Unfair Contract Terms Act 1977 in this case.

Legal case: *Timeload Ltd v British Telecommunications plc (1995)*

Timeload purchased the freephone number 0800 192 192 from British Telecommunications plc (BT). It hoped to establish a free telephone enquiry service. BT were using the number 192 for its own service so tried to terminate the Timeload service. BT was using an exemption clause in its standard contract, which allowed it to terminate services. The Court of Appeal, using the Unfair Contract Terms Act 1977, declared this unreasonable.

Another important case that used the provisions of Unfair Contract Terms Act 1977 is the following

Legal case: *Smith v Eric Bush (1990)*

A surveyor tried to limit liability when he made an inaccurate assessment of a house. The court felt that the task was not particularly difficult and any reasonably competent surveyor should have had no significant problems in surveying the house accurately. The court however did make the important point that if the task was particularly difficult it would not be unreasonable to limit liability providing the customer was clearly aware of this situation.

2 European legislation on exemption clauses

You may remember from your AS course that delegated legislation is often used to meet requirements of European law. The European Directive on Unfair Terms in Consumer Contracts came into effect in 1993 meaning that all European Union (EU) member states had to pass domestic legislation to meet the Directives requirements.

The UK responded to this Directive by passing the Unfair Terms in Consumer Contracts Regulations Act 1994. This had the effect of updating the Unfair Contract Terms Act (UCTA) 1977. This Directive was aimed not just at unreasonable exemption clauses, but any term that was considered unfair. The new legislation went beyond what was reasonable or unreasonable to what was fair or unfair. This widened the issues the courts could consider and strengthened the position of consumers in the European Union, forcing businesses to adopt fairer contracts overall.

The Unfair Terms in Consumer Contracts Regulations 1999 updated the previous 1994 legislation and brought UK legislation more in line with the language of the European Union. The 1999 legislation is very similar to the 1994 legislation: the key difference is the expansion in the number of institutions that can play a part in enforcing the regulations.

Examples of the terms covered in the legislation include:

- terms which exclude liability for death

- terms which the customer had no opportunity to look at before they were bound by them
- terms which allow amendments to the contract by the seller to the disadvantage of the customer
- terms which exclude the customers statutory legal rights.

The Directive does not allow interference on terms that have been agreed by the two parties, even if afterwards it may be seen that the terms are unfair. If the central terms to the contract have been clearly written or communicated and the consumer agrees then this will form a binding contract. The courts will of course interfere if terms are illegal.

Key differences between UCTA 1977 and the Unfair Terms in Consumer Contracts Regulations 1999

UCTA 1977 deals with unreasonable exemption clauses, whereas the Unfair Terms in Consumer Contracts Regulations 1999 deals with broader issues of unfairness. In addition, UCTA 1977 includes the possibility of companies being consumers, whereas the Unfair Terms in Consumer Contracts Regulations 1999 looks at consumers as human beings, not companies.

3 Common law on exemption clauses

The courts may examine these limitation or exemption clauses and agree with them, modify them, or disregard them completely. Three key issues have to be answered.

- Is the exemption term part of the contract?

  The exemption term must be incorporated into the contract in the normal way. The key issues to consider are whether it was obvious that the exemption term was in the contract, whether the consumer had a past history with the business and should have known of the exemption, and whether the exemptions were brought to the notice of the consumer before or during the making of the contract. The key issue is whether parties know what they are getting into.

  ### Legal case: *Olley v Marlborough Court Ltd (1949)*

  Mrs Olley booked into a hotel but unfortunately had her belongings stolen. The hotel tried to avoid liability by saying that there was an exemption clause on the back of the hotel room door. The courts decided that the contract had been made when Mrs Olley signed in at reception and that the exemption clause was not part of the agreement she had entered into.

  The exemption term must be brought to the attention of the consumer in a reasonable way. There may be difficulties here given the specific parties involved. A young enthusiastic law student may well read the small print on all agreements with relish; a tired traveller may not be so interested. Small print really is small print for some.

The party attempting to limit their exposure must incorporate the exemption term into the contract. There are three main ways this can be achieved.

- Signature agreement to exemption clause

If a party signs a contract the terms are established even if the person has not read the contract. This principle comes from an important case called *L'Estrange v Graucob (1934)* and is extremely important for contract law purposes, although the consumer does now have more statutory protection in the form of implied terms than they did in 1934.

Legal case: *L'Estrange v Graucob (1934)*

A woman bought a vending machine on hire-purchase. She signed the agreement but did not read the small print of the contract which excluded all liability if there were any problems with the item. The machine proved to be defective but the court felt that there was no remedy available to her, she had signed the agreement even if she failed to realise the significance of what she had done.

The *L'Estrange v Graucob (1934)* rule does not stand up, however if there has been misrepresentation as the following case illustrates.

Legal case: *Curtis v Chemical Cleaning and Dyeing Co (1951)*

The claimant took a wedding dress to be cleaned by a professional cleaning company. The dress was made from satin and had a number of sequins and beads stitched into the fabric. When the assistant asked her to sign an exemption clause the claimant asked what it covered and was told that it excluded liability for the sequins and beads. The dress was stained during the process and when the claimant complained she was told the exemption clause actually covered staining as well. The Court of Appeal found in the claimants favour. The statement by the assistant, although not intending to be untruthful, had the effect of cancelling the exemption clause.

- Time of notification of exemption clause

Normally the incorporated term must be given to the customer either before or at the time the contract becomes effective. If notice of the exemption is given after the contract has been formed there are two situations to consider:

1 it may be too late in that the event being excluded has already happened or

2 possibly the customer may not want to contract on that basis or may wish to attempt a suspension of the exemption clause.

The following is a leading case in this area:

Legal case: *Thornton v Shoe Lane Parking (1971)*

The claimant parked his car in a Shoe Lane Parking car park. There was an automatic machine at the entrance, which dispensed tickets, and payment was made at this point. The ticket contained small print, which referred to terms and conditions displayed within the car park. One of these included an exemption clause relating to injury of customers. The claimant was injured in the car park when he later returned to pick up his car and he sued Shoe Lane Parking. The Court of Appeal struck out this exemption clause on two grounds.

1 The exemption was too wide ranging and if it was to be enforced it would have to be very publicly seen.

2 The contract was formed at the ticket machine and the claimant had no chance to see the exemption clause before the contract was formed.

● Reasonable notice of exemption clause

If the exemption clause is to be effective it must have been given to the claimant in an effective way. The courts will take three key issues into consideration on this.

1 How was the notice of exemption given?

2 When was the notice given?

3 How unusual was the exemption in the circumstances of the trade?

The following cases show some of the issues that have arisen.

Legal case: *Thompson v LMS (1930)*

The claimant was given a ticket, which said 'Excursion, for conditions see back'. On the back of the ticket was an instruction to see conditions printed on the railway company's timetable, which cost 6d (about 2½p) to buy. The claimant could not read and was injured during the journey. There was an exemption clause on injury contained in the conditions. The Court of Appeal however found in favour of the Railway Company.

Group activity

Comment on the *Thompson v LMS (1930)* case. Do you think the notification was reasonable? How else might notification be given of these exemption clauses?

Do you think the exemption terms in the following contract were brought to the consumer's notice in a reasonable way?

Legal case: *Parker v South Eastern Railway (1877)*

Ms Parker left her bag at the left-luggage office of South Eastern Railway. She was given a receipt, which contained a limitation clause. The courts decided that she had indeed had notification of the limitation clause even though she had not read it.

- Is the issue a consumer brings to court covered by the exemption clause?

The courts use two guiding rules to decide whether the matter the claimant has brought to court is covered by the exemption clause.

1 Main purpose rule

If the term defeats the main purpose of the contract then it will not be allowed to stand. The following case illustrates the point.

Legal case: *Glynn v Margetson (1893)*

A clause in a contract allowed a ship to call at other ports on its way home in order to pick up other cargo. The ship had a contract to deliver oranges from Malaga to Liverpool but the captain decided to use the clause to go into the Mediterranean to pick up extra cargo, thus lengthening the total journey and jeopardizing the quality of the oranges. The oranges were found to be past their best when they were finally delivered. The contract had stipulated that the goods were to be delivered 'in good condition'. The clause was not allowed to stand.

There are ways around the main purpose rule, but these clauses must be very clearly brought to the attention of all concerned so that each party can take a fully informed and calculated risk.

2 *Contra proferentem* rule

If there is an ambiguity in an exemption clause then the *contra proferentem* rule will give the benefit of the doubt to the injured party. This may be because the party who put the clause in may have deliberately worded it in such a way to produce an ambiguity and thus unfairly confuse the other party.

An important exception to this is the famous *L'Estrange v Graucob (1934)* rule (see page 175) that says that parties are bound by the terms of a contract even if they have not read it. This ruling implies that a well-written and reasonable clause, even if it contains ambiguity, may be allowed to stand by the courts.

The *contra proferentem* rule can be seen operating in the following case.

Legal case: *Houghton v Trafalgar Insurance Company (1954)*

The Trafalgar Insurance Company refused to pay out on a car accident as a clause in the contract excluded their liability if too much load was being carried. The car that should have held five passengers actually had six on board when the accident happened. The insurance company claimed that this amounted to excessive load but the Court of Appeal ruled that 'load' should refer to goods and not people. The insurance company was ordered to pay out since they had interpreted the exclusion clause too widely.

Oral statements

One of the parties, or an employee of one of the parties, may make an oral statement that contradicts an exemption clause in a contract.

Legal case: *Mendelssohn v Normand (1970)*

A customer was told to leave his car unlocked by a garage attendant. Goods were stolen from the car but the garage rejected liability on the grounds of an exemption clause. The court ruled that the oral statement had effectively destroyed the exemption clause.

Group activity

Try to find six exclusion clauses when you next go shopping or in advertisements for products or services. They should be fairly easy to find, particularly where goods are being offered for special promotions.

Key statutory legislation covering exemption terms

1 Unfair Contract Terms Act (UCTA) 1977

This was the first key piece of legislation in this area and focuses on business liability and definition of what a consumer is. Legislation excludes death or personal injury exemptions, restricts other liability to what is reasonable and limits exemptions on non-performance of contract.

2 Unfair Terms in Consumer Contract Regulations 1994

This legislation applies to any term that is not personally negotiated with the consumer. It therefore covers virtually all terms in all contracts with a consumer. This legislation applies to all unfair terms and not just exemption clauses.

3 Unfair Terms in Consumer Contract Regulations 1999

This has updated the 1994 Regulations and in particular increased the number of institutions, which have power to implement legislation.

1. What is the point of an exemption clause and a limitation clause?

2. What is a term?

3. What is the main purpose rule and the *contra proferentem* rule?

4. What does the Unfair Contract Terms Act 1977 and the Unfair Terms in Consumer Contracts Regulations 1999 do?

5. What are the main legislations passed in the UK?

6. What factors do the judges take into account when deciding what is reasonable?

7. Outline the facts in *George Mitchell (Chesterhall) Ltd v Finney Lock Seeds (1983)*.

8. Name the key European Directive in this area.

9. When did the European Directive on Unfair Terms in Consumer Contracts come into effect?

10. What effect does an oral statement have on an exemption clause?

Exam question

Examine the effectiveness of statutory legislation in controlling unfair exemption clauses.
[50 marks]

Exam answer guide

Knowledge and understanding [20 marks]
- ✓ Define exemption clauses
- ✓ Identify key legislation in the area of exemption clauses:
- ✓ Unfair Contract Terms Act 1977 UCTA. Quote *George Mitchell (Chesterhall) Ltd v Finney Lock Seeds (1983)* and *Phillips Products v Hyland (1987)*
- ✓ Unfair Terms in Consumer Contracts Regulations 1994
- ✓ Unfair Terms in Consumer Contracts Regulations 1999

Analysis and evaluation [25 marks]
- ✓ Assess the impact of statutory legislation on exemption clauses
- ✓ Compare this to common law rulings such as *Olley v Marlborough Court Ltd (1949)* and *Parker v South Eastern Railway (1877)*

Presentation [5 marks]
- ✓ Structure your work in a logical and well-planned way. Employ good quality and clear English in your writing. Make use of punctuation and correct spelling in your answers.

MODULE 2575

Law of contract 2

Privity of contract

Why do I need to know about privity of contract?

Privity became established for very sound reasons as it was felt that only those who wished to enter into a contract should be bound by it. You could not drag an unsuspecting party into the agreement without their knowledge or permission. The other side of the coin was that the third party could not enforce an agreement even if it was to their benefit. Over time, methods were devised to avoid the restrictions of privity and eventually statutory law was put in place to avoid the worst aspects of the doctrine. Common law was to remain active in this area to protect the rights of those who needed it.

Privity of contract

1 Privity: nature and function

Only those actually involved in a contract can have obligations or rights under it. The key reason for privity is to avoid the imposition of obligations on third parties. Obligations entered into must be done freely and with intent to form legal relations. This avoids the possibility of a third party becoming obligated by an agreement they had nothing to do with. Third parties, even if they benefit from the contract, do not have rights to enforce contracts entered into by other parties.

There are two key points to the rule of privity.

1 Obligations cannot be enforced on a third party

This is relatively uncontroversial. No one would like to find out that they were legally obligated to perform terms in a contract without voluntarily doing so. Person A cannot contract person B without their agreement.

2 Benefits cannot be claimed by a third party

This is more troublesome. If the contract has been made to benefit a third party, the third party has no right to enforce it if it goes wrong: only the person who signed the contract has this right.

Legal case: *Tweddle v Atkinson (1861)*

Two fathers made a contract to give money to their newly married son and daughter. Mr Tweddle senior had given the money but then died. Mr Atkinson did not come forth with his share and was taken to court by his son-in-law. The court ruled that the son-in-law was a third party and could not enforce the contract even if it was to his benefit.

There has been a major change in the whole area of privity brought about by some major statutory legislation – the Contracts (Rights of Third Parties) Act 1999. This piece of legislation protects those who are beneficiaries of a contract that has been specially made for them.

The case below illustrates the issue of privity.

Legal case: *Dunlop Pneumatic Tyre v Selfridges (1915)*

Dunlop sold tyres to a wholesaler called Dew. There was a contract that included a clause that tyres were not to be sold under a certain minimum price. Dunlop were keen to keep prices reasonably high in a bid to secure high profit margins and to build the public perception that its tyres were of a superior quality. Dew sold the tyres it bought from Dunlop onto Selfridges under the same agreement. Selfridges, however, chose to reduce prices and sell them under the agreed price. Dunlop tried to sue Selfridges but privity of contract meant that this was impossible. The only party Dunlop could sue was Dew, and the only party who could sue Selfridges was Dew. Dew wisely chose not to sue its important customer, Selfridges.

The case of *Dunlop Pneumatic Tyre v Selfridges (1915)* seems a reasonable decision. The problem arises when the third party is to receive a benefit from the contract such as that in *Tweddle v Atkinson (1861)*.

There are times when the courts ignore the principle of privity to establish a more just outcome.

Legal case: *Jackson v Horizon Holidays (1975)*

Mr Jackson was disappointed by the amenities provided during a holiday in Sri Lanka. He sued the company, Horizon Holidays, who argued that the contract was only with him so he could not claim for the disappointment suffered by other members of his family. Lord Denning allowed the full claim. This was a controversial move since it seemed that Lord Denning was creating new law from his position in the Court of Appeal.

Group activity

Get hold of some brochures from holiday companies and identify the process unhappy customers have to go through to make a complaint.

---

2 Established exceptions

Married Women's Property Act 1882

If a life assurance policy was made for the benefit of a spouse (husband or wife) or for children, the Married Women's Property Act 1882 would allow the spouse or children to sue for the benefit of the policy. In other words, they can enforce a contract made in their favour even if they did not form the contract themselves.

Law of Property Act 1925

Property rights can be allocated to people under this act even if they were not originally involved in the contract.

Road Traffic Act 1988

All drivers have to be insured by law for accidents they may cause to others. This type of insurance is known as third party cover. If a person is the victim of a road accident, they can make a claim on the negligent driver's insurance even if they themselves were not party to the contract between the negligent driver and their insurance company. This statutory protection is very important as it means that ordinary members of the public are protected against injury and damage to their property.

Collateral contracts

Judges create collateral contracts when they wish to get around the doctrine of privity for reasons of justice. The case of *Shanklin Pier Ltd v Detel Products Ltd*

(1951) (see page 147) is a good example. Collateral contracts involve creating a contractual relationship by bringing another party in where they did not exist in the original agreement.

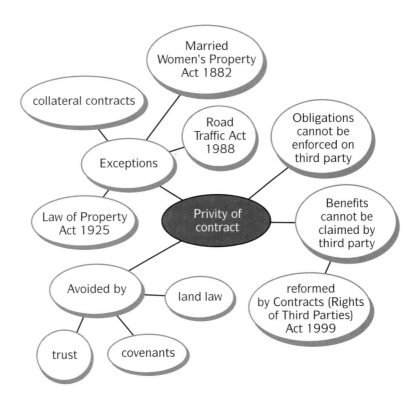

Privity of contract

3 Avoiding privity

There are ways that those who wish to avoid privity can do so. The main ways of doing this are trusts, covenants, and the creative use of land law applied to goods other than land.

Trusts

A trust is created when someone takes on a duty to administer property for the benefit of another. If a trust is held on someone, they may be able to show that they have contractual rights to an agreement that has been set up for their benefit. Therefore, if A asks B to do some work for C and A and C have a trust relationship, then C may be able to enforce their benefits from the A and B agreement via the trust. The courts were happy to enforce trust-like arrangements even when they were not expressly stated in a contract. The following case illustrates one approach to the issue.

Legal case: *Les Affreteurs Reunis SA v Walford (1919)*

The chartering of ships between owners and hirers was brokered by Walford. The owners of the ships agreed to a clause which gave Walford three per cent commission, which was effectively held on trust. Walford sued the owners and received payment even though technically he was not party to the agreement between owners and hirers.

On the other hand, courts have sometimes been more rigid and have not implied trusts even when the result may be seen as very harsh.

Legal case: *Re: Schebsman (1943)*

Schebsman worked for a company and, wishing to protect his wife and children, entered into an agreement that stated they would be paid in the event of his death. He later died and his family tried to sue for the money when the money was not paid. The courts decided that the doctrine of privity should prevail since they did not want to create trusts where trusts had not been intended.

The courts have been reluctant to use one area of law to foil the intentions of another area – in this case, to use trust law against contract law and the privity element.

Covenants

A covenant is an agreement contained in a deed that promises something or restricts something. These agreements, often attached to land, may carry on with the land regardless of owner. The promises or the restrictions become attached to the land and later owners may have covenants enforced against them. The following case is an example of a restrictive covenant.

Legal case: *Tulk v Moxhay (1848)*

The central garden area of Leicester Square in London was sold by Tulk to Elms. There was a restrictive covenant in the contract, which stated that the garden area was not to be built upon: it was to be preserved for the benefit of the residents who lived on the square. Elms sold it to Moxhay who knew of the restriction but nevertheless intended to build on the garden area. Tulk, the original owner, took Moxhay to court and despite not being party to the sale of the land between Elms and Moxhay was able to stop the development through the use of injunction.

Land law and other applications

At the beginning of this unit you studied the implications of *Dunlop Pneumatic Tyre v Selfridges (1915)* in terms of privity. Dunlop could not sue Selfridges because of the existence of the wholesaler Dew, who was the one with the contract with Dunlop. The fact that parties may wish to attach special conditions, which apply to products and services they supply, is a common commercial practice, but possibly one which is not in the best interests of the eventual consumer. The following case attempted to use the decision in *Tulk v Moxhay (1848)* to enforce an outcome.

Legal case: *Toddy v Sterious (1904)*

Toddy was a tobacco manufacturer. They tried to ensure that wholesalers sold their tobacco on at a minimum price and then on to the retailer with the same restriction. The eventual retailers did not go along with the agreement and were sued using the *Tulk v Moxhay (1848)* case. The court, however, decided that the manufacturer had no rights over the retailer.

4 Statutory reform – the Contract (Rights of Third Party) Act 1999

Privity is sometimes seen as an inflexible principle and there have been attempts to reform the law in relation to it. The Contract (Rights of Third Party) Act 1999 is one such move. The main provision is that if a third party is clearly identified in a contract, they may be able to enforce their own benefits even if they were not party to the original agreement.

The Contract (Rights of Third Party) Act 1999 allows the enforcement of a third party contract if:

- the contract expressly provides that they may do so

- the contract confers a benefit on that person.

There are some conditions that limit the entitlement to enforce the contract.

- The contract must be clear that the benefit is for the third party.

- The parties who made the contract intended the third party to be allowed to enforce the contract.

- The third party must be identified in the contract by name, description, or as a member of a recognized group.

The Act allows justice when justice is needed in third party contracts, but the common law rules are such that those third parties who are not willing to be bound by contracts they know nothing about are effectively protected. The present situation seems to work well with rights and also with flexibility.

1 Define privity.

2 What is the main reason for privity?

3 What are the two key points to privity?

4 Outline the case of *Tweddle v Atkinson (1861)*.

5 Outline the case of *Dunlop Pneumatic Tyre v Selfridges (1915)*.

6 What are the established exceptions to privity?

7 How can privity be avoided?

8 Compare the cases of *Les Affreteurs Reunis SA v Walford (1919)* and *Re: Schebsman (1943)*.

9 Outline the case of *Tulk v Moxhay (1848)*.

10 Outline the Contract (Rights of Third Party) Act 1999, including rights and conditions.

Exam question

Examine the advantages and disadvantages of the principle of privity in contracts. [50 marks]

Exam answer guide

Knowledge and understanding [20 marks]

✓ Define the nature of privity

✓ Outline aspects of obligations on third parties and benefits to third parties

✓ Quote *Tweddle v Atkinson (1861), Dunlop Pneumatic Tyre v Selfridges (1915)* and *Jackson v Horizon Holidays (1975)*

✓ Note established exceptions, such as the Married Womens Property Act 1882, Law of Property Act 1925 and collateral contracts

✓ Illustrate ways of avoiding privity, such as trusts, covenants, land law

✓ Outline the Contracts (Rights of Third Parties) Act 1999

Analysis and evaluation [25 marks]

✓ Weigh up the advantages and disadvantages of privity and give your opinion on principle

✓ Assess the impact of the Contracts (Rights of Third Parties) Act 1999

✓ Comment on cases that illustrate the advantages and disadvantages of privity

Presentation [5 marks]

✓ Structure your work in a logical and well-planned way. Employ good quality and clear English in your writing. Make use of punctuation and correct spelling in your answers.

UNIT 2

Vitiating factors

Key points

1 Effect of void and voidable contracts
2 Mistake
3 Misrepresentation
4 Duress and undue influence

Why do I need to know about vitiating factors?

Vitiating factors are those that bring about the cancellation of a contract. There are a variety of reasons for this, some of which are mistakes and some of which are deliberate. You must understand the cause and effect of void and voidable contracts including mistake, misrepresentation, and duress and undue influence. You must remember that contracts are sometimes made in the harsh reality of commercial pressures and there may be an incentive for one side or the other to take advantage. On top of this there are many opportunities for either party or their legal representatives to make genuine errors of judgement or procedure that lead to problems later on.

Misrepresentation

1 Effect of void and voidable contracts

There are a number of factors that may cause a contract to fail and these are known as 'vitiating factors'. Even if a contract has been drawn up correctly and seems to be watertight, there may be factors that mean genuine consent has not occurred. If this is the case, the contract is void and becomes worthless. The key factors that vitiate or invalidate a contract are:

● mistake

● misrepresentation

● duress and undue influence

● illegality.

Contracts must be entered into freely. If a person has been threatened with some form of punishment if they do not enter into a contract, the whole basis of the agreement is undermined. The courts will not enforce a contract if it has not been freely entered into. This means that the contract is no longer binding on the two parties to the original contract.

The vitiating factor present will determine whether the contract is void or voidable. There are important differences between the two.

● **Void**

If a vitiating factor makes a contract void, it will have the effect of wiping the slate clean and the contract will be non-existent. The innocent party can then walk away from the bad deal completely. The courts will not enforce a contract that is void. It may be void due to the fact that it is illegal or has been formed without proper capacity (both parties must understand the nature and consequences of the contract). A common area for void contracts is restraint of trade where an employer, or former employer, attempts to limit what their employee, or previous employee, can do. Two cases illustrate this, one claimant is more famous that the other.

Legal case: *Schroeder Music Publishing Co Ltd v Macaulay (1974)*

A powerful music group drew up a contract with a young songwriter, which was very much in their favour. The music company would pay royalties if they used the music but reserved the right to extend the contract if the royalties paid to the writer exceeded £5,000. The court felt that the contract was unfair to the songwriter and declared it void.

Another, more famous, songwriter had less good fortune in the courts when he too tried to escape from the confines of a contract he had signed with a large music group.

Legal case: *Panayiotou v Sony Music Entertainment (UK) (1994)*

Panayiotou (George Michael) had signed a contract with CBS records in 1988, which meant an agreement to produce eight albums over fifteen years. The contract also meant that Michael could only record for CBS and he would receive a twenty percent royalty. CBS was eventually taken over by Sony. Michael claimed that the contract was void because it was so unreasonable. Michael used European law in his submissions. The court however felt that since he had expert legal advice and had taken a payment in 1990 it was not a restraint of trade. The contract was therefore not void.

- **Voidable**

  If a vitiating factor makes the contract voidable, the innocent party can choose to go ahead or not. A small disadvantage may be ignored, but if the contract is substantially not in their interests, they may cancel the whole thing and possibly get a new contract drawn up which is fairer. This element of choice is what makes voidable contracts different from void contracts. Voidable contracts are capable of being put aside but the injured party may wish to proceed, possibly with amendments to the agreement. The following case from 2000 shows how an injured party may seek the courts permission to set aside the contract or to not uphold their obligations in the matter and allow the other side to sue for payment. They might also of course choose to continue with the contract as it was.

Legal case: *Spice Girls v Aprillia World Service (2000)*

The Spice Girls pop band had five members but after disagreements one member of the band, Geri Halliwell, left the group on 29 May 1998. During that year the band had signed a contract with a scooter company called Aprillia, which agreed to sponsor a tour in return for the rights to use images and logos of the band in their scooter advertisements. A written contract was signed on 6 May 1998 that referred to all members of the band. A commercial was shot, which the company was allowed to use until March 1999. When Geri Halliwell left the band the company felt they had signed the contract under misrepresentation. The full facts had not been given to them and they felt the arrangement, and the material they had been promised, was not what they were expecting. They refused to pay. The Chancery Division of the High Court felt that by allowing Geri Halliwell to participate in filming the advertisement they were implying to the company that she would be with the band until March 1999. The group knew of the impending split and were therefore liable for misrepresentation. The Spice Girls were ordered to pay £428,000 to Aprillia in damages. This included the cost of filming the commercial and also the costs incurred by the company in abandoning a special Spice Girls scooter. This machine was to feature all five Spice Girls and was to be called 'Spice Sonic'. Aprillia could have continued with the arrangement but chose not to. The contract was voidable due to misrepresentation

We will look at a number of other cases of voidable contracts in the following sections, all are caused by mistake, misrepresentation, duress or undue influence.

2 Mistake

A mistake may occur before or during the formation of a contract. A mistake may make a contract void or voidable. Common mistake occurs when both the parties to the contract believe the same false assumption. There are four main classes of mistake.

1 Mistake concerning the existence of the subject matter

Where the subject of the contract no longer exists prior to the contract being formed then the contract becomes void. The situation is known as *res extincta* meaning 'the item is destroyed'.

Legal case: *Scott v Coulson (1903)*

A life insurance contract was made on someone called Mr Death who had already died. Clearly the subject matter was non-existent, that is, Mr Death. This meant that the contract was void.

2 Mistake over the quality of the subject matter

Essentially this means that if a bad bargain is entered into this is no excuse for voiding a contract.

Legal case: *Leaf v International Galleries (1950)*

A painting was thought to have been painted by a famous English painter called Constable by both buyer and seller. It later transpired that the painting was not by this painter and therefore worth considerably less. The painting was nevertheless a good copy and the court decided that the contract related to the painting itself and not necessarily to whom it was painted by.

3 Mutual mistake

There may be a mistake concerning the subject matter. The contract is void if one party thinks the contract is about *X* and the other party thinks the contract is about *Y*. They are said to be at cross-purposes and this is known as mutual mistake.

Legal case: *Raffles v Wichelhaus (1864)*

A contract was made to buy a cargo of cotton on board a boat called *Peerless* sailing from Bombay to England. Coincidentally, there were two ships called *Peerless* sailing from Bombay with cotton on board. The only difference between them was that one set sail in October and the other in December. The courts decided the contract was void since the confusion would have been impossible to sort out.

4 Unilateral mistake

Mistake concerning the person may happen where one of the parties mistakes the identity of the other. The contract may become void if the identity issue is relevant to the contract itself. Often one of the parties may have been deliberately misled as in the following case.

Legal case: *Cundy v Lindsay (1878)*

Cundy supplied handkerchiefs to a firm called Blenkarn whose premises were 37 Wood Street. Cundy mistakenly thought that he was dealing with a well-known and respectable firm named Blenkiron, whose premises were also in Wood Street at number 123. Blenkarn were in fact con men. The House of Lords voided the contract between Cundy and Blenkarn based on the mistake.

Mistake concerning documents

If parties sign a document in writing, they are generally bound by its terms and conditions. There are two important exceptions to this:

1 *Non est factum*

If a person is tricked into signing something that they never would have signed if they knew of its real details, they can claim *non est factum*, meaning 'not my deed'.

Legal case: *Foster v Mackinnon (1869)*

An elderly man signed a document that he was told was a guarantee. It was in fact an agreement to give money to a con artist. The court allowed the elderly man's plea of *non est factum*.

This protection is only accepted in very strong cases. People might well try to use it to avoid contracts they simply regretted.

2 Rectification

If two parties make verbal agreements and then draw up a contract that does not completely reflect their oral intentions, the court may rectify the contract. In other words, the courts may attempt to modify the contract to reflect what is perhaps actually going on. The following case illustrates this point.

Legal case: *Joscelyne v Nissen (1970)*

A father and daughter formed an agreement verbally which was afterwards put into a written contract. The father would pass his business to the daughter and she would pay certain bills. Some time later there was a dispute when the daughter had stopped paying some of the bills. There had been evidence that the bills had been paid for some time so the court rectified the contract. In other words, the court changed the written contract to reflect the real situation.

3 Misrepresentation

Representations may occur before a contract is drawn up and some may actually appear in it. Representations are statements made before or during the formation of the contract. If a person signs a contract on the basis of some of these representations that later turn out to be untrue, this is known as 'misrepresentation'.

A misrepresentation **is not**:

● an opinion

If a person qualifies a statement with 'I think. . .'or 'I suppose. . .', this may be called an opinion. Many television adverts contain these sorts of 'get-out clauses'. For example, 'Carlsberg is probably the best beer in the world' – clearly a matter of opinion!

Legal case: *Bisset v Wilkinson (1927)*

The contract involved land for a proposed sheep farm in New Zealand. Neither buyer nor seller knew anything about sheep and the land had never supported sheep. The seller gave his opinion during the negotiations that he thought 2000 sheep could probably live on the land. This turned out not to be the case. The court decided that since he knew nothing about sheep it was a mere opinion and not the statement of someone who knew the facts.

● a commendation

A commendation is similar to a recommendation and not a fact. Sometimes it can be difficult to spot since the professional may be well versed in the way a commendation can be disguised as fact. They may be seen as 'sales patter' rather than statements of cast-iron fact.

Legal case: *Dimmock v Hallet (1866)*

Estate agents selling a farm described a piece of land as 'fertile and improvable'. The court felt that this was really sales patter rather than a statement to be taken as a firm statement of fact.

The law has since tightened up on what estate agents can say when describing property, although it is unlikely that we will see the end of phrases such as 'cosy' and 'has great potential'.

● a promise of future intentions

A promise of future intentions is not generally taken as a misrepresentation, however, if a person promises certain actions but has absolutely no intention of carrying them out, the case may be taken to court. If, for example, on buying a house the previous owner promised to cure some damp and fix the back wall which was falling down and then does not do it, it may be seen as misrepresentation.

Legal case: *Edington v Fitzmaurice (1885)*

A business offered shares in the company stating that the money was going to be used for expansion and improvement. The money was in fact used to pay off old debts. The Court of Appeal ruled that this was fraudulent misrepresentation as the owners of the business never intended to invest in the way they had promised.

- a statement of the law

  As people have equal access to the law it is assumed that both parties can check legal statements made and action cannot be taken by one party against another in this area. The only exception is when professionals such as solicitors make statements that are not true. This can then become misrepresentation and is actionable.

Silence and misrepresentation

If a seller does not reveal key issues that might affect the buyer's decision to buy or not, the expression *caveat emptor* applies. This means 'let the buyer beware'. It is up to the buyer to make a thorough investigation and not the seller to provide those details. The key case is shown below.

Legal case: *Fletcher v Krell (1873)*

A governess was employed who had been previously married but was now separated. In Victorian times she would not have been employed if this fact had been known. The question was not asked and she did not reveal the truth. The employer took the case to court on the grounds of misrepresentation. The claim failed as the governess was under no duty to reveal what was not asked for.

There are some exceptions to this rule, however, which are important to note.

Changed circumstances

Changed circumstances may alter the relationship between the parties fundamentally and the initial basis of the contract.

Legal case: *With v O'Flanagan (1936)*

A medical practice was being sold, but between the first negotiations and the contract being signed, most of the patients had gone elsewhere and therefore the income from the business was substantially reduced.

Deliberate cover up

If a seller deliberately conceals a defect of a product they are selling then this may amount to misrepresentation.

Legal case: *Schneider v Heath (1813)*

A boat was being sold which had a rotten hold. The seller submerged that part of the boat so that it would not be seen and give the game away. The contract was duly voided.

Non-verbal communication

If a seller nods his head or smiles in answer to a question, this may be misrepresentation.

Misleading statement

If in answer to a direct question the seller gives a half-true statement, this may amount to misrepresentation.

Legal case: *Dimmock v Hallet (1866)*

An estate was going to be sold containing a number of farms that were rented out to farm tenants. The buyer asked whether the farms had tenants and the seller said that there were tenants for all the farms. He did not tell the buyer that the tenants were about to leave, which would mean a fall in rental income for the estate.

Fiduciary relationships

The word 'fiduciary' relates to the concept of trust. If there is a fiduciary or other strong relationship between various parties, this may affect the contract. Relationships might include father and child, solicitor and client, doctor and patient, and so on.

Uberrimae fidei

Uberrimae fidei means 'of utmost good faith'. This means that all material facts must be disclosed and if they are not then the contract is void. *Uberrimae fidei* goes against the concept of *caveat emptor* (let the buyer beware). *Uberrimae fidei* is often used in buying life insurance where the company could not possibly check into the medical histories of all its customers. The customer is under an obligation to tell the company all relevant facts.

There are four main types of misrepresentation.

1 Fraudulent misrepresentation

The definition of fraudulent misrepresentation came in the following case.

Legal case: *Derry v Peek (1889)*

A transport company hoped to run steam-powered tramcars in Plymouth. The permission of the Board of Trade was required. The company thought this was a mere formality and when it issued its prospectus in order to raise money it said the Board of Trade had given permission. The Board of Trade did not in the end give such permission and the company went bust and investors lost money. The case went to court under the tort of deceit but the court decided that the company had not deliberately set out to be dishonest. A fraudulent misrepresentation would be a statement that is made:

1 knowingly, or

2 without belief in its truth, or

3 recklessly as to whether it is true or not.

This means that a person is guilty of misrepresentation if they make a statement that they know is untrue when they make it and one party has deliberately set out to mislead the other.

Fiduciary relationships involve trust between two parties.

2 Negligent misrepresentation using common law

If a special relationship exists between two parties where the first party will rely on a statement made by the second party, then negligent misrepresentation at common law may occur. The party giving the advice will have to have some professional or specialized interest in the contract drawn up. The case of *Hedley Byrne and Co v Heller & Partners Ltd (1964)* is often quoted when discussing negligent misrepresentation. The misrepresentation is not deliberate but negligent.

Legal case: *Hedley Byrne and Co v Heller & Partners Ltd (1964)*

Hedley Byrne relied upon a recommendation made by a bank called Heller & Partners Ltd on a business called Easipower. Easipower defaulted on money it owed to Hedley Byrne and a claim of misrepresentation was made against Heller & Partners Ltd. The claim would have won if it had not been for a minor legal technicality. The case is, however, used as a statement of the current position of the law in this area of negligent misrepresentation.

The *obiter dicta* of the Hedley Byrne case is used in later cases although it is not strictly binding. *Obiter dicta* relates to supporting arguments made by judges during a case. It is not binding but can be used as persuasive precedent in later cases.

Another supporting case of this situation is the following.

Legal case: *Esso Petroleum Co Ltd v Mardon (1976)*

The Esso Company sold one of its petrol stations to Mardon stating that the outlet should sell approximately 200,000 gallons of petrol per year. During the formation of the contract the local authority made changes to the location that meant the capacity of the petrol station would be reduced. In the end only about 100,000 gallons were being sold and Mardon fell behind with the rent. Esso sued and Mardon counter-sued. Mardon claimed that Esso had not told him about the significant changes and this meant negligent misrepresentation had occurred. The *obiter dicta* of Hedley Byrne was applied to this case and Mardon won.

3 Negligent misrepresentation using statute law

Negligent misrepresentation using statute law is made possible by Section 2(1) of the Misrepresentation Act 1967. This section allows the innocent party to claim damages from the other party if they think misrepresentation has occurred. The party who is being accused must prove that they believed the disputed statements to be true when the contract was drawn up and had reasonable grounds for that belief. The burden of proof is on the accused party to prove that they told the truth.

Legal case: *Howard Marine and Dredging Co Ltd v A Ogden and Sons (Excavations) Ltd (1978)*

A company needed to dump clay at sea and therefore had to hire some large barges. The barge owner's company overestimated the capacity of the barges: they had got the capacity from an official source that was in fact wrong. The true capacity of the barges was kept at the head office of the company. The Court of Appeal found the barge company had misrepresented using Section 2 of the Misrepresentation Act 1967. There must have been 'reasonable grounds' for any facts stated by the company.

4 Innocent misrepresentation

Innocent misrepresentation is the other extreme to fraudulent misrepresentation. Here the party who is accused of misrepresentation can prove that the statement was true as far as they were concerned and they had reasonable grounds for believing it was true.

Legislation

Section 2 Misrepresentation Act 1967

The misrepresentation was not made fraudulently, unless he proves that he had reasonable grounds to believe and did believe up to the time the contract was made that the facts represented were true.

The case of *Howard Marine and Dredging Co Ltd v A Ogden and Sons (Excavations) Ltd (1978)* shows how difficult this can be to prove.

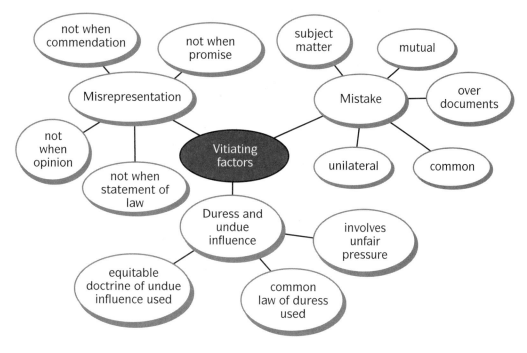

Vitiating factors

4 Duress and undue influence

Contracts require genuine consent from each of the two parties as to the formation and execution of a contract. If there has been unfair pressure placed on one or both of the parties, then the courts will cancel the contract. They do this under the common law doctrine of duress and the equitable doctrine of undue influence.

Duress

Duress is common law and once related to the threat of violence or constraint to one party in the contract or their close relatives. This definition has widened with the passage of time and now covers the concept of economic duress. Economic duress involves taking advantage of someone when they are having financial difficulties. This is probably far more common now than the threat of violence. The problem the court has is in deciding what is economic duress and what is simply the operation of free-market forces. Farmers in the UK have complained for some time that supermarkets have forced prices down and pushed their own profits up. This may be to the advantage of the consumer and some would say that it is the capitalist system in operation.

The first case to hear the newly coined economic duress concept was the following.

Legal case: *North Ocean Shipping Co v Hyundai Construction Co (1979)*

The builder of a ship raised the price during construction by ten per cent. The buyer was in negotiation to charter the ship to an oil company and therefore reluctantly accepted the price increase. Eight months after the ship had been delivered, the buyers tried to get the ten per cent back by claiming economic duress. The courts agreed but said that they had waited too long therefore establishing affirmation of the modification. In other words, the time delay meant that the modified contract was confirmed.

Undue influence

If the matter does not amount to duress but pressure has been brought which is unfair, the innocent party may apply for an equitable solution. This is known as the doctrine of undue influence. The courts may modify the contract or set it aside. There are two main scenarios.

1 No pre-existing relationship

The burden of proving undue influence rests with the party making the accusations.

2 Pre-existing relationship – fiduciary relationship

If there is a situation where one party is known to the other and is in a position of trust with the other, the more powerful of the two must prove there has been no undue influence. The law does not assume that this has automatically happened but it is a possibility that must be explored. The party who has been accused must 'rebut the presumption', meaning denying any wrongdoing as far as the contract was concerned.

Legal case: *Allcard v Skinner (1887)*

A nun joined a convent and gave the convent her savings. She later left the order to join another. After some time had elapsed she was told that she could have brought her savings with her. There was a presumption of fiduciary interest between the Mother Superior and the nun. Unfortunately she had waited too long and the money could not be returned to her.

Banking cases

Banks hold a very powerful position over individuals and businesses. They are a special study by themselves, given their unique position of power. In some examples it may be clear that there is a fiduciary relationship (a relationship of trust) between client and banker but in others it may be less certain. For many people a bank manager is someone they never see. The world of electronic transfers of money; debit cards and cash machines has removed the necessity of seeing a personal figure. Some people however, may have close and interrelated relationships based on years of business and so trust has built up. If advice is given in these circumstances there can sometimes be problems. The following case illustrates some of the dangerous ground banks sometimes have to cover.

Legal case: *Lloyds Bank v Bundy (1974)*

A father and son shared the same bank. The son ran into difficulties and the father acted as a guarantor for the son, using his farm as security. The son's financial position deteriorated and the father's farm was in danger of being repossessed by the bank. The father made the claim that the bank should never have allowed the position in the first place. The Court of Appeal agreed that there was 'undue influence' and the father won his case.

Other banking cases followed and developed some of the principles first seen in *Lloyds Bank v Bundy (1974)*. Some were good news for banks as in the next case but some brought bad news and prompted the need for greater care when dealing with clients of the bank. An important aspect began to emerge from the cases, which was the fact that banks could rebut the accusations against them by suggesting to the clients that they seek independent financial advice. This would remove or certainly reduce the possibility of undue influence.

Legal case: *National Westminster Bank v Morgan (1985)*

Mr Morgan's business was under great pressure and to rescue it he approached National Westminster Bank for a loan. They did agree but insisted that the family house jointly owned by Mr and Mrs Morgan should be used as security in the event that the business failed. Although the bank agreed to the loan they had reservations about the viability of the business, which were passed on to the couple. Mrs Morgan had no great faith in the business either and asked to speak to the Manager of the bank in private but this never actually happened. The signature confirming the use of the house for security on the loan was taken in the presence of Mr Morgan. The business did fail and sometime later Mr Morgan died. Mrs Morgan claimed that undue influence had been used in the transaction. In this case however the court felt that the bank and Mr and Mrs Morgan did not have a fiduciary relationship. Both Mr and Mrs Morgan were deemed fit to make up their own minds and in addition the bank had cautioned against the loan. In addition the arrangement was not to her disadvantage since the business may have been saved. There was therefore no undue influence and no duty on the bank to suggest to the couple that they should seek independent advice.

The *National Westminster Bank v Morgan (1985)* case produced two important points. Lord Scarman, one of the judges on the case, stated that,

- the fiduciary relationship must be one where one party exhibits some dominance over the other
- the transaction which involves the fiduciary relationship must be to the disadvantage of the weaker party.

The *BCCI v Aboody (1990)* case greatly increased the scope of court intervention in cases of undue influence even if the bank was not directly involved.

Legal case: *BCCI v Aboody (1990)*

Mrs Aboody was totally dominated by her older husband in financial matters. The courts found that there had been undue influence on Mrs Aboody even though it might not have been to her disadvantage. The court heard that the undue influence may not have been intentional.

The case produced two important points that were confirmed in later cases. Undue influence was seen to come in two varieties.

1 Class 1 actual undue influence

The parties have no special relationship and the party who is claiming that there has been undue influence must prove this to be the case.

2 Class 2 presumed undue influence

The parties have a special relationship. This might be parent, child; guardian, ward; teacher, student; doctor, patient. These types of relationship will be presumed to be fiduciary. If other relationships exist of a similar nature but do not fall into the typical list then the claimant must show proof and the defendant must disapprove.

Another important case involving the banks responsibility to look after the interests of the weaker party was *Barclays v O'Brien (1993)*. Here the banks were not even directly involved in the undue influence but were expected to take action to prevent its possible consequences. There are clear links between this case and the *BCCI v Aboody (1990)* case. In fact the key points in *BCCI v Aboody (1990)* were confirmed in *Barclays v O'Brien (1903)*.

Legal case: Barclays v O'Brien (1993)

Mrs O'Brien believed her husband when he told her that he needed £60,000 for a short time to support his ailing business. She signed papers agreeing to the loan, which used the family house as security. The loan grew to £135,000 and when it was left unpaid the bank tried to seize possession of the house. Mrs O'Brien went to the Appeal Court and claimed undue influence. The court ordered that the amount repayable to the bank should only be the first sum agreed to by Mrs O'Brien, £60,000. The bank took the case further to the House of Lords. The House of Lords decided that as Mrs O'Brien was an intelligent and capable woman there was no undue influence. However they also stated that there had been misrepresentation and banks in these cases had a duty to make sure that the weaker party in the arrangement should have independent advice. The banks have a duty to ensure that no undue influence or misrepresentation has occurred. In Mrs O'Brien's particular case the House of Lords ordered that the whole sum owed by Mrs O'Brien should be put aside. She would have to pay nothing back to the bank.

Restraint of trade

A contract may try to curb a person's liability to seek employment or enter into a business enterprise that is closely related to the previous employers interests. For example, if a hairdresser set up a salon 100 yards away from their previous employer, it might encourage previous customers to change allegiance. For public policy reasons, however, such limitations are closely monitored so as to prevent abuse. All contracts that have such limitations in them will be void unless there are strong reasons to have them incorporated. These reasons include the following.

- The protection of a trade secret

  There may be patent and copyright laws that protect inventions and devices as well as employment contract clauses that prevent key workers from moving to rival firms and revealing confidential commercial matters.

Legal case: *Foster v Suggett (1918)*

A company had a secret process for the manufacturing of glass. A manager who worked in the business was prevented by his contract from working in the same field for a competitor for five years after the end of his contract with his existing employer. The court felt that this was valid given the information and experience the manager had acquired in his post.

- The protection of a customer base

  Employees who leave a particular employer may have made valuable connections that they might later profit from at the expense of the original employer.

Legal case: *Fitch v Dewes (1921)*

A solicitor's clerk was prevented from working within seven miles of his previous employer's practice. The court felt this was reasonable given the nature of the work carried out by the firm and the number of clients in the area.

On the other hand –

Legal case: *Office Angels v Rainer-Thomas (1991)*

The defendant had worked for a company supplying office staff to businesses. Their contract prohibited them from enticing any previous clients of the firm for a period of six months after their contract had ended. The court felt that this was unreasonable since it covered many thousands of firms that Office Angels had dealt with.

● The strategic importance of the business

There may be important military, economic, or political reasons for the continuation of a particular business.

Legal case: *Nordenfelt v Maxim Nordenfelt (1894)*

A restraint on trade was upheld on a business that supplied arms and ammunitions and no other firm was allowed into the same market for 25 years. Even to this day, licences have to be sought to conduct such business. Some important rules came out of this case.

1 A party wishing to restrain trade must show reasons why.

2 The party restraining trade must show that the restrain is reasonable between the parties and in terms of public interest.

3 A restraint will only be upheld if it shows it upholds the legitimate rights of the other party.

The courts may not necessarily void the whole contract but may amend it, if possible, to make the overall effect more reasonable. The following case illustrates such a point.

Legal case: *Esso v Harper's Garage (1968)*

Esso had an agreement with the garage that only Esso petrol would be sold. The garage felt that the term of twenty-one years was too long a period to be tied into the agreement. The court agreed and reduced the period to four years.

Statutory protection against restrictive practices

There are statutory protections on the restraint of business. One of the most important is the Restrictive Trade Practices Act 1976, which makes restrictive practices illegal unless they are approved by the Director General of Fair Trading. Another statutory piece of legislation is the Resale Prices Act 1976, which outlaws attempts by suppliers to force the imposition of minimum prices on their customers. These statutory matters may well make some clauses in contracts illegal, or they may be made illegal by common law rulings.

Quick revision questions

1 Which factors invalidate a contract?

2 What is the difference between void and voidable?

3 What are the four main classes of mistake?

4 Which two exceptions are there to parties being bound by mistakes in written documents?

5 Outline misrepresentation and what is not included as misrepresentation.

6 What are the main exceptions to silence as a misrepresentation?

7 What are fiduciary relationships?

8 What does *uberrimae fidei* mean?

9 Name the four types of misrepresentation.

10 What is duress and undue influence? Illustrate your answer with examples.

Exam question

Analyse the key ways a contract may fail. [50 marks]

Exam answer guide

Knowledge and understanding [20 marks]

✓ Show differences between void and voidable
✓ Mistake and four classes: subject matter existence, quality of subject matter, mutual mistake and unilateral mistake quote *Scott v Coulson (1903)*, *Leaf v International Galleries (1950)*, *Raffles v Wichelhaus (1864)* and *Cundy v Lundsay (1878)*
✓ Misrepresentation: Quote *Bisset v Wilkinson (1927)*, *Dimmock v Hallet (1866)*, *Edington v Fitzmaurice (1885)*, *Fletcher v Krell (1873)*, *With v O'Flanagan (1936)*, *Schneider v Heath (1813)*, *Derry v Peek (1889)*, *Hedley Byrne and Co v Heller & Partners Ltd (1964)*, *Esso Petroleum Co Ltd v Mardon (1976)* and *Howard Marine and Dredging Co Ltd v A Ogden and Sons (Excavations) Ltd (1978)*
✓ Duress and undue influence: Quote *North Ocean Shipping Co v Hyundai Construction Co (1979)*, *Allcard v Skinner (1887)*
✓ Present banking cases such as *Lloyds Bank v Bundy (1974)*
✓ Refer to restraint of trade cases such as *Office Angels v Rainer-Thomas (1991)* and *Esso v Harpers Garage (1968)*

Analysis and evaluation [25 marks]

✓ Assess importance of each of the vitiating factors
✓ Evaluate the decisions on the quoted cases

Presentation [5 marks]

✓ Structure your work in a logical and well-planned way. Employ good quality and clear English in your writing. Make use of punctuation and correct spelling in your answers.

UNIT 3

Discharge of contracts

Key points

1 Performance
2 Agreement
3 Frustration
4 Breach

Why do I need to know about discharge of contracts?

Discharge relates to the successful carrying out of contractual obligations so that both parties receive the benefit they hoped for when they formed the contract itself. There may, however, be times when this successful discharge is not possible. In these circumstances both parties must come to an agreement between themselves or with the use of alternative dispute resolution or use the courts to find a satisfactory outcome. This may involve cancellation of an existing contract, the formation of a new contract, or some other solution. There are elements of performance, agreement between the parties, frustration, breach and anticipatory breach involved in the discharge of contracts.

Frustration: Taylor v Caldwell

1 Performance

There are a number of ways in which a contract may come to an end, the first is called performance. This means that the parties involved in the contract have carried out all the obligations required by that contract exactly and completely. The following case shows failure to do this in the extreme.

Legal case: *Cutter v Powell (1795)*

A sailor died whilst on a voyage and his widow tried to claim his wages for the part of the journey where he was working and doing his job. The court felt that he had not completed his contract until he arrived at the ship's destination. The widow was unsuccessful in her claim.

An equally harsh case from 1921 illustrates the power of the buyer when using the law.

Legal case: *Re: Moore and Co v Landauer (1921)*

Consignments of fruit were ordered in boxes of 30. When the delivery came it was found that some of the boxes contained the tins in two-dozen boxes. The same quantity that was ordered was delivered in total. The buyer refused to accept the consignment citing the law, which stated that the delivery description must tally with the actual delivery.

There are, however, a number of exceptions to the performance requirement.

Severable contracts

Severable contracts contain obligations which can split one from the other. This means that payment may be due for various stages as they become complete. Employment contracts are a good example. Employees are not paid after 25 years worth of service, they are paid weekly or monthly. Builders are often paid in the same way so that they do not run into cash-flow problems.

Prevention of performance

If one party prevents the other from completing their contractual obligations, the innocent party may be able to claim compensation for the work done up to that point. This is known as suing or *quantum meruit*, which means 'as much as he deserves'.

Voluntary acceptance of partial performance

One party may voluntarily agree to accept partial performance of a contract although it did not start out that way. They will then accept and pay for the work done up to that point. They will have turned an ordinary contract into a severable one.

The story of contractual difficulties between builders and householders is seen in an old case from 1898.

Legal case: *Sumpter v Hedges (1898)*

A builder was contracted to do £565 worth of work that included building two houses and a stable for horses. The builder disappeared after completing only £333 worth of the work. The householder had to complete the buildings by himself and he used materials discarded by the original builder. The builder then reappeared and sued *quantum meruit* for the work that he had completed and for the remaining materials. The builder lost as far as the work was concerned. The householder did *not choose* voluntarily to complete the work, as he had no choice when the builder vanished. The builder, however, recovered the costs of the materials, since the householder had a choice on that issue.

Substantial performance

If the most important parts of a contract have been completed satisfactorily, the party who has done the work will be able to claim their money less the amount of any outstanding work. This will only apply to warranties or innominate terms. Any major term of the contract not completed may allow the innocent party to claim rescission (setting the contract aside) or damages.

Legal case: *Boone v Eyre (1779)* ~~back in the day~~ *out of date*

A plantation was being sold complete with slaves. When the new owners took possession they found that the slaves had gone. The case went to court and the decision reached was that the contract had been substantially completed regardless of the slaves.

Two more recent and perhaps more relevant cases are the following.

Legal case: *Hoeing v Issacs (1952)*

A decorator worked on a job worth £750. £400 was paid up front, but the householder was unhappy with the work and refused to pay the remaining £350. The court felt that the job had been substantially completed and the decorator was entitled to his fee less the amount needed to get the decoration to the householder's satisfaction, which was a mere £56.

The following case uses the judgements made in *Hoeing v Issacs (1952)* to determine the verdict.

Legal case: *Bolton v Mahadeva (1972)*

A central heating engineer installed a £560 system. It was found to be defective as it failed to heat the house properly and emitted dangerous fumes. The cost of putting the system right would be £174. The judge ruled that the work had not been substantially carried out using the case of *Hoeing v Issacs (1952)*. In that case the £56 repair was only 7.5 per cent of the total cost of the job. The repair in this case was 31 per cent, a much bigger proportion.

Vicarious performance

Vicarious performance involves a third party doing the work another person has been contracted for. If a person books a hairdressers appointment with the star hairdresser, will the trainee do? Clearly not. In this contract the buyer is paying for the experience and talent of a particular person. If, for example, a contract involves removing a skip that had been used for building work, the company that removes it is less important. The key point to consider with vicarious performance is whether the buyer's interests have been prejudiced.

2 Agreement

If both parties want to end the contract before it is finished they may do so. What they have freely entered into they can freely leave, providing both parties agree. There are two issues to a successful agreement taking place on a contract: consideration and paperwork.

Consideration

Consideration has to be given to make a contract binding in the first place. When cancelling a contract between two parties consideration must once again be seen so that the new situation can be binding on both parties. If a builder is contracted to build a new kitchen and a loft extension and the householder decides not to go ahead with the loft, the contract can be cancelled if both agree. The builder does not build the loft and the householder does not pay the £10,000. These two elements would be the consideration for the agreement.

Paperwork

The official documentation will depend on what the two parties want.

Partial discharge of contract

Any minor changes of contract must be done in writing. Normally a second agreement is drawn up that includes changes and anything left over from the first contract that needs to be included.

Complete discharge of contract

If the two parties wish to cancel the contract completely they can do this verbally.

Cancellation of first contract and replacement with second contract

The first contract can be cancelled verbally but the second must be drawn up in writing.

3 Frustration

If the contract comes to an end through no fault of either party, it is known as frustration and the obligations of the contract are cancelled. The first major case involving this concept was *Taylor v Caldwell (1863)*. Prior to this case the obligations of a contract were absolute and there were no possible excuses for one party to escape their obligations. The Taylor and Caldwell case demonstrated that the rules were being relaxed and allowed a bit of flexibility and common sense when no one was to blame.

Legal case: *Taylor v Caldwell (1863)*

A series of big concerts were planned using the Surrey Gardens and Music Hall. Less than a week before the concerts were due to begin the building was burned to the ground and the concerts could not go ahead. The party who organized the music and hired the building sued. The courts decided that the contract was frustrated through the fault of no one and the owners of the buildings were not forced to pay damages.

Situations that cause frustration

- The performance of the contract is impossible. If the sports complex at Manchester had been struck by lightning and destroyed in 2002, the Commonwealth Games would have been impossible. The *Taylor v Caldwell (1863)* case illustrates this.

- A performer gets ill. The band Oasis had a car crash in the US, which made it impossible for one of their concerts to go ahead. The ticket purchasers got a replacement but the owners of the venue lost out on a night's takings. (It is possible, however, that the venue had an insurance policy for such eventualities.)

- Death of one of the parties. Clearly it would be impossible to ask a dead builder to finish off your extension. In this case the contract is discharged. Exceptions to this may be possible if the contract does not involve a personal service. The estate of the dead person may discharge the contract in certain circumstances.

- If one of the parties tries to use frustration to evade a contract that is turning out to be unprofitable, they will find themselves still liable to performance.

Legal case: *Davis Contractors v Fareham Urban District Council (1956)*

A building contractor was commissioned to build 78 houses for Fareham Council. The price was £94,000. The company had promised to take eight months to finish the job. Labour shortages slowed down the job and the price shot up to £115,000 and took 22 months. The building contractor tried to get out of the contract by claiming the lack of workers amounted to frustration. The courts decided that this would have been a normal risk in the building industry and something for which the building firm should have made allowances.

- The performance of contract would be illegal. If the law changes after a contract has been made but not fully completed, it will be frustrated. The parties will be unable to perform and so discharge the contract. This might involve a change to food legislation by the Foods Standards Agency that is designed to protect human health. The legislation may come in quite quickly if it is a serious issue, or give notice to avoid the problem of contracts being frustrated. An outbreak of foot and mouth disease in the UK in 2001/2 prohibited the movement of various animals and the destruction of large numbers of cattle. Various contracts would have been frustrated in these circumstances of agricultural emergency and government restrictions.

- The performance of the contract would be worthless. If events change so dramatically that the performance of the contract would be a waste of time for all concerned then frustration may be argued. Two famous cases come from the coronation of Edward VII in 1901, just after the death of Queen Victoria. Special events had been organized around the country but, unfortunately, the King fell ill and most were cancelled. Two cases went to court and clarified the area of frustration and pointless events.

Legal case: *Krell v Henry (1903)*

Rooms had been booked in one of the most desirable points on the coronation procession, Pall Mall, leading up to Buckingham Palace. The person who booked the rooms hoped to rent them out to wealthy individuals who wanted a good view of the events around the palace. The contract made no mention of the coronation and the good view, but clearly that was the intention. The Court of Appeal ruled that the cancellation of the coronation had made the hiring of the rooms pointless. The court said the cancellation went to the root of the contract and the contract was cancelled.

A similar case with a different result was the following.

Legal case: *Herne Bay Steam Boat Co v Hutton (1903)*

A boat was hired with the intention of watching the review of the navy to be carried out by the King. The coronation was cancelled since the King was ill, which meant that the review was also cancelled. The court ruled that the cancellation of the review of the navy did not stop the sightseers enjoying a pleasurable boat tour. It did not go to the root of the contract and so the contract was not frustrated.

Group activity

Give reasons why the judges gave different rulings in the two 'coronation' cases. Were the rulings fair?

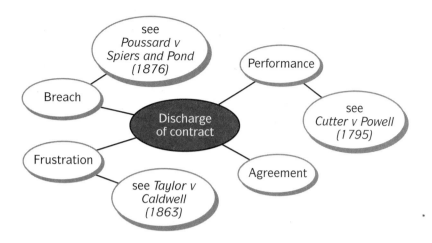

Discharge of contract

Law Reform (Frustrated Contracts) Act 1943

The Law Reform (Frustrated Contracts) Act 1943 was a welcome relief to the law on frustration and moved a, sometimes, very inequitable situation into a fairly balanced one. Before the Law Reform (Frustrated Contracts) Act 1943 all movement on the contract ceased at the point of frustration. This meant that any money that had been paid could not be reclaimed, and any duties owed were now cancelled. This was particularly unfair if one of the parties had paid upfront for services which were then not provided.

A slight improvement occurred via the decision in the Fibrosa case of 1942. This case involved a contract with a firm in Poland who could not complete the contract since the country had been invaded by the Nazis and no trade was permitted with the enemy. The ruling here meant that any payments made would be returned provided the other party had not carried out any of their obligations. If it had completed some of the contract, however, this meant no money would be refunded. The 1943 Act changed the situation entirely and ordered that money could be returnable, any expenses connected with the job were recoverable, and if a significant benefit had been received then compensation could be granted.

4 Breach

If one of the parties to the contract does not perform their obligations properly or fails completely, this is known as breach of contract. The innocent party can either reject the entire contract, known as repudiating, or it can claim damages. Two main situations can arise.

1 Term not complied with

If a term in a contract is not performed or defectively performed, the innocent party has a choice of either repudiating the whole contract or claiming damages. As they are the ones who have been wronged, they have the flexibility to choose which they prefer. The case of *Roussard v Spiers and Pond (1876)* demonstrates the issue of 'term' (see page 194).

2 Minor item (warranty) not completed

The innocent party can only claim damages on a warranty not being complied with. As the other party has complied with most of the contract, it would be unfair to them to have the contract cancelled as they may lose money over an insignificant issue.

The warranty issue is illustrated by another case involving an opera singer.

Legal case: *Bettini v Gye (1876)*

The claimant was an opera singer who could only attend three days of rehearsals rather than six but recovered for the performance. The court felt that this was a breach of warranty and the case was solved using damages. The singer won the case.

The breach of contract may be actual or anticipatory. If an actual breach of contract has happened, the innocent party would be able to sue for non-performance and claim damages. If the innocent party is warned that a breach is about to take place, this is known as anticipatory breach of contract. Here the innocent party could also sue for damages.

Legal case: *Hochster v De La Tour (1853)*

A courier was employed to accompany groups of travellers on their holidays. The contract he signed, however, was cancelled before the start date. He needed money to cover him for living expenses during the time he would have been employed so he sued for damages and was successful.

[handwritten margin notes:]
opera singer a missed final rehearsal and previous performances of opera

opera producer dismissed singer stating breach of conditions

HELD: failure of singer went to root of matter

d allowed 2 repudiate contract

singer lost case.

Quick revision questions

1 What is performance?

2 What did *Cutter v Powell (1795)* illustrate?

3 What exceptions are there to the performance rule?

4 What forms a successful agreement?

5 What does frustration of contract involve?

6 What does *Taylor v Caldwell (1863)* show?

7 What situations cause frustration?

8 Outline the *Davis Contractors v Fareham Urban District Council (1956)* case.

9 What conditions cause a breach of contract?

10 Outline two cases that illustrate failure to perform, warranty and term.

Exam question

Discuss the main ways a contract may be discharged [50 marks]

Exam answer guide

Knowledge and understanding [20 marks]

✓ Define and show understanding of:

✓ Performance. Quote *Cutter v Powell (1795)*, *Re: Moore and Co and Landauer (1921)*

✓ Agreement. Mention paperwork, partial and complete discharge

✓ Frustration. Quote *Taylor and Caldwell (1863)* and *Davis Contractors v Fareham Urban District Council (1956)*. Coronation cases *Krell v Henry (1903)* and *Herne Bay Steam Boat Co v Hutton (1903)*

✓ Breach. Quote *Bettini v Gye (1876)* and *Hochster v De La Tour (1853)*

Analysis and evaluation [25 marks]

✓ Comment on the fairness of cases quoted in each of the four sections. Were decisions made by courts the right ones?

Presentation [5 marks]

✓ Structure your work in a logical and well planned way. Employ good quality and clear English in your writing. Make use of punctuation and correct spelling in your answers.

Remedies

Why do I need to know about remedies?

Millions of contracts take place every year and the vast majority of them take place smoothly and to everyones satisfaction. When they do not it can cause great stress and even financial loss. The courts are prepared to step in to make sure those who do not fulfil their contractual obligations do not injure the innocent party. The key aim of the courts however, is to see that contracts work if at all possible. You should be aware of the common law remedy of damages, how it is used and how they are calculated. In addition to common law the innocent

Trading standards enforce legislation

party may avail themselves of an equitable remedy. You will need to understand the concepts of rescission, rectification, injunctions and specific performance. Finally this unit looks at the area of consumer contracts, which is where the vast amount of contractual obligation in the legal system actually takes place. There is outline of the protection afforded to the consumer and where they can seek legal redress.

1 Common law remedies

There are a number of ways in which the common law can offer a solution to problems with contracts, although none are perfect. The courts are keen to make contracts work and therefore awards made by the courts often amount to an admission of failure in that the contract has not been performed to completion. The key common law remedies are:

- the award of unliquidated damages which is based on the actual loss suffered by the parties
- the award of liquidated damages which is a sum agreed by the parties when the contract was formed
- the award of quantum meruit which is a sum based on the amount of work actually completed.

Damages

If a party who has entered into a contract feels that they have been unfairly treated they may seek a remedy known as damages. Damages are normally a financial payment and try to compensate the wronged party. Damages can sometimes be administered by the person themselves or more often by the courts. The main remedy the common law provides is damages.

What are damages for?

Normally a party may be able to claim damages if there has been partial or complete failure to complete the performance of a contract. Usually they attempt to compensate for financial loss. There are also a number of related issues that are important to understand.

- Punishment

Damages are not designed to punish the party that has not performed. The courts will therefore only take the loss suffered by the injured party into consideration rather than any gain made by the offending party.

- Mental suffering

The courts traditionally did not allow claims for mental suffering but there has been some leeway recently. A number of cases involving breaches that have ruined a special event or day have been allowed. Wedding transport in *Chandle v East African Airways (1964)*, breakdown that ruined a special day out in *Bernstein v Pamson Motors (1987)* and wedding photographs in *Diesen v Sampson (1971)*. Damages are obviously not available for commercial contracts (the mental suffering of companies).

- Non-financial loss

The rise of the holiday trade has brought many parties to the courts for settlement on disappointing vacations. The classic case is *Jarvis v Swans Tours (1973)*.

Legal case: *Jarvis v Swans Tours (1973)*

A holiday was booked for Switzerland which promised yodelling, afternoon teas and a 'house party'. None of these items materialised in a way that could be called satisfactory. The claimant was awarded half the contract price in terms of damages but Lord Denning raised this on appeal. He felt that such a long journey and such disappointment demanded a more robust financial settlement.

The thinking of the courts here is that recreation is about carefree days in the sun and not about haggling with companies over disappointing experiences.

Liquidated and unliquidated damages

As we have seen this is an attempt to compensate the innocent party using money. This may seem the quickest and easiest way of sorting out a disagreement but it may leave the innocent party in a weak position. They may be desperate to see the completion of the contracted work. Damages can be of two main types:

- liquidated

These damages involve sums of money which are already known by the two parties. The amount may already be included in the details of the contract.

- unliquidated

Here the amounts are unclear and the parties have not agreed to a sum. If action goes ahead in the court there may be a number of outcomes.

1 Substantial damages that are an attempt by the court to reflect the true loss incurred by the innocent party.

2 Nominal damages where the court awards a small amount of damages to the innocent party signalling that they have won the case but the court feels it would be unfair to give them a big payout.

3 Exemplary damages show the displeasure of the court and give the innocent party a very large payout. They are rarely used. The courts normally see their task as correcting issues and putting the innocent in a position where he was before the breach. The courts also protect against appeal dragging out the proceedings.

Limitations on the recovery of damages

● Causation

The chain of events may be broken by intervening events. This will mean that the defendant may be able to claim protection and limit their exposure to damages.

Legal case: *County Ltd v Girozentrale Securities (1996)*

County Ltd asked Girozentrale Securities to approach investors to persuade them to buy shares in a Public Limited Company. Girozentrale Securities breached their contract and County Ltd were left with a £7 million debt partly caused by Girozentrale Securities failures. The court ruled that although the debt was produced by a number of factors Girozentrale Securities was the main cause, they were found liable and had to pay damages.

● Remoteness

If the defendants breach was relatively minor but caused a great deal of financial loss to the claimant the courts may limit the defendants exposure to damages.

Legal case: *Hadley v Baxendale (1954)*

A shaft that drove a mill was sent away for repair. Without the shaft the mill could not function and no profits could be made. The date of the delivery for the repaired shaft was missed and the claimants sued for the profits they lost between the promised date of delivery and the actual date of delivery. The court felt that the mill should have had a spare shaft for such a situation and they had not made it clear to the defendant that the shaft was of vital importance to the continued operation of the business. The case produced two important points.

1 The defendants would be liable if their breach of contract and its consequences arose from the 'usual course of things'. In this case however it would have been usual for a mill to have a spare of such an important item such as a shaft.

2 The defendants would have been liable if there had been specific discussion and agreement during the formation of the contract that the breach would have had serious consequences, which the defendant would then be responsible for. No such discussion took place.

The mill owners lost their case.

Two further cases emphasize the issue of remoteness and explore the situation where abnormally high losses are created by the defendant's breach of contract. The House of Lords discussed the two cases in relation to one another when they focussed their attention on this important area despite the fact that they were heard twenty years apart.

Legal case: *Victoria Laundry (Windsor) Ltd v Newman Industries (1949)*

Victoria Laundry were keen to take on a lucrative government contract but needed to expand their business first. They signed a contract with Newman Industries for a large second hand boiler and stated clearly that they needed the item at once. Both parties were therefore clear about the need for a speedy completion of the project. The boiler was unfortunately late due to damage caused when it was being dismantled and Victoria Laundry took Newman Industries to court for damages, they claimed for two sets of losses.

1 £16 per week loss from work they would have taken on apart from the government contract

2 £262 per week loss from work they failed to complete on the government contract.

The court decided that although the defendants knew that the boiler was needed quickly they did not know about the lucrative government contract and therefore could not be held liable for this. They were however ordered to pay damages for the lost £16 per week on the other work. As a result of the case it was decided that only losses, which could be 'reasonably foreseeable', could be claimed as a result of a breach of contract.

Legal case: *The Heron II (1969)*

This case also looked at the issue of abnormal losses. A ship the Heron II sailed for Basra with a consignment of sugar that was to be sold on arrival. The journey was expected to take 20 days but the Captain strayed from the normal route and in the end the journey actually took 29 days. The price of sugar had in the meantime dropped in Basra and the claimants in the case sued the shipowner for the loss in profit. The shipowner had breached the contract agreed and the House of Lords decided that it would have been obvious that the sugar was to be sold 'in the normal course of events' and therefore within the 'contemplation of the parties'. A key problem that arose in this case was deciding the probability that the parties would have contemplated the event. The House of Lords decided that the consequence of the breach had to be 'liable to result' rather than just to be 'reasonably foreseeable'.

- Mitigation

The defendant may have good reasons for non-performance of their contractual obligations. The court may take a lenient view and limit their exposure to damages.

The leading case in this field in *Brace and Calder (1895)*.

Legal case: *Brace and Calder (1895)*

A man was employed by a four person partnership but five months afterwards the partnership was dissolved as two members wished to retire. The two remaining partners offered to re-employ the man on the same conditions he had enjoyed with the original set up but he refused. Technically a breach of contract had occurred when the man was made redundant from the original deal but the court felt that as he had refused a perfectly adequate alternative offer of employment there was only an award of nominal (a small amount to indicate that the person was technically right) damages.

Basis of assessment

- Restitutio in integrum

Damages may attempt to put the innocent party into the position as if the contract had been satisfactorily completed. This is known as restitutio in integrum This of course is not perfect since the party wanted the contract to perform a particular function but given that is impossible the next best alternative is money in most cases.

- As if contract had never existed

Another method of assessing is to put the parties back to the position before contracts were formed.

- The market

Under this the injured party would claim the difference between what would have been paid under the contract and what it would now cost if it were to be bought.

- Contributory negligence

Contributory negligence involves taking into account any part the innocent party had in bringing about the unwanted situation. This is not possible for cases of breach of contract at the moment but the Law Commission have put it forward as a possibility for the future.

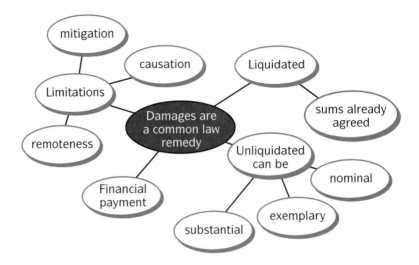

Damages are a common law remedy

2 Equitable remedies

Equity law is used when common law fails. In the past the failure could have been caused by common law being too rigid or not moving forward with the times. Equity is now a body of principles, which can be used by all courts, but when there is a conflict between equity law and common law equity law takes priority. Unfortunately equity is now as often as rigid as common law at times. The Chancery Division of the High Court was historically associated with equity law but it now also uses common law.

There are four main types of equitable solution to a problem with contract law. They are:

- rescission
- specific order performance
- rectification
- injunction.

Rescission

This involves cancelling of the contract. This may disadvantage the party who is seeking a solution to a breach in contract. Rescission can be used when there has been misrepresentation. Misrepresentation can occur when there has been a mistake, when there has been carelessness or when there has been fraud. The order from the court is to try to return the parties to their pre-contract state. If this is not possible, because events have moved on significantly, then rescission is not possible.

The Misrepresentation Act 1967 allows misrepresentation providing it is reasonable. This is because many contracts are highly complex and innocent misrepresentation may creep in by mistake. The courts will normally attempt to make a contract work if possible.

Specific order performance

The court orders the party who is in breach of contract to finish their part of the contract. This is sometimes to the benefit of the innocent party but may result in longer-term problems. Relationships can be soured by court action and the contract may be fulfilled in a less than satisfactory way. This could mean additional legal moves.

There are some very good reasons for courts not to order specific performance:

- unfair contracts
- suffering to the claimant would arise
- inappropriate contracts.

Rectification

Contracts may be amended to highlight the true intentions of each party. The breach may have been caused by a communication breakdown in the original contract. A more carefully drafted and considered document in court should lead to a successful completion.

Injunction

An injunction stops a party acting out a breach of contract. There are a number of types of injunction.

- A prohibitory injunction is an order not to do something. The court may order a builder not to cut down some important trees due to protected wildlife living there.
- A mandatory injunction is an order to do something. This might be an order to take down an extension to a house that is blocking a neighbours access.
- An interlocutory injunction is an order to stop something happening before the case is heard in court. This might relate to preventing a local authority commencing building work on a public area.

The most common type used in a breach of contract case is probably a interlocutory injunction. It stops events rolling forward until a court has considered the issues and given a judgement.

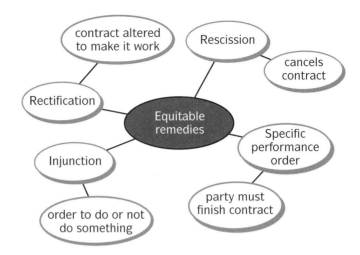

Equitable remedies

3 Advice on consumer contracts

Although many contracts are made between businesses and businesses and between businesses and government and other public bodies, the vast majority of contracts involve consumers. A number of key pieces of legislation can now be used by consumers to make sure their rights are protected when they are dealing with retailers and businesses and there are a number of places where ordinary consumers can get advice about their contractual rights.

The role of local authorities

Central government has a part to play in protecting the consumer when it passes statutory legislation such as the Sale of Goods Act 1979, the Consumer Protection Act 1987, the Trade Descriptions Act 1968 and the Unfair Terms in Consumer Contracts 1994. The enforcement of much of this is left to the local authorities and the local courts if necessary.

There are two key departments of the local authority with responsibility for consumer issues:

- the Trading Standards Department
- the Environmental Health Department

The local authority funds both departments and both have powers to carry out investigations, inspections and work connected to consumer complaints. There are almost 500 local authorities and as many retailers have shops all over the country, duplication of work is avoided by liaison with the Department of Trade and Industry.

If investigations or inspections uncover serious violations of consumer law, both trading standards and environmental health have the power to prosecute. The maximum fine available for such offences is £5000 or up to two years in prison.

Although the Trading Standards and Environmental Health department have prosecution powers often consumers simply want a solution to their grievance. Alternative dispute resolution is encouraged where retailer and consumer can meet in less formal circumstances to iron out their difficulties. If this is unsuccessful consumers have the right to pursue the matter through more formal and possibly more expensive and time-consuming channels, that is, through the courts.

In the wake of several scares about the quality of food the government formed the Food Standards Agency, which was to represent both the interests of consumers and the food industry. Some saw this as a conflict of interests but the Food Standards Agency believes it is possible to represent both interest groups fairly.

Consumer legislation

The key pieces of statutory legislation available to local authorities are the following:

Sale of Goods Act 1979

A key piece of legislation, which gives the consumer protection on a number of fronts. It covers consumers in terms of the quality, description, title and sample. The last two items relate to whether the seller actually owns the article for sale (title) and whether any examples (samples) shown to the consumer match the goods actually supplied.

Trade Descriptions Act 1968

Another important and effective piece of legislation passed to protect the rights of consumers against business fraud is the Trade Descriptions Act 1968. Section 26 obligates local authorities to enforce this law.

Consumer Protection Act 1987 Part III

This Act is enforced by Trading Standards. Part III covers misleading pricing information designed to defraud consumers.

Food Safety Act 1990

Food poisoning and restaurants hotels shops that sell food. BSE, listeria, salmonella and various other unpleasant bugs have all caused national concern. Legislation is becoming tighter in this area as patterns of consumption change and more and more people eat out.

Weights and Measures

Local trading standards often make investigations in this area testing quality and quantity sold to consumers. Weighing machines for example are tested to make sure consumers are not getting less than they pay for.

Trading standards

The Trading Standards Office of every local authority has officers committed to giving advice to both consumers and businesses about consumer protection and how the law supports fair-trading. Key areas of involvement are:

- fair trading
- metrology
- consumer safety
- quality.

In addition there is a code of practice that hopes to give advice to traders on how to avoid breaking the Consumer Protection Act 1987. If the law is broken, traders can be prosecuted by Trading Standards Department or the Office of Fair Trading.

Traders can obtain information from Trading Standards Offices directly or can become members of the Trading Standards Institute. This organization is in constant contact with domestic and European government and the Confederation of British Industry. The TSI offers events, regular updates on changes to the law and a campaigning arm that aims to improve the quality of consumer legislation that consumer and businesses have to deal with.

The Office of Fair Trading can refer major cases to the Competition Commission. The Secretary of State for Trade and Industry can also prohibit the supply of certain goods and services if they are deemed dangerous.

Other sources of advice

The Consumer Association, *Which*?

The Consumer Association (CA) is an independent group which acts on behalf of the consumer. It has a magazine called *Which*? that investigates products and businesses and tries to give impartial and accurate information to consumers.

Citizen's Advice Bureau

A large network of bureaus around the country give advice on a huge range of legal and consumer issues.

Law centres

There are around 50 centres in the country normally in areas of most need. Staff in these centres usually have wider legal training than the Citizen's Advice Bureau staff.

Local solicitors

Legal advice will be offered for a fee but some offer pro bono (for free) advice and services such as calls for information.

Libraries

Often contain leaflets produced by local authorities and copies of the Consumer's Association publication *Which*?

Internet

A proliferation of sites is now available including the government's justask. The private sites are often connected to solicitor's numbers as a means of obtaining business.

Independent charities

Many independent charities target specific ethnic groups to give support to these communities who sometimes fall outside the mainstream support systems.

Consumer programmes

The most famous is *Watchdog* from the BBC but many local programmes cover issues of consumer interest.

Magazines and newspapers

Many local and national newspapers offer advice from financial services to raising awareness of poor quality products.

Trade unions

As part of their package of services many trade unions offer a set time with the union solicitor on issues of general interest.

Trading Standards Institute

There is an umbrella organization called the Trading Standards Institute which offers advice to trading standards officers and other professionals in the field. The organization also takes an active role in relevant legislation both domestic and European to ensure high quality consumer law.

4 Action on consumer contracts

The consumer has a number of options available if they feel they have been treated unfairly by a business:

Complaint to local authority trading standards office

Local authorities provide a service known as trading standards office.

Action in the county court

There are a number of possible actions the consumer may take to the local county court if they have a dispute with a business.

- The small claims court this is available for disputes ranging from 1p to £5000.
- Fast track for disputes ranging from £5000–£15,000
- Multi track for disputes over £15,000 or particularly difficult cases.

High Court

The High Court is seen as a last resort since the cost of the High Court would put off most ordinary consumers pursuing a case. Their case may, however be backed by a local Citizen's Advice Bureau or other organization if there is a general point of consumer law that needs clarification.

Office of Fair Trading

The Office of Fair Trading (OFT) is responsible for more general areas of consumer protection particularly involving large businesses. The OFT can refer cases to the Competition Commission.

Ombudsman

The ombudsman is an official appointed to investigate individual's complaints, especially against public authorities. Consumers can avail themselves of the ombudsman in a range of different areas. The most prominent is in the financial services sector but there are ombudsmen also set up to deal with the provision of legal services and conveyance. Other industries in the private sector have organized similar schemes to allow consumers the opportunity to put their grievance to an independent source. The ombudsman will be looking at procedures and attempting to see if proper process has been afforded the customer rather than exploring the facts of the case.

Web activity

Got to www.heinemann.co.uk/hotlinks to find more information on ombudsmen.

Regulatory bodies

In addition to formal methods, consumers may have the right to make complaints to trade bodies who will investigate and attempt to come to an agreement between consumer and the member business, such as the Association of British Travel Agents (ABTA) and the Master Builders Federation (MBF).

Quick revision questions

1 What is the purpose of damages?

2 Outline the key elements of *Jarvis v Swans Tours (1973)*.

3 What are the differences between liquidated and unliquidated damages?

4 What are the key limitations on damages?

5 What does Restitutio in integrum involve?

6 Outline the processes of rescission, specific performance order and rectification.

7 What does an injunction do and name the main forms of injunction available.

8 List the key pieces of consumer legislation available.

9 How can consumers get advice on statutory protection?

10 What court processes are available to consumers?

Which method of remedy is most effective?

a Common law remedy

b Equitable remedy.

[50 marks]

Exam answer guide

Knowledge and understanding [20 marks]

✓ Define the common law remedy of damages

✓ Consider limitations on damages such as causation, remoteness, mitigation

✓ Show how damages are calculated

✓ Define quantum meruit and restitution

✓ Refer to specific performance and injunctions

Analysis and evaluation [25 marks]

✓ Assess whether common law or equity provide the most acceptable solution to the wronged party

Presentation [5 marks]

✓ Structure your work in a logical and well-planned way. Employ good quality and clear English in your writing. Make use of punctuation and correct spelling in your answers.

Law of contract examination

Examination questions for OCR

What do I need to know about the contract law exam?

The examination board produces a guide which examiners use when they mark your essays and case studies. This section shows you what examiners are told to look out for in students work. There are three main stages to securing a good grade.

Knowledge and understanding

Recall, select, deploy and develop knowledge and understanding of legal principles accurately and by means of example and citation.

What do I need to know about knowledge and understanding?

When examiners are marking your script they look out for certain things. The first is your level of knowledge of law and how well you understand that knowledge. Law is a difficult but interesting subject where you are required to make sense of some very difficult ideas. This knowledge and understanding is the first step on the road towards getting a good grade.

It is important that you have a good understanding of the basic ideas of law; this will help you to find the modules easier to handle. If you do not understand something it is important to ask your teacher, another student or read another book, which might be able to explain the idea in a way you might understand more easily. Remember it will be difficult at first, but keep on trying it will click into place!

There are three ways you can show the examiner that you have covered the course and have understood some of the key points.

- **Quote relevant legal cases**

The use of cases to back up your arguments is crucial to examination success. All law made by judges is made by using cases and law made by Parliament is tested in the courts which also produces a case. Use index cards (small pieces of card to carry around with you and read whenever you can) and build up a library of cases. It is best to do this gradually and look at them often. For example the following cases would show your knowledge of invitation to treat and the concept of offer: *Carlill v Carbolic Smoke Ball Company (1893)*, *Fisher v Bell (1961)* and *Pharmaceutical Society of Great Britain v Boots the Chemist (1953)*. Examiners will give you credit for using these types of cases to show your knowledge.

- **Quote statutory legislation**

Use important pieces of law passed by Parliament that you know; in most topics there will be one. The government is keen to make laws that reflect its interests and the job of Parliament is to look carefully at the ideas suggested by the government to make sure they are fair. Index cards with key pieces of Parliamentary law will help with this. Legislation such as The Unfair Contract Terms Act 1977 and the Sale of Goods Act 1979 for example should be understood and put on index cards for future use.

- **Quote key legal ideas**

Concepts such as privity in contracts and vitiating factors need to be defined and explained. Again you can make a set of index cards, which hold these key ideas. Eventually you will find that the more you know the more links you will see between cases, Parliamentary law and legal ideas.

Display analysis, evaluation and application

Analyse legal material, issues, and situations, and evaluate and apply the appropriate legal rules and principles.

What do I need to know about analysis, evaluation and application?

There are a lot of marks to be gained in this section. The first skill you must display is analysis. This is something you do all the time in other areas of your life, when you look at the pros and cons of buying something such as choosing a holiday or which college to go to. There are two main ways you can look at analysis in your law work.

Analysis

1 Break a complicated idea down to help understanding

For example an important idea in contract law is that of consideration. You need to break this idea down into smaller parts and give examples which show your understanding. There are five rules which break this down into simpler units. You need to show that consideration must pass between the two parties, it cannot be past, must be sufficient, cannot be illegal and cannot be an existing duty. Consideration is much easier to understand if you define the term and then illustrate the five rules.

2 Develop a flow of ideas

To do this you must see connections between different ideas and put them altogether. Linking how the courts see social and domestic arrangements and how the courts see commercial arrangements for example would show a flow of ideas.

Evaluation

The examiner is interested in your views on legal issues. Giving your view is also known as evaluation; other words for evaluation are opinion, conclusion, recommendation or judgement. Evaluating legal issues or cases will help you to get marks.

An example of evaluation

Student evaluation

Although minors have been protected by the decisions in various cases and some statutory legislation, the passing of the Minor's Contracts Act 1987 evened up the balance. This legislation began to give some well-deserved protection for adults who formed contracts with minors. This was an important and welcome change.

This gives some information about the issue, points out some issues and then gives an opinion. Never forget to include an evaluation and practice forming a view about everything you hear!

Application

This involves thinking about which law or cases you would use in a particular situation.

If a situation is exploring the rights of consumers some key pieces of legislation to apply might be the Sale of Goods Act 1979 and the Consumer Protection Act 1987. An associated case that might be used could be *Priest v Last (1903)* involving a defective hot water bottle.

Applying points of law will give you credit with the examiner.

Display communication and presentation

Present a logical and coherent argument and communicate relevant material in a clear and effective manner using appropriate legal terminology.

What do I need to know about communication and presentation?

There are a number of points to this but the key element is to make sure you plan your answers effectively so that your answer is logical, easy to follow and answers the question. You must use legal vocabulary in your answer so it is important that you build up your knowledge of key legal terms, when you use a new term for the first time in your work make sure that you define it accurately.

Another way to pick up marks is by taking care with grammar, punctuation and spelling. You can improve this before the examination by plenty of reading and making sure that you take notice of feedback from your teacher. Make a list of commonly used legal terms and write them on an index card. Pay particular attention with the few Latin phrases you will need to know. Examiners notice these particularly. Show how professional you can be by paying some attention to these details.

For assessment criteria used for examination questions, see the end of the section 'Criminal law examination' on page 135.

Examples of contract law questions

1 Examine the level of protection that a minor receives in the area of contract law. [50 marks]

Answer guide for Question 1

- Define the legal concept of a minor.
- Exceptions to common law on contracts for minors.
- Explain necessary goods and services using Section 3(2) of the Sale of Goods Act 1979.
- Use *Nash v Inman (1908)* to illustrate necessaries.
- *Clements v London and North West (1894)* and *De Francesco v Barnum (1890)* to illustrate benefits for minors.
- Explain the Minors Contracts Act 1987.
- Compare case law protection and statutory protection.

2 Outline and evaluate the use of innominate terms in contracts. [50 marks]

Answer guide for Question 2

- Explain innominate terms, conditions and warranties.
- Explain innominate via *Hong Kong Fir Shipping Company v Kawasaki Ltd (1962)*.
- Explain conditions and warranties via *Poussard v Spiers and Pond (1876)*.
- Outline effects of breach in each case. Explain void and voidable.
- Outline use of Sale of Goods Act 1979 in deciding terms.
- Evaluate the effects of courts and statute law on this area of law. Consider justice delivered from using innominate terms.

3 David had just opened a nightclub called 'The Lantern Lodge' and was interested in buying some ovens so that he could serve late-night dinners to clubbers. Robert was an old friend and business acquaintance who had exactly the type of oven that David needed. Robert had indicated that he would take somewhere in the region of £2500. David phoned Robert and offered £2000 for the ovens leaving a message on the answer machine, adding that there was no need to reply if the £2000 was satisfactory. Robert was happy with this but a week later found out that David had changed his mind and had decided to order food from a catering company instead.

David entered a written contract with Carlton Caterers. He would pay a fixed sum up front for their services of £10,000. In return, Kerry Caterers would agree to respond to any additional food requests within twenty-four hours. In the first six months David was not very happy with the service offered. Two birthday party's had been ruined due to food not turning up as requested. Customers were unhappy and several potential clients cancelled celebrations at the club. David cancelled the contract and demanded that Carlton Caterers return the £10,000.

Explain the contractual issues and consequences of the various agreements made in this case. [50 marks]

Answer guide for Question 3

- Explain the elements of a valid contract with particular focus on agreement and intent to cause legal relations.

- Explain the rules on offer and acceptance. Of particular interest are rules on offer and counter offer, and acceptance by silence.

- Explain the remedy of damages if there has been a breach of contract.

- Explain the classification of a contract: express terms, implied terms, conditions and warranties.

- Explain rules on breach of contract with regard to what is a term and what is a warranty, and possibility of innominate terms.

- Explain remedies available depending on whether terms or warranties have been broken.

- Explain and evaluate rules on offer and acceptance.

- Explain and evaluate the rules on consideration.

- Explain and evaluate the rules on intent to create legal relations.

4 How does the legal doctrine of frustration bring justice to parties involved in a contract? [50 marks]

Answer guide for Question 4

- Definition of frustration.

- Outline the various circumstances where frustration may occur.

- Explain when frustration may not be used.

- Outline the effect of the Law Reform (Frustrated Contracts) Act 1943.

- Outline common law on frustration.

- Evaluate the effect of frustration in terms of justice to either party.

5 Evaluate the ways in which a contract may be discharged.   [50 marks]

Answer guide for Question 5

- Define discharge of contract.
- Discharge by performance. See *Cutter v Powell (1795)* and *Re: Moore and Co and Landauer (1921)*.
- Exceptions to performance. Severable contracts, prevention of performance, voluntary acceptance, and so on. See *Sumpter v Hedges (1898)*.
- Discharge by agreement.
- Discharge by frustration, see *Taylor v Caldwell (1863)*. Explain other situation that causes frustration, that is, death.
- Discharge by breach, see *Poussard v Spiers and Pond (1876)*.

Special study paper

Why do I need to know about the special study paper?

This book will look at general issues of advice for the special paper. The advice outlined will be relevant to any criminal/contract synoptic paper you will take with OCR, even after January 2005. You will look at the materials presented to students for the session June 2003–January 2005 as an example of what to look for. The questions for the special paper change for each session of the examination but they are all based on the currently live source material. Note that Question 1 is based on a theme that relates to work covered in your AS course and is examined in Question 1 of both the contract and criminal special papers.

1 Preparation for the special paper

Do not try to question spot – this is impossible. There are, however, things you can do before the day of the examination.

The paper is synoptic so you must have a strong working knowledge of both AS and A2 module material. There is no new material to be learned in the synoptic OCR papers, but you do need to be able to apply the legal knowledge, concepts and principles you have already learned to new material found in the source material via the questions asked on the examination paper. Obviously, the key concepts you have studied in criminal/contract law need to be given full use in this paper.

Read the source material as soon as you get it: this will allow you to look out for issues in the press and on television that might cast further light on the issues discussed in the sources. Early reading of source material will also allow work done during your course to be linked. The earlier and more you read the material, the more relationships you will see in the material. Do not spend all year reading the material or you will suffer from over-preparation and fatigue, which will make your answers wooden. Keep your work in perspective and read around the issues to build knowledge and confidence.

Look for themes and relationships between the sources. The *Williams v Roffey (1990)* case explored in Source 7, for example, forms the substance of Source 10, where the judgement is looked at in even more detail. *Stilk v Myrick (1809)*, briefly mentioned in Source 7, is again expanded in Source 10.

2 What kind of questions will be asked?

The paper has four questions:

Q1 An essay type question based on a theme from your AS material.

Q2 An essay type question based on the issued source material.

Q3 An essay type question based on the issued source material.

Q4 A question based on a short criminal/contract law scenario given in the examination question.

Question 1 will be an essay type question based on a theme taken from the AS course and explored in Source 1 of the material in your booklet. For the June 2003–January 2004 paper, for example, the theme is the development of the law via flexibility or lack of it using judicial precedent in the Court of Appeal and the House of Lords.

Questions 2 and 3 require you to have knowledge of the cases, legislation and issues explored in the sources. The questions require you to spot legal themes and issues and have the ability to discuss them and then evaluate them. In the June 2003–January 2004 paper, for example, the theme is consideration in contract law.

Question 4, the mini case study scenario, requires you to apply your knowledge of criminal/contract law to a simple given situation on the examination paper. This application question will revolve around the themes explored in the source material.

3 What are the examiners looking for in the special paper?

Examiners will be looking for analysis and evaluation backed up with cases, legal principles, relevant legislation, and knowledge and opinions on recent developments. The very best candidates will be able to combine their own knowledge of criminal/contract law with the source material to explore principles under discussion. Examiners will be looking for sound knowledge of any relevant legislation and the ability to pick the key cases and appreciate their broader significance.

The process of trying to predict questions is a waste of time for the special papers. The number of potential questions would be vast and any hope of intercepting the examiner's mind on the question itself would be futile. The process of trying to predict legal theme or issue is, however, a fruitful use of time. Each source will provide possibilities for research. Look at this as an opportunity to find out more about law and so not only help you in your synoptic special paper, but also other module examinations.

As soon as you receive the source material read it thoroughly and discuss it with fellow students, if possible, and your teacher.

Key points for the synoptic paper

- Do not waste time trying to guess what questions will come up.

- Search for legal themes in each of the sources.

- Know the material intimately and the associated cases and legal material.

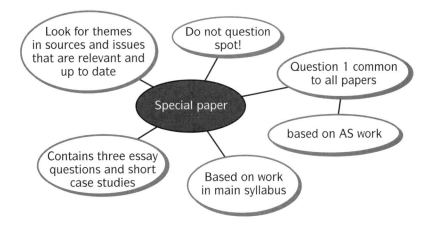

Special paper

4 Issues of interest in the Common Question 1

Question 1 on the contract and criminal paper examines a theme from your AS studies. All students must do this Common Question 1.

Source 1

Extract adapted from *The Discipline of Law* by Lord Denning, Butterworths, pp. 291–7

Lord Denning was one of the key judges working in the Court of Appeal. He often irritated the House of Lords by commenting on issues they felt were more properly theirs. One of his great creations was the doctrine of promissory estoppel used in contract law. Denning was always keen to see a just outcome and was prepared to go against convention to achieve this.

The extract explores the fundamental idea of *stare decisis*. The appeal court was released from this constraint to a certain extent by the *Young v Bristol Aeroplane Ltd (1944)* case. This allowed the Court of Appeal some flexibility when three situations arose.

1 When a previous case was wrong due to ignorance of the law. This is also known as *per incuriam*.

2 Where two conflicting previous decisions conflict with one another.

3 Where the House of Lords has superseded the judgement with a judgement of their own.

The House of Lords was also given an element of freedom from the use of the Practice Statement issued in 1966. This meant that the Law Lords could create new decisions and not be bound by their own previous decisions. This allowed the possibility of legal development, but it was used very sparingly in the first few years.

Denning's plea in this source is for the use of commonsense and bravery by the lawyers and judges who may find themselves holding on to the security of judicial precedent. Denning feels that justice is best served by fresh decisions on new cases wherever applicable. The only problem was that the Practice Statement 1966 only applied to the House of Lords and not to the Court of Appeal, which hears much more cases each year. Lord Denning was dismayed by this deliberate decision to exclude the Court of Appeal.

5 Issues of interest in the criminal source material

Source 2

Extract adapted from the judgement of Lord Lane, Lord Chief Justice in *R v Graham (1982)* 74 Cr. App. R 235 (Court of Appeal Criminal Division)

The source material for the criminal special paper revolves around the concept of self-defence and duress using charges of murder and non-fatal offences against the person. The case of *R v Graham (1982)* involved a married homosexual man who lived with both his wife and his gay lover. Graham was threatened by his gay lover, King, and strangled his wife. The court felt that the threats were not serious enough to allow a defence of duress. The case is extremely important as it produced a two-part test on the issue of duress.

1 Did the defendant fear death or serious injury?

2 Would a person of reasonable firmness have reacted in the same way as the defendant to the threat?

Here you will see both subjective (part 1) and objective (part 2) criteria used.

Source 3

Extract adapted from the judgement of Lord Hailsham LC in *R v Howe (1987)* 1 AC 417

Lord Hailsham was an important judge who also served as Conservative Lord Chancellor to Mrs Thatcher. The source material considers the balance between the threat made and the use of force to defend one self. *R v Howe (1987)* is an important case in the area of duress as a defence to a crime. Duress can be used as a defence to all crimes except treason or murder. Duress occurs if threats of serious harm or death make the act of the defendant one that is not really voluntary because of the threat. In *R v Howe (1987)*, Lord Hailsham outlines the issues as a concession to human frailty. The defence allows a person to make a choice between the 'lesser of two evils'. If the defence is accepted, the defendant can walk free as it is a complete defence. This case is important in that it creates precedent that duress is not available to charges of murder.

Source 4

Extract adapted from the judgement of Lord Griffiths in *R v Howe (1987)* 1 AC 417 HL

In the case of *DPP for Northern Ireland v Lynch (1975)* the defendant was found guilty of aiding and abetting in the attempted murder of a policeman, rather than charged with attempted murder itself. Lord Griffiths departs from the *DPP for Northern Ireland v Lynch* judgement by reiterating that duress is not available as a defence for murder or attempted murder.

Source 5

Extract adapted from the judgement of Lord Jauncey in *R v Gotts (1992)* 2 AC 412 HL

Duress is seen as a complete defence to a crime, but Lord Jauncey is asking for it to be seen as a mitigating factor. This would allow judges the flexibility to look at the individual circumstances and still sentence the defendant using the defence of duress or discharge them. He also calls for it to be reviewed in serious crimes other than murder. Lord Jauncey feels that an attempted murderer should not be able to a defence which is not available to a murderer. This case is important in that it creates precedent that duress is not available to attempted murder.

Source 6

Extract adapted from *Criminal Law Text and Materials* by Clarkson and Keating, Sweet & Maxwell, pp. 328–9, 335–6

This source reflects on what may or may not amount to the threats that may be considered serious enough to warrant a defence of duress. Previous cases seemed to suggest that only the threat of serious harm or death were to be considered enough to warrant duress. In *Valderrama-Vega* the defendant received death threats but also was under pressure from financial sources and the threat of disclosure of his homosexuality. The court ruled that the jury was entitled to look at the whole situation and not just the threats of physical violence. As the jury had been instructed to look only at the threat issue as duress for the crime of importing cocaine for a mafia-related organization, he was acquitted.

Valderrama-Vega was instructed by the people threatening him exactly what crime he had to commit. In *Cole*, however, the defendant was threatened by moneylenders, but he decided his own crime. The court, therefore, felt the defence of duress was not available to him. There was an insufficient link between the threat and the crime.

Two young women, Linda Hudson aged seventeen and Elaine Taylor aged nineteen, had been called to give evidence against a violent individual, Jimmy Wright, who had wounded another man in a Salford pub. Before they were to give evidence the two were threatened by a friend of Jimmy Wright's who said the two girls would be 'cut up' if they gave evidence. They saw the friend of Wright's in the public gallery of the court when they were to give evidence and decided that they would refuse to identify Wright as the assailant. The judge charged the girls with perjury stating that the defence of duress was not available to them as they were in the safety of the courtroom. Their convictions were quashed on appeal as the Court of Appeal decided that it would have been impossible for the police to protect the two girls twenty-four hours a day and the threat was actually a very real one.

Source 7

Extract adapted from *Principles of Criminal Law* by Duncan Bloy and Philip Parry, Cavendish, pp. 259–60

The defence of duress is not available to those who voluntarily join a gang. They have put themselves into the position they find themselves in. In *R v Sharp (1987)* the defendant was charged and convicted of manslaughter, robbery and attempted robbery. He had voluntarily joined a gang, which had robbed a post office and killed the sub-postmaster. Sharp tried to use duress as a defence saying that one of the gang had threatened to blow his head off if he did not take part in the robbery. The court found him guilty and the Court of Appeal upheld the conviction.

The case of *R v Shepherd* was distinguished from Sharp. The gang had not been a violent one when Shepherd had joined it and there was no evidence that they would have threatened violence if he wanted to leave. The court felt that they would allow duress as a concession to 'human frailty'.

Source 8

Extract adapted from *Criminal Law* by Michael Jefferson, Pitman, pp. 236–9

Duress involves a defence to a criminal charge where the defendant, their family, or other persons, were threatened with death or serious injury. The defence has developed via the cases above. Another development has been the defence of duress by circumstances. The key difference is that the threat comes not from threats of serious injury or death from a person, but by the circumstances the defendant finds themselves in. A key case in this area is *R v Conway (1989)*. The defendant had a passenger in his car that had just escaped from a gun attack. Two men approached the car and the defendant, thinking they were involved with the earlier incident, drove dangerously away from the scene. The two men approaching the car were in fact police officers but the defence was allowed.

Before the development of duress of circumstances, via the *R v Willer (1986)* and *R v Conway (1989)* cases, there was another defence available which the courts seemed unwilling to use. The defence was called necessity and involved doing something which avoided a worse evil. Duress of circumstances and necessity seem to all intents and purposes the same thing.

Source 9

Extract adapted from the judgement of Lord Justice Kennedy in *R v Pommell (1995)* 2 Cr. App R. 607

The defendant in *R v Pommell (1995)* had confiscated a weapon from a friend who had been intent upon using it. Pommell had intended to hand the gun over to the police, but as it was early in the morning he decided to wait until the next day. In the meantime, police arrived at Pommell's house and arrested him for possession of a gun. The judge denied a defence of duress, but on appeal the court decided that the time delay was understandable given the lateness of the hour when the gun was taken by Pommell from the original owner.

Source 10

Extract adapted from *Criminal Law Text and Materials* by Clarkson and Keating, Sweet & Maxwell, pp. 357–8

The legal area of duress, duress of circumstances and necessity developed as courts began to see that life was complex and behaviour did not always fit into neat categories of good and bad. There would be some behaviour, which on the surface looked wrong but on further investigation was attempting to do the greater good. The Law Commission's work in this area shows the complexity of the matter and the unexpected consequences that often arise when the law is changed. The Commission's proposals seem to have swung from one extreme to the other when the results of the change were more properly considered. The courts have been the forum for the development of the defence of duress rather than statutory provisions that might have come from the Law Commission's proposals.

Source 11

Extract adapted from the judgement of Lord Justice ward in *Re: A (Conjoined Twins) (2000)*, New Law Journal, 6 October 2000, pp. 1453–4

In the difficult and moving case of J and M in *Re: A (Conjoined Twins) (2000)* the conjoined twins clearly stretched the issue of necessity to its limits. An innocent human being, M, was to be denied the right to life to allow her sister, J, the right to life as only one could live or both could die. The question was clearly one of 'which was the lesser of the two evils?' This question is one that relates to cases you have looked at in the previous sources, which consider the issue of duress, duress of circumstances and necessity.

Source 12

Extract adapted from *The Manchester Conjoined Twins Case* by Christopher F Sharp QC, New Law Journal, 6 October 2000, pp. 1460–2

Walker LJ, Ward LJ, and Brooke LJ investigated the doctrine of necessity using the case of the conjoined twins above. One of the problems that needed to be considered was the decision in *R v Howe (1987)* that there was no defence to murder in the form of necessity. This proved to be a difficult issue for the courts since the conduct of the doctors without the permission of the courts might have been seen as unlawful however well intentioned.

Walker LJ believed that each case needed to be looked at on its own merits and in the absence of legislation by Parliament the law would develop in this way.

Ward LJ looked at the possibility that circumstances would arise which would be so extreme that the ruling in *R v Howe (1987)* could be suspended. His conclusion was that the law should allow 'an escape' in order that the lesser of two evils should prevail.

Brooke LJ set a three-part test that it was hoped would answer the difficult question.

1 'The act is needed to avoid inevitable and irreparable evil.' The evil to be avoided in this case was the possibility that both girls would die and that at least one of them could have lived.

2 'No more should be done than is reasonably necessary for the purpose to be achieved.' The doctors in this case had an enormous medical task in front of them that could not in fact have guaranteed one hundred per cent the survival of either of the twins. What was known, however, was that if intervention did take place at least one would die and possibly even both.

3 'The evil inflicted must not be disproportionate to the evil avoided.' The evil inflicted was the inevitable death of the weaker twin. The evil avoided was the almost certain death of the stronger twin. The question posed is a difficult one, which requires great wisdom to get right.

6 Issues of interest in the contract law source material

Source 2

Extract adapted from the judgement of Patterson J in *Thomas v Thomas (1847)* 2 QB 851

The *Thomas v Thomas (1847)* case revolved around a husband and wife agreement. The husband wanted the wife to be able to live in the house owned by him when he died. He charged her £1 a year rent, which was well below the market rate even for those times. The court felt that even though it was inadequate for normal purposes, it was sufficient consideration for a contract. The key issue about consideration is that it is a legal issue rather than an economic one. As long as courts see something moving from one party to another they will probably accept the existence of a legal contract.

It is important that you have good quality definitions and understanding of the words 'sufficient' and 'adequate'. Sufficient is all that is required by the courts. It must be capable of recognition. Adequate may apply to reality where parties are hoping for a bargain that makes it worthwhile for them to go to the trouble of forming a contractual relationship.

Source 3

Extract adapted from *Cheshire, Fifoot & Furmston's Law of Contract* by Furmston, Butterworths, pp. 84–7

Freedom to contract is essentially fundamental to the law of contract. Courts will not normally look at the equity of contractual relationships unless one party expressly takes the matter to court to complain of such an issue. Parties, if they hold the capacity to form contracts, will be assumed also to have the ability to weigh up their own financial or other interests. The case of *Chappell & Co Ltd v Nestle Co Ltd (1960)* illustrates the point of what should or should not be the value of a consideration.

The Nestle Company were undertaking a promotion, which included offering a record in return for money and three wrappers of chocolate. The company banked the money but the wrappers were thrown away as they had no monetary or intrinsic value to the company although they had significance in terms of consideration. The House of Lords decided an important legal point during the case: the wrappers alone could be regarded as consideration even if they were not adequate. They were sufficient in legal terms.

Source 4

Extract adapted from the judgement of Lord Sommerville in *Chappell & Co Ltd v Nestle Co Ltd (1960)* AC 87

Lord Somerville was the judge in the case of *Chappell & Co Ltd v Nestle Co Ltd (1960)*. In his judgement he underlines the freedom of the contracting parties to choose what they believe is to be taken as consideration. It may be of no value on the free market, but if they choose to accept it as of value to them then that is all that matters. The chocolate wrappers in the case were actually thrown away. The court was not concerned. All that mattered was that Nestle had decided that that was the consideration that was of importance to it. As he says in the judgement: 'A contracting party can stipulate for what consideration he chooses.'

Source 5

Extract adapted from *An Outline of the Law of Contract*, by GB Treitel, Butterworths, pp. 32–3

There are five key rules on consideration in contract law.

1 Consideration must move between promissor and promissee.

2 Consideration must be sufficient but does not have to be adequate.

3 Consideration must not be illegal.

4 Existing duty cannot be consideration.

5 Consideration must not be past.

The last point on consideration is explored in Source 6. Although past consideration is no consideration, the source identifies the fact that there is some flexibility possible on this rule to take account of commercial realities. It may not be possible, for example, to agree a price for some jobs until they are finished. The courts are keen to make contracts work and rules such as this one are only used when appropriate to the situation.

Source 6

Extract adapted from *The Law of Contract* by Paul Richards, Pitman, pp. 49–50

This source looks again at the notion of past consideration and draws our attention to *Roscorla v Thomas (1842)* and *Re: McArdle (1951)* and then goes on to explore in more detail *Lampleigh v Braithwaite (1605)*.

In *Roscorla v Thomas (1842)*, a horse had been described by the seller as 'sound and free from vice' after the sale had gone through. The court felt that the later statements could not be used to change the price. Consideration had already been completed.

The *Re: McArdle (1951)* case dealt with a family who built a granny flat for an elderly relative. Other members of the family promised to pay for some of the work after they had seen it. They failed to pay and the case ended up in court. The court felt that past consideration was not valid.

The *Lampleigh v Braithwaite (1605)* case illustrates a case that was enforceable in the courts. A pardon was obtained and the recipient promised £100 after release. Although the consideration happened after the release, the court felt that it would have been reasonable to expect expenses to be paid.

Source 7

Extract adapted from *Key Issues in Contract* by John Adams and Roger Brownsword, Butterworths

Williams v Roffey (1990) is a classic example of the judiciary attempting to bring law into the real world of commercial decisions and situations. The economy was suffering from a recession, which lasted until the end of 1992, and businesses were facing problems of survival. The case revolved around a building company who had promised some carpenters extra money to pay for materials. They finished the work but the builders failed to pay. The court decided that the carpenters were entitled to the extra payment above the agreed price.

The complex summary of the Glidewell case needs to be simplified. The best chance of quick and effective understanding is to put all six details onto a flow chart and show the interrelationships.

Again, references to *Stilk v Myrick (1809)* and *Williams v Roffey (1990)* need to be related to later sources particularly Source 10.

Source 8

Extract adapted from the judgement of Lord Scarman in *Pao On v Lau Yiu Long (1979)* 3 All ER 65 PC

The source revolves around the situation where completion of an existing contractual duty can also be seen as consideration for a third party. The case is a notoriously difficult one to understand, but the principle involved can be explained via two other famous cases.

Scotson v Pegg (1861) saw the claimant contracted to supply a cargo of coal to a third party or to any customer that the third party instructed it to be delivered to. Under the agreement Scotson delivered coal to Pegg who agreed as part of the deal to unload the coal upon delivery. Pegg refused to accept that this was consideration since there was already a contract with the third party. The court decided that the consideration from Scotson was the delivery and the consideration from Pegg the unloading.

Shadwell v Shadwell (1860) involved the claimant suing the estate of his wife's uncle. The uncle had promised a payment if the claimant, a young barrister, married the niece. £150 was promised per year until the barrister was earning £600 per year, which he never reached. The allowance from the uncle was not always paid and when the uncle died the barrister sued the estate for the arrears. The court felt that marrying the niece was a consideration and the pleasure or relief the uncle enjoyed from the arrangement was a consideration.

Source 9

Extract adapted from the judgement of Viscount Cave LC in *Glasbrook Brothers v Glamorgan County Council (1925)* AC 270 HL

During a strike a colliery asked police for extra support. When the time came to pay for this extra work they refused to pay saying that the police had an existing public duty to provide such protection. The issue revolved around consideration. The court felt that the police had promised consideration in the extra and special way they had completed their duties, which was beyond the limitations imposed by existing public duty not being consideration for a contract.

Source 10

Adapted from the judgement of Purchas LJ in *Williams v Roffey (1990)* 1 All ER 512 CA

The *Stilk v Myrick (1809)* case is used to try to understand the issues in *Williams v Roffey (1990)*. The *Stilk v Myrick (1809)* case involved eight sailors who promised to cover for two others who had deserted the ship. They were promised a share of the wages of those who had gone. When the money was not paid the case went to court. The court decided that they had done nothing more than their duty and were not entitled to payment. Contrast this case with *Hartley v Ponsonby (1857)* where seventeen sailors deserted ship leaving nineteen to cope. In this case the court decided the sailors were owed their money. The *Williams v Roffey (1990)* case builds on the two earlier cases.

Source 11

Extract adapted from the judgement of Russell LJ in *Williams v Roffey (1990)* 1 All ER 512 CA

Given the apparent unfairness in *Stilk v Myrick (1809)* over the want of consideration, the courts are much more likely to look for even the smallest evidence of consideration to make a just outcome more possible. A good question to ask is why was there a more equitable decision in *Hartley v Ponsonby (1857)* when the circumstances were similar to that in the *Stilk v Myrick (1809)* case? *Williams v Roffey (1990)* attempts to bring the law up to date without dismissing the idea of consideration.

Source 12

Extract adapted from *Law of Contract* by WT Major and Christine Taylor, Pitman, pp. 53–7

A pre-existing duty may come from three sources.

1 Existing contractual duty as in *Williams v Roffey (1990)*.
2 Existing public duty as in *Glasbrook Brothers v Glamorgan County Council (1925)*.
3 Out of a contract with a third party as in *Pao On v Lau Yiu Long (1979)*.

If the party concerned does nothing more than what the contract or what their public duty says they should do, there is no further consideration. Situation three, concerning a contract with a third party, normally results in the creation of consideration.

Acts of Parliament

Legal cases

Index